RICHARD
DYER-BENNET

RICHARD DYER-BENNET

The Last Minstrel

Paul O. Jenkins

Foreword by Bonnie Dyer-Bennet
Afterword by Andrew Schulman

UNIVERSITY PRESS OF MISSISSIPPI
Jackson

www.upress.state.ms.us

The University Press of Mississippi is a member of the Association of
American University Presses.

First printing 2010
∞
Library of Congress Cataloging-in-Publication Data

Jenkins, Paul O.
Richard Dyer-Bennet : the last minstrel / Paul O. Jenkins ; foreword by
Bonnie Dyer-Bennet ; afterword by Andrew Schulman.
p. cm. — (American made music series)
Includes bibliographical references and index.
ISBN 978-1-61703-205-9 (cloth : alk. paper) 1. Dyer-Bennet, Richard.
2. Folk singers—United States—Biography. I. Title.
ML420.D978J46 2010
782.42162'0092—dc22
[B]   2009015241

British Library Cataloging-in-Publication Data available

FOR ALL JENKINSES AND ALL DYER-BENNETS,
BUT ESPECIALLY BONNIE, BROOKE, AND MEL

Contents

ACKNOWLEDGMENTS
IX

FOREWORD
Bonnie Dyer-Bennet
XI

INTRODUCTION
XV

CHAPTER 1.
Master and Pupil
3

CHAPTER 2.
New York
23

CHAPTER 3.
Early Recordings
40

CHAPTER 4.
Aspen Interlude and Life on the Road
54

CHAPTER 5.
The Blacklist
66

CHAPTER 6.
Dyer-Bennet Records
78

CHAPTER 7.
The Lovely Milleress and Stony Brook
104

CHAPTER 8.

The *Odyssey* of Richard Dyer-Bennet

117

CHAPTER 9.

The Legacy of Richard Dyer-Bennet

124

AFTERWORD

Richard Dyer-Bennet as Guitarist
Andrew Schulman

132

DISCOGRAPHY

137

REPERTOIRE

143

NOTES

157

REFERENCES

168

INDEX

172

Acknowledgments

This book would not have been possible without the assistance of Bonnie Dyer-Bennet. Her timely and tireless cooperation made this book possible.

Other members of the Dyer-Bennet family have also freely given their time. These include Mel, Dick's widow; Miriam Jr., his sister; Brooke, his daughter; David, his nephew; and Mary, his sister-in-law.

Elias Lien was very helpful.

Thanks to Craig Gill of the University Press of Mississippi for his faith in the project.

I wish to express my gratitude to a number of Dick's former students who granted me interviews: Andrew Schulman, Lesl Harker, Val Sigstedt, Will Holt, and Ruth Buell.

Folk music legends Pete Seeger and Oscar Brand took time out from their still-busy schedules to speak with me about Dyer-Bennet.

My knowledge of Sven Scholander was helped immensely by Liz Slaughter-Ek's translation of Leif Bergman's biographical sketch of him, written in Swedish.

Thanks to the archivists of the New York Public Library for providing me with hundreds of newspaper clippings about Dyer-Bennet.

F. Jason Torre, university archivist at SUNY Stony Brook, was very helpful in providing student evaluations of Dyer-Bennet as professor.

I am indebted to Sven-Erik Lundgren of Swedish Broadcasting Resources for providing me with samples of Sven Scholander's existing recordings.

Thanks to Ingrid Scholander for help with information about her grandfather.

Sven Aas provided valuable help with the scanning of the book's images.

Jeri Shea of the Taft Union High School District sent me information on Miriam Dyer-Bennet Sr. Thanks, too, to Pete Gianopulos, a student of Miriam's at Taft Junior College.

Harvey Cort gave graciously of his time.

Stephan Chodorov unearthed the videotape of the 1962 WCBS program.

Thomas Stern provided many additions to the discography.

College of Mount St. Joseph librarians Char Gildea and Julie Flanders assisted me in obtaining materials from other libraries that were vital to my research. Nicole Freire, interlibrary loan librarian at UC Santa Barbara, was also quite helpful.

Thanks to my College of Mount St. Joseph colleagues Tim Lynch, Elizabeth Barkley, Tiffany Owens, Gene Kritsky, Darla Vale, Jeff Hillard, Ron White, Eileen Wedig, Phil Amalong, John Trokan, Jack Hettinger, Chris Boland, and Carol Herzog.

Matt Le Tissier and Dennis Bergkamp provided inspiration.

Thanks to my wife, Mary, for her love and emotional support, and to my son, Tom, for bringing me so much happiness.

I am forever indebted to my brothers, Clay and Hugh, and my sister, Carol, for numerous life lessons.

Finally, thanks to my parents, Owen and Barbara, for bringing music into my life.

FOREWORD

On Christmas Day of 1955 or 1956, when our family was still living in the first home my parents ever owned—a twenty-four by twenty-four–foot bungalow in the middle of the woods—our breakfast was interrupted by the arrival of a neighbor, a farmer who lived up the road a couple of miles and from whom we sometimes bought hay for our horse.

He banged on the door, demanding loudly that Dad come home with him immediately because there were some people there who did not believe him when he told them Dad was a friend of his. The man was, as Dad described him later with some amusement, "drunk as a skunk."

But Dad, being Dad, agreed to go with him, sensing that would be the most expedient way to handle the situation. Given the man's state of inebriation, the pick-up truck ride up the slippery hill to the farm was apparently a bit unsettling, but once there, Dad met the farmer's doubting friends, had a drink with them, and was brought safely home again to continue our Christmas festivities.

To the farmer, Dad was both a neighbor and the fellow who sang a benefit once a year for the local Congregational Church (Dad's only connection with any church). I do not know if he attended any of those concerts or if he just figured Dad must be famous because he was a performer and therefore someone whose acquaintance was worth boasting about.

My parents had bought land and built their first little house in a then quite out-of-the-way corner of the Berkshires, primarily so that Dad could have the privacy and quiet he needed when he was not on tour. But in the 1950s and 1960s, especially during the summer, hardly a week went by without the appearance of an unfamiliar car making its way slowly down our long driveway. The car would come to a stop and the couple inside (it was almost always a couple) would remain in their seats for a moment, gazing at our house.

As I remember, it was my mother who most often dealt with the strangers, telling them as politely as she could that, yes, this was the home of Richard Dyer-Bennet, and no, he was not available to talk with them, or sign an autograph, or pose with them for a picture. Once in a great while, Dad would handle the visitors himself and send them away after a conversation whose length depended on his mood and what their arrival had interrupted.

Growing up, I found these interruptions of our privacy intolerable. Why couldn't these people leave us alone? Nor did I enjoy having to wait around backstage after a concert while fans swarmed eagerly around my father, asking him the same questions I had heard asked countless times, when I knew that what Dad needed was to get out of there and have something to eat. The child in me is still resentful; my adult self is more tolerant, having been in the position once or twice of waiting backstage in hopes of shaking the hand of an actor I greatly admired.

Of course I was proud of him and proud to be in the audience surrounded by people who so clearly loved his work. I loved it myself, after all. But I sometimes wished our family could move anonymously through the world, unnoticed by other people. And now, years after his death, I have that anonymity and I find it bittersweet.

Throughout most of my life, as often as not, mention of my surname would result in the question, "Are you by any chance related to Richard Dyer-Bennet?" In recent decades, this has occurred with less and less frequency, due to the gradual attrition of the people who once composed my father's large and loyal audience.

His earliest fans, who were his own age or close to it, are now in their eighties and nineties. The next age cohort was made up, to a great extent, of college students; he performed at colleges and universities many times each year. And apparently, many of the children of members of both of these groups grew up hearing my father's recordings. But as the times and musical tastes change, the number of people who know anything at all about Richard Dyer-Bennet is dwindling.

When Paul Jenkins approached the family for our assistance with this book, he said that he hoped that by telling the story of my father's career he might re-awaken interest in both the man and his music. For many fans from the early days, such a book would provide some glimpses into the life of someone they knew only from hearing him in concert. Most of them probably would not have known about the stifling effect the McCarthy-era blacklist had on my father's career, that he taught for years in the drama department of a university, that he translated and performed one of Schubert's song cycles, or that he had hoped to record Robert Fitzgerald's beautiful translation of Homer's *Odyssey*.

The family has a dozen large boxes of letters, programs, itineraries, contracts, fan mail, and photographs from which Paul drew to help piece together this story. But quite apart from this memorabilia, Paul's diligent and inspired research led him to material that even my father was unaware of, such as the family background of Dad's model and mentor, the Swedish minstrel, Sven Scholander.

My father is long gone, and with him that voice, tinged with something from his first five years in England, something from his years in Canada, and his particular blend of earnestness, inquisitiveness, and humor that so enriched the stories he used to tell about his experiences. His singing voice can still be heard in recordings, his speaking voice in Jill Godmilow and Susan Fanshell's documentary film, *The Odyssey Tapes*; but to capture a sense of his aesthetic, musical, political, and ethical integrity—the man, in three dimensions—in the absence of the man himself, was a daunting task indeed.

Paul also had to convince three stubborn women who are still as protective of Dad's privacy, legacy, and interests as we ever were (my mother, my sister Brooke, and myself), that he had a sense of what was unique about the man; what he strove for in his performances and recordings, and why; his originality; and his perfectionism.

With much patience and skill, Paul has made his way through all these obstacles and told the story of my father's career in a way I think will bring back fond memories to those who remember him and awaken interest in those who never heard him.

BONNIE DYER-BENNET, 2008

INTRODUCTION

Richard Dyer-Bennet's younger brother John and his wife Mary were my parents' best friends. Every so often John would give our family one of Richard's recordings. It was thanks to John that I grew up listening to RDB *1, 5, 6, 7, 10*, and *1601*. Perhaps it is because I have always been familiar with Dyer-Bennet's recordings that I am surprised that most others born after 1950 are not.

Initially it was Dyer-Bennet's material, those marvelous folk songs that have stood the test of time, that held my interest. As a teenager I began to poke around libraries to find more information on "The Bonny Earl of Morey," "Lord Rendal," and "Barbara Allen." These songs haunted me, possibly because each concerned the death of its protagonist. As I grew up and heard other artists perform the same songs, however, I realized that it was not only the songs themselves but Dyer-Bennet's interpretations that made them so memorable. Nobody brought the same drama to a song the way Dyer-Bennet could.

Still, it was only after Dyer-Bennet's death in 1991 that I began to want to learn more about the life of this singularly talented artist. I interviewed John Dyer-Bennet and taped all of his brother's albums that my family did not already own. After John lent me access to his collection of newspaper clippings, I began my research in earnest. Printed accounts can only tell one so much, of course, so I asked John if he would be willing to give me the address of Richard's widow, Melvene (Mel). John advised me that Mel was still deep in mourning and that it was too soon to make such overtures.

In 1993 I completed a nineteen-page biographical sketch of Dyer-Bennet and created a web site based on it (richard.dyer-bennet.net/). After sending her a copy of my work, I spoke with Mel in 1995 and found her still somewhat reticent. Many others, she told me, had written articles about Dick, but each of these accounts contained so many factual errors that she had grown leery of any subsequent requests. She did provide me with a great deal of information, however, and corrected many errors in my manuscript. I did not think that further efforts would prove very fruitful, so the project became dormant.

As the years passed I was gratified to receive many enthusiastic emails from readers of my Dyer-Bennet web site. I recognized in them kindred spirits—others eager to learn more about the singer whose work we so revered. One such message in 2005 encouraged me to try my luck with the Dyer-Bennet family again. This time I contacted Bonnie Dyer-Bennet, Richard's daughter, who had written a wonderful biographical essay on her father to accompany the liner notes to the Smithsonian-Folkways CD release of *Richard Dyer-Bennet 1*. Bonnie proved receptive, and we began a lengthy email correspondence. Eventually I was able to visit Bonnie and her husband, Steve, in Massachusetts in order to begin to sift through the family archive of information about Richard's life and career. While the sheer volume of documents, letters, and articles was daunting, I dove in with all the enthusiasm of a pilgrim finally granted access to Mecca. The more I learned about Dyer-Bennet's life and what a popular performer he had been in the forties and fifties, the more I wondered why no one had trod this path before me.

Dyer-Bennet was a modest man, not given to self-promotion. Although he published two songbooks and recorded the cream of his repertoire with an eye toward the future, he was decidedly less interested in sharing his personal life with the public. Only when performing did Dyer-Bennet enjoy being in the public eye. It was the songs he wanted people to remember, not the singer. In this respect Dyer-Bennet shared Rudyard Kipling's notion that

> *And for the little, little span*
> *The dead are borne in mind,*
> *Seek not to question other than*
> *The books I leave behind.*

I grant that readers of my book will learn more about Dyer-Bennet the singer than Dyer-Bennet the man, but given Dyer-Bennet's personality, this seems entirely appropriate. He was an interesting man who led an interesting life, but most interesting of all was his music. Dyer-Bennet practiced an old European art, minstrelsy, for listeners in his adopted country of America, most of whom were not familiar with the term or his material. They knew what they liked, however, and one of my objects is to show how popular Dyer-Bennet was in his heyday. He was a performer who made a real connection with his audience, and his art should not be forgotten. Dyer-Bennet played an important part in the folk song revival of the twentieth century. While today's audience has chosen to embrace another approach to folk music, it is important to remember the alternative that singers like Dyer-Bennet presented.

The desire to categorize artists is understandable, but it is not always possible to accurately assign them to a particular movement, style, or genre. This is certainly the case with Dyer-Bennet. One of many who tried to classify those who perform folk music was Ellen Stekert. Her essay "Cents and Nonsense in the Urban Folksong Movement: 1930–1966" is just one example of the potential pitfalls such schemata face. Stekert identifies four groups of folk singers. The first "is composed of the traditional singers—singers who have learned their songs and their style of presentation from oral tradition as they grew up."[1] Woody Guthrie, Lead Belly, and Sarah Ogan Gunning are some of the names she includes in this group. The second group she labels "imitators," those who have "taken time to learn the skills of those whom they have admired."[2] She cites the New Lost City Ramblers and John Hammond (son of the Columbia Records executive) as exemplars of this rather uncomplimentary categorization. The third group she calls "utilizers." "This conglomeration of people is loosely held together by the fact that they have taken folk material and have altered it in the light of accepted city aesthetics."[3] The Weavers and the Kingston Trio are two such groups who altered folk songs in their "tune, text, and style of presentation."[4] The final group she names the "new aesthetic," those "whose clientele scorned the Kingston Trio and felt art singing too sterile and inhibited."[5] Stekert includes Joan Baez, Judy Collins, and Peter, Paul and Mary in this category. Where does Dyer-Bennet fit in this scheme? Stekert places him (along with Alfred Deller) in a subset of the "utilizers" she dubs "art utilizers." That is, Dyer-Bennet and Deller have "picked and utilized their material in the light of art song performance."[6]

Such classifications are, of course, generalizations at best, and usually far from satisfactory. Any artist resents the limitations implicit in such categorization. Certainly Dyer-Bennet would cringe at the phrase "art utilizer." So how did he describe himself? I begin my study of Dyer-Bennet with a thorough examination of the life and music of the Swedish minstrel Sven Scholander, because Dyer-Bennet repeatedly classed himself as a minstrel and pointed to Scholander's art as what he wished to practice. In a sense, Dyer-Bennet's career began with his trip to visit the aging minstrel in 1935. Up to this time he had sung and studied singing, but it was only after meeting Scholander that he understood just what he wanted to do with his talent.

A few other notes of explanation may prove helpful to the reader. Since other biographers—Joe Klein on Woody Guthrie and David Dunaway on Pete Seeger— have painted vivid pictures of the New York folk scene of the 1940s, I have chosen not to elaborate further on it in my second chapter. Robert Cantwell's *When We Were Good* and Richard Reuss's *American Folk Music and Left-Wing Politics* are two other fine books I recommend to readers who wish to know more about the period. I have been content to examine Dyer-Bennet's place in this fecund period.

Chapters 3 and 6 detail Dyer-Bennet's recorded repertoire. These songs constitute Dyer-Bennet's legacy, and it is important to understand not only their provenance but also the singer's approach to them. Chapter 3 treats songs Dyer-

Bennet recorded for commercial labels from 1941 to 1954, chapter 6 those he chose to include on his Dyer-Bennet record releases (1955–64). Some of the minstrel's early releases are quite obscure, and their omission from chapter 3 indicates that I have never heard them.

I direct those readers who desire a more in-depth analysis of Dyer-Bennet's singing to Conrad Osborne's essay, "The Voice of a Genuine Original," included in the booklet that accompanies the CD release of *Richard Dyer-Bennet 1*. Similarly, guitar players should consult Andrew Schulman's essay included as an afterword to this book.

I have attempted to let Dyer-Bennet speak for himself as often as possible. I quote at length his 1961 article, "A New Age of Minstrelsy," and the valuable liner notes he included with each of his Dyer-Bennet records releases.

Like any biography, mine is incomplete, and for this I beg the reader's indulgence. Some unanswered questions remain. Why, for example, did Dyer-Bennet cease making recordings for his own label after the release of *Richard Dyer-Bennet 13* in 1964? If he was so encouraged by the improvements Cornelius Reid had brought to his voice in 1968, why did Dyer-Bennet not return to the studio? Why did the *Odyssey* project remain incomplete? Certainly Dyer-Bennet's declining health is partially to blame, but I gained the impression that much more—if not all—of the project could have been captured on tape.

In the end, I can only hope that my work comes close to matching the high standards Richard Dyer-Bennet established for his own endeavors. All errors in the text are my own.

RICHARD
DYER-BENNET

Chapter 1

Master and Pupil

There once was a ship that sailed upon the sea . . .

"I found him living quietly in the suburbs of Stockholm. He was seventy-five years old, and not much was left of his voice. Nevertheless, when he took his lute in hand and began *The Golden Vanity* I heard a kind of singing I had never dreamed of. He looked straight at me and spun tale after tale as though singing out of his own life. He sang of soldiers, sailors, young lovers; he sang dialogues between mother and daughter, altercations between birds and animals, descriptions of mountain and countryside. A pageant of the ages seemed to pass before my eyes, and it was all evoked by the husky voice of this old man and by his simple but exactly appropriate accompaniments on the lute."[1]

Such is Richard Dyer-Bennet's description of his first meeting with Sven Scholander, the singer who would serve as his master and greatest inspiration. The year was 1935, and Dyer-Bennet had used an unexpected inheritance to travel from Berkeley to Sweden (first by freighter via the Panama Canal, and then by bicycle) with the express purpose of tracking down the famed minstrel. What he found was an old man who proved reticent to perform for the young enthusiast. He was retired, Scholander reasoned, his voice but a whisper of its past glory. Eventually Scholander called for his lute, however, and sang a few songs from his old repertoire. "It wasn't a man singing at all," Dyer-Bennet would later write, "it was simply a man telling you a story—and, my gosh, how you believed him! Yet it was as polished, as consonant with the music, as absolutely right as the Budapest String Quartet."[2]

It is impossible to overestimate the importance of this visit on Dyer-Bennet. Time and time again in liner notes, interviews, and articles Dyer-Bennet sang Scholander's praises. "I have since heard many singers to the lute and guitar, some quite competent, but no one to compare with Scholander. His fusion of poetry, melody, and harmonies on the lute made each song seem a perfect work of art. His singing moved me beyond anything I had ever experienced, and even as I recall the hearing, my scalp prickles."[3] Scholander seemed to be singing directly to young Dyer-Bennet. "With a narrative song, a song with which you are communicating consciously and openly and overtly, communicating a certain content to a listener requires another attitude. And few singers have it. Scholander had it."[4]

The art Scholander practiced, and that Dyer-Bennet wished to resurrect for an American audience, was that of the minstrel, someone not necessarily of the folk who expressed in song emotions and themes understood by both the privileged and the humble, the higher classes and the true folk. Dyer-Bennet's presentation of these songs was more artistic and refined than that of peers Woody Guthrie, Pete Seeger, or Lead Belly. He wanted to perform songs of the past for a contemporary audience, hopeful that his style would most clearly reveal their beauty. Considering the scope of these ambitions, Dyer-Bennet's achievements are admirable. Only nine years after his meeting with Scholander he became the first solo performer of his kind to appear in Carnegie Hall. Dyer-Bennet's performances acquainted his audiences with folk songs from both the American and English traditions long before they became fashionable.

Indeed, one can claim with some certainty that Dyer-Bennet was one of the major figures who paved the way for the so-called folk boom in the United States of the mid-1950s and early 1960s. His influence can be heard in the work of Joan Baez, Judy Collins, Cynthia Gooding, and dozens of others. Had his career not been interrupted in midstream by the blacklist, Dyer-Bennet would certainly be much better known than he is today. His musical achievements are many. One result of the boycott against him was the creation of his own recording label. Again in this regard, Dyer-Bennet stands at the forefront of the industry. Later in his career he made two bold attempts to make great art more accessible to his audiences, initially by performing Schubert's *lieder* in English, and then by reciting Homer's *Odyssey* in live performance.

Dyer-Bennet's life is characterized by continual striving toward ideals. When he picked up the lute, and later the guitar, he was determined to master them. He did not perform a song in public until he felt sure he understood its every nuance and could express it musically. Oscar Brand, a Canadian singer and contemporary of Dyer-Bennet, recalls one example of Dyer-Bennet's perfectionism. If perhaps colored by nostalgic hyperbole, Brand's comments provide a useful portrait of the singer's pursuit of perfection.

> One day he was rehearsing, and I came up to the door, knocked, and he said "come in" and went back to rehearsing. And what he was rehearsing was "John Henry," one of his great songs. I thought it was kind of funny at the time. I didn't have the approach that I have now. Dyer-Bennet was working on one line: "this hammer'll be the death of me, Lord, Lord, this hammer'll be the death of me." And I waited for the rest of the song. Then he started again: "this hammer'll be the death of me, Lord, Lord, this hammer'll be the death of me." Now Richard went over that line, about four or five times, and it looked to me as if he was going to go on for another half an hour. I went back across the street, made some phone calls, did some work, and about two hours later came back, knocked at the door—"come in"—and he was still sitting at the same place and he was still singing "this hammer'll be the death of me, Lord, Lord, this hammer'll be the death of me." Over and over again. I was astonished because it never occurred to me that these songs were like jewels that had to be polished continually, over and over again until you get it just right. I come from a different background, singing in the streets, singing in Canada, in the saloons, very often without an instrument. I was astonished that anybody would put that much work into one single line of music. But Richard Dyer-Bennet was demanding. He was not easily satisfied; he had to do it over and over again until it was just right. He was a specialist, a diamond cutter. He took a song that he thought was a diamond and he started working on it so it sparkled and so all its facets were perfect and it shone out to the world. I don't know of many people who can do that.[5]

English by birth, Dyer-Bennet performed his art mainly for American audiences. His foreign birth and unusual approach to folk music served to heighten his individuality, his "differentness," and while these struck some as inappropriate, Dyer-Bennet never compromised his vision. If he, an Englishman with a trained voice, wanted to sing "Go Down Moses," then by God he would sing it, and in his own way. If his politics ultimately hurt his career, he made no apologies for them, and had no regrets for practicing them as he saw fit. Similarly, while Dyer-Bennet's interest in providing a good upbringing for his children may have halted the tremendous momentum he had established early in his career, he would certainly have taken the same actions if given another chance.

Since the practice of minstrelsy in its European tradition colored much of Dyer-Bennet's approach to his music, it is appropriate to briefly examine its history and some of its practitioners who especially influenced him. As Dyer-Bennet would later note, "I may not be a particularly gifted exponent of my way of singing, but the way itself is valid, has a great tradition, and should be understood."[6] Writing in 1765, Thomas Percy charmingly defined minstrels as "an order of men in the middle ages, who subsisted by the arts of poetry and music, and sang to the harp verses composed by themselves, or others. They also appear to have accompanied their songs with mimicry and action; and to have practiced such various means of diverting as were much admired in those rude times, and supplied the want of more refined entertainment."[7] Early in the tradition, most minstrels sang their own compositions, but as the art matured, they more frequently began to sing pieces composed by their peers. Percy's essay outlines the heyday and sad decline of the minstrels in Western Europe. Successors to the bardic tradition, minstrels made their living mainly by entertaining nobles. While not as venerated as their northern European counterparts, English minstrels were "yet highly favoured and protected, and continued still to enjoy considerable privileges."[8] Some were provided with homes, others with positions at court. By Elizabeth's reign, however, the minstrels' reputation had deteriorated to the point that they were included among "rogues, vagabonds, and sturdy beggars" who could be punished for "wandering abroad."[9] Put another way, they gradually became known less as distinguished artists and more as mere entertainers.

One of Renaissance England's most accomplished musicians was John Dowland (1563–1626). Dyer-Bennet greatly admired Dowland, and if not strictly a minstrel, Dowland's skills as a composer and lutenist make him comparable to one. A brief biographical sketch provides a useful example of the dynamic and roller-coaster careers minstrels often led. It seems probable that Dowland's early musical education resulted from an attachment to an aristocratic household. Further youthful training in France led Dowland to convert to Catholicism, a decision that was, he believed, largely to blame for his inability to gain a permanent position at Elizabeth's court. Dowland's skill on the lute was legendary, prompting contemporary Richard Barnfield to declaim that his "heavenly touch upon the lute doth ravish human sense."[10] Dowland's appointment as lutenist to the court of King Christian IV of Denmark in 1598 paid well, but did little to soothe his injured pride. He was apparently a very sensitive and volatile man, many of whose compositions—"Flow My Tears," recorded by Dyer-Bennet in 1959, and "In Darknesse Let Me Dwell," to name but two—reflect the fashionable melancholy of the period. In 1597 Dowland published his highly successful *First Booke of Songes*, which enjoyed four reprintings in sixteen years, and helped to ensure his legacy.

Finally, after years of disappointment, Dowland was granted a position at the court of England's James I in 1612. Dowland's prestige in his native land at last matched the acclaim he had long enjoyed on the Continent. He was awarded a doctorate from Oxford and continued to publish settings for his compositions until his death. Dowland's popularity among practitioners of the lute has never abated. Julian Bream (b. 1933) recorded a great many of Dowland's works in the 1960s, as did the rock singer Sting in 2006. Sting describes Dowland as "our first alienated singer-songwriter,"[11] and while this characterization is perhaps simplistic, it is not far from the truth. Dowland was paranoid, jealous, and insecure.

The Swedish minstrel Carl Michael Bellman (1740–1795) also played an important role in Dyer-Bennet's career, for he was Scholander's inspiration. After struggling for years to earn a living through his music, Bellman finally found favor with King Gustavus III, who created a special position at court for him. Yet it was Stockholm's gutters, not its palace, that inspired Bellman. During his residence there, Stockholm was a city of 70,000 inhabitants and 700 taverns. Bellman's most famous collection of songs, *Fredman's Epistles* (1790), is "a collection of fictional letters portraying imaginary scenes in the lives of known contemporary drunkards and loose women"[12] that delighted both the bluebloods and the riffraff. Bellman's method was to set new words to popular melodies. His use of pastoral motifs and classical allusions betray him as a man of the Enlightenment. A true artist, Bellman often employed complex metrics and has become recognized as "Sweden's Shakespeare of the Guitar Song." In his subject matter, Bellman can be likened to Brueghel, Dickens, and Hogarth. His songs teem with life. As Paul Britten Austin wrote in his introduction to an English edition of *Fredman's Epistles*, "Not since the gods drank and fought in Valhalla have mortals disported themselves with scantier inhibition."[13]

The following verse from "Epistle Number 2" provides a good example of Bellman's art.

> So screw up the fiddle,
> Come, fiddler, quick I say!
> Dearest sister gay
> Never say me nay,
> Say but yes and we'll be jolly!
> Sit down, man, don't dawdle,
> Caress thy silver string,
> Let the fiddle sing
> Till the rafters ring,
> Nor break it in thy folly!
> Thou sweatest!—A bath
> Of brandy be thy solace,
> For underneath this roof
> Is Bacchus' palace!

Bellman was most at home with composition. His voice was slight and he did not particularly enjoy performing. When he did perform, however, Bellman demanded absolute silence. A gifted mimic, he sang not only words, but also the "characteristic timbres of waldhorn, flute, oboe, bass viol . . . indeed every instrument to perfection."[14] While still beloved in Sweden, Bellman's poetic songs have proved untranslatable and he is now known outside Sweden only to the cognoscenti.

Sven Scholander made it his lifework to preserve Bellman's art by reintroducing it to European concertgoers. Indeed, many of his performances were described as "Bellman evenings." Born in 1860, Scholander grew up in a home bursting with music and creativity. Brothers Torkel, Erik, and Göran all sang, while sister Anna became an artist. Scholander seems to have inherited little from his mother, a tranquil follower of theosophy. Scholander's father, on the other hand, was a huge personality. Fredrik Wilhelm (F. W.) Scholander possessed an amazing array of skills. His principal pursuit was architecture. His lectures on Renaissance and medieval architecture at the Swedish Art Academy were legendary. Nicknamed the Swedish Michelangelo, Scholander *père* was also a proficient watercolor painter and poet. His *Collected Writings*, published in 1881, ran to three volumes and include poems, stories, and plays. Scholander paints a vivid picture of his father as a man who "during his entire life had understood how to make the most of every minute of the day in order to get the biggest possible meaning of his life. He rested after one piece of work by immediately throwing himself into another."[15]

But if young Sven delighted in his father's various displays of virtuosity (including his performances as puppeteer), he was also intimidated by the man's legendary temper, something he himself would inherit. As a boy, Sven would often display his anger by beating his head against the floor or even stabbing himself with a fork. On a happier note, Scholander also picked up from his father the gift of improvisation, his love of children, and his musical ability. Scholander recalled how his father would often sit outside after dinner and entertain neighbors with his bass voice and guitar. Not surprisingly, many of these pieces were his own compositions and were published by the family as an addition to F. W.'s collected writings. Dozens of these songs would later make their way into his son's—and thus Dyer-Bennet's—repertoire.

Sven Scholander heard his first Bellman songs at fifteen. His description of the moment recalls Dyer-Bennet's own first encounter with Scholander. It was "the most remarkable experience of my youth, which more than anything else laid the groundwork for my future."[16] The singer that evening, Edward Björklund, sang Bellman's songs in an appropriately dramatic fashion, and this left a distinct impression on Scholander. Even more weighty, however, were the songs' lyrics. "Bellman's words and images crowded that moment into the innermost center of my being, fastened there, and changed me and gave a new direction to my future."[17] Bellman immediately become young Scholander's obsession. Not everyone shared his enthusiasm for this new interest. Bellman's bawdy tales of life in Stockholm were far different from the songs F. W. had sung, and Scholander's grandmother, for one, was appalled by them. Still, the die was cast.

After F. W.'s death in 1881, Scholander left Sweden to study architecture in Paris and Italy. It quickly became clear, however, where his real vocation lay. During any available break from work he would pull out the volume of Bellman songs he always carried in a back pocket. Scholander also "attended, as a spectator, singing lessons for the famous Italian Delle Sedie, and he learned a selection of older and newer French folk songs in the artistic circles he moved in. He would never pursue more in-depth studies in music theory and music history, but the musical environment in which he was raised would have given him a good general musical education and an extensive repertoire even outside of the folk genre."[18]

All that remained now was for Scholander to master the lute, the instrument with which Bellman had accompanied himself. Scholander's first instrument was his father's forbidden guitar, which he played on the sly. When F. W. inevitably caught him in the act, however, his only punishment was to force his son to practice on the instrument for at least two hours a day. A year later, Scholander was given his own guitar, and at nineteen he purchased a battered lute. He had it repaired, but quickly grew dissatisfied with its peculiar tuning. "The lute had, in addition to 6 counter bass strings, 8 strings on the handle. These were tuned in A-major, which meant that the 5 below followed the A-major scale from A to E: A, H, C-Sharp, D, E; whereupon the pure A-major tri-chord A, C-Sharp, E followed."[19] Scholander subsequently always tuned his lute in the manner of a guitar; he states with characteristic modesty:

> And with that, I also managed a sweeping modernization of the instrument. The old tuning screws of wood were replaced with mechanical metal screws, a metal or wooden section gave the much stronger counter bass strings (made of steel instead of the much earlier sinew) the most necessary support, the throat was made thinner and more suitable for 6 instead of the earlier 8 strings, and the counter bass' capotasto-device was eliminated. And thus, it was named the "Scholander-lute" after me, a "fait accompli"—a name which really related more to the fact that I was the first to give new life to the old Swedish lute than to my modernizing interference.[20]

While some critics—spurred by this characterization of Scholander as reviver of the lute—were later to call the instrument a "lute guitar," Scholander always fiercely insisted on his right to be called "singer to the lute." Besides these technical enhancements, Scholander's chord inversions and bass passages distinguished his accompaniments from those traditionally practiced. Indeed, one contemporary German reporter later even went so far as to say that in Scholander's hands, the lute resembled an entire orchestra.

It would be 1892, however, before Scholander felt confident enough in his art to move his performances from private homes to the concert stage. His early repertoire consisted of Bellman songs and French *chansons*. "His art was completely developed already at his debut and would not change afterwards, only be fine-tuned over the years."[21] It is noteworthy that, in his first "concert evening" Scholander performed two pieces Dyer-Bennet would eventually incorporate into his own repertory: "Le brave marin" and "Le veritable amour." While already comfortable with French songs, it would be some time before Scholander would perform German songs in concert. More than fifty songs from two of Bellman's most popular collections, *Fredman's Songs* and *Fredman's Epistles*, would remain central to his programs. Eventually his repertoire would grow to include more than a thousand songs.

Like Bellman before him, Scholander possessed a real gift for composition. He would often take verses by German and Swedish authors and write melodies for them. The works of Swedish author Dan Andersson (especially his *Vårkänning, or* Spring Feeling) were particular favorites of his. "Scholander's own melodies often ripple with cheerful fancies. They are for the most part considerably more melodic and harmonically complicated than the folk songs that were a part of his program—and the smoothly changing harmony in the melody of, for example, Körner's *Sängerleben* brings to mind Schubert and Schumann. With their rhythmic pauses and quick leaps between high and low tones, Scholander's earlier melodies place an especially great demand on the performer, and it seems as if their main purpose was to win public acclaim as performance pieces for Scholander himself."[22]

As a man, Scholander was a fascinating mixture of conceit and self-doubt. Renowned for his public displays of self-assurance, he also privately (in letters to his wife) disparaged his voice and his "little art." One critic rather unkindly, but quite poetically, described his singing this way: "he has an affliction in his throat, which he chooses to believe is something which might be called a voice, but which is more like the sound which arises when one scrapes a rusty nail against a grater."[23] Indeed, Scholander would sometimes refer to himself as "der stimmlose Troubadour" (the voiceless troubadour). He would usually begin concerts by apologizing for his voice, and in concert programs would remind his listeners that it was not the voice or the instrument that were important, but rather the text itself. Like his pupil Dyer-Bennet, Scholander's diction won great praise. "Even from the beginning, however, the critics agreed that Scholander, for all his tuneful failings, was still a master of phrasing and composition. It was mentioned as something new and notable that his audiences could really hear every word of the lyrics."[24] Scholander also advised attendees to familiarize themselves with the lyrics, provided in concert programs, so as to maximize their enjoyment of the songs. (In like manner, Dyer-Bennet would later include lyrics to all his songs on his recordings). It is not surprising, then, that, both in concert and on recordings, Scholander would often introduce each song and its origin before performing it.

Part of Scholander's success was due to his acute business acumen and skill in self-promotion. These attributes saw his career gain steady momentum until he was invited to perform for the royal houses of Sweden, Denmark, and Germany. Still, it was with a more common audience that he found his greatest success. What delighted his patrons most was his ability to dramatize the events in a song. In Scholander's hands, each song became a little play, which demanded no little effort; by performance end, his shirt was soaked with perspiration. Scholander noted in a letter to his wife that one critic had dubbed him "the world's foremost artist of facial expressions." Others referred to him as a "magician" and a "spell-master." Scholander was known on occasion to use his lute as a prop to imitate a gun, or to serve as a swinging church bell. His voice might mimic the heralding sound of a trumpet one moment and an animal the next, all in the service of the song. Scholander was thus able to bring the characters in his songs to life for the audience.

While dozens of examples are available, three (the first two of which concern Bellman songs) must suffice here. "In the depiction of Corporal Boman's funeral one saw not merely all the funerary pomp, but one believed oneself, the entire time, to be a part of the procession, listening to the rumble of the drum, which half comically, half sorrowfully accompanied the gossip in the alley, where the procession passed."[25] "Who has ever performed the 38th epistle 'Undan ur vägen' [Get out of the way] like he did? He stood at one end of the stage and let the audience see the funeral procession go by without moving from the spot. And the audience *saw* the procession. Without any need on his part to resort to large gestures."[26] "Scholander isn't just a singer, he is also a good actor, and that is why he can infuse such life into his songs. One both *sees* and *hears* the characters that appear in them—it could be a French miller or a Swedish bohemian figure from many centuries ago. And the singer doesn't give us just one character in each song, there could be a swarm of such figures and he has the ability to portray them all regardless."[27] Scholander's renown as an actor even led to a major role as Sintram in the Swedish epic movie, *Gösta Berlings Saga* (1924), which starred Greta Garbo. Still, not all critics were impressed with Scholander's flamboyant style, and according to newspaper reports, some younger audience members were known to have snickered in secret at his theatrics.

Even during the later stages of his career, critics praised Scholander's unrivalled ability to connect with an audience, and his contagious joie de vivre. "Scholander is an Amateur in the best sense of the word. He seems to get as much pleasure from his singing as the audience sitting in the hall. Thus his art gains much from the indescribable improvisational style that he undertakes, so that the listeners come to forget that they are sitting in a concert hall."[28] Unlike earlier artists such as Dowland, Scholander "was partial to choosing songs which preach happiness and contentment in life."[29] The following lyrics are thus typical:

I am not afraid of the troublesome,
If the sky is overcast.
Instead I'll sing a tune to comfort
And soon comes sun and Spring.

It is important to stress how new and different Scholander's art seemed to his audiences. His singing style was unique, as was his lute playing, and he was instrumental in reawakening a nation's admiration for Bellman. Bellman's songs were then being performed only in choral settings; Scholander's solo approach led listeners back to the composer's intended presentation. It is indeed no exaggeration to state that Scholander set the standard for a new movement in European folk music. "We should not forget—Stockholmers forget easily—that Sven Scholander was the first, who with the lute, with song and declamatory performances gave the impulse for a modern troubadour style. His famous style of performing has gained many imitators, but Scholander still stands as the initiator in this area — admitted as such nearly everywhere in Europe."[30]

Richard Dyer-Bennet's road to Stockholm and Scholander began in Leicester, England, where he was born October 6, 1913, his parents' first child. One of the oldest cities in England, Leicester is the largest in the East Midlands and had a population of 227,200 in the census of 1911. Dyer-Bennet's father, Richard Stewart Dyer-Bennet (1886–1986), was trained at Woolwich to become an army officer. He rose to the rank of major and during World War I became brevet colonel. Originally the family name was simply "Dyer." Indeed, throughout Dyer-Bennet's singing career, the press delighted in noting that he was listed in *Burke's Peerage* as a cousin of Sir John Ludovick Swinnerton Dyer. Dyer-Bennet himself rarely referred to this fact. Richard Sr.'s father, Frederick Stewart Hotham Dyer, added "Bennet" as an additional surname at the request of a Mr. Bennet who, being childless, made Frederick an heir to his estate upon that condition.

Dyer-Bennet's mother was born Miriam Wolcott Clapp in Illinois in 1890 and was raised in California. Richard Sr. and Miriam met in England while she was visiting school friends she had met in France. If not terribly happy, their union was prolific. The family grew to include four sons Richard, John (1915–2002), Fred (1917–1991), and Christopher (1920–1985), and one daughter (Miriam, born 1922). While both Richard Sr. and Miriam Sr. were fond of music, neither received any formal training. Still, music filled the house night and day. As a young child, Dyer-Bennet was given music boxes and recalled humming their tunes happily until he learned them by heart. His first exposure to professional singing came from listening to recordings on the family's Victrola. Dyer-Bennet later recalled that "the voices of Caruso, Scotti, De Gogorza, Chaliapin, McCormack, Galli-Curci, and Schipa were my constant companions, though I had then no thought of becoming a professional singer."[31]

While many singers may have colored Dyer-Bennet's musical foundation, the one most similar to and most influential on the young singer was certainly John McCormack (1884–1945). McCormack began his career singing ballads of his native Ireland before turning to the operatic stage. While successful as an opera singer, McCormack was never comfortable with the acting aspect of such performances and eventually returned to his first love. It is as a singer of songs like "I Hear You Calling Me" and "The Last Rose of Summer" that he is best remembered. Songs in the McCormack repertoire that Dyer-Bennet would eventually record include "Oft in the Stilly Night," "Molly Brannigan," "Plaisir d'Amour," "All Mein Gedanken," "The Garden Where the Praties Grow," "Down by the Sally Gardens," "She Moved Through the Fair," and "Kitty, My Love, Will You Marry Me?"

Speaking with Studs Terkel in 1955, Dyer-Bennet noted: "My repertoire is in many ways similar to John McCormack's. His programs went back and forth from straight art song to folk song, traditional songs. I think McCormack must have simply learned any songs that he felt he wanted to sing, that he longed to sing."[32] Other similarities between Dyer-Bennet and McCormack exist. Both were born in the United Kingdom but eventually settled in the United States and became citizens there (Dyer-Bennet on his twenty-first birthday). Both were natural singers who were not given voice lessons until they were young adults. Both were popular with audiences but sometimes snubbed by purists. Indeed, one critic went so far as to state that McCormack was "a singer of popular ballads and tunes who prostituted his greater accomplishments for wider and commercial application of lesser, sometimes worthless material."[33] If McCormack brought an opera singer's voice to folk ballads, Dyer-Bennet brought to them a lesser voice, but a new refinement.

An anecdote from young Richard's life gives us a glimpse of what the boy was like. In 1959, J. C. Reid wrote Dyer-Bennet from Canada, reminding him that they had met forty-two years previously.

Your mother, I believe, was a very kind-hearted lady who was devoting considerable time to a hospital for convalescent soldiers in the hamlet of Bakewell, and I
had preceded to Bakewell to visit a brother who was quite badly broken up with
shell-shock, etc and your mother was very kind to him, and I met her through my
brother and she invited us to her home. When I went to your door you opened
it and the following is my recollection of your welcome: "I presume you are Sgt.
Reid and in the absence of my father, Major Dyer-Bennet, who is in His Majesty's
Service on the Continent, I make you welcome." You ushered me to the library or
living room and tried to put me at ease and told me that your mother was delayed
and was upstairs dressing and perhaps I would like to see the garden to which you
took me. There you explained the different flowers and plants and asked me a few
questions about our flowers in Canada which I could not answer.[34]

Such poise and social grace would remain with Dyer-Bennet his entire life.

Major Dyer-Bennet retired in 1919 and moved the family to Canada. Canada
was a popular destination for Englishmen after the war, and, like many others,
Major Dyer-Bennet was granted a subsidy by the government to farm in its western provinces. The family settled in Chilliwack, British Columbia, and began to
raise chickens. Located on the Fraser River near the border of the United States,
the small community consisted then of only 1,700 residents. Years later Dyer-
Bennet recalled his arrival in Canada. "I remember that first very cold cold of
Canadian winter: the railroad trip across continent to the West Coast, the look
of the snow-covered Rockies (an unbelievable sight for so small a boy), and the
green shutter shades on the railroad sleeper."[35] What an adventure it must have
seemed for one so young.

It quickly became apparent, however, that Major Dyer-Bennet's rather romantic venture was doomed to failure. The marriage became strained as well. Changed
markedly by his experiences in the trenches, Major Dyer-Bennet became more
and more difficult to live with. Though a divorce was not finalized until 1929,
Richard Sr. left the family in 1923 to lend assistance to the victims of the horribly
destructive Japanese earthquake of the same year. The family saw little of him in
the following years, but Richard Jr. corresponded regularly with his father and
spent four days with him in England on his way to Sweden in 1935. Major Dyer-
Bennet traveled from Japan to Australia and would later reside in Oakland, Reno,
and Ojai before eventually returning to England in the early 1950s, where he died
in 1986. He remains a rather mysterious figure. In a 1938 letter to his mother,
Dyer-Bennet's description of his father lends some explanation. "All his life has
built up an essential conflict in his nature. He tries to find the key to things, sets
up a self-supposed course of reasonable action, and then follows it even when it
rides rough-shod over others' feelings and in opposition to his own emotional

make-up. . . . The result is always that he hurts someone and is himself hurt."[36] By all accounts Richard Sr. possessed considerable personal charm. According to his daughter Miriam, he was not a "here and now person," but rather one who "dreamed of larger schemes with little regard for the necessary details of their accomplishment."[37] Though he had no formal academic background, Richard Sr. was something of an amateur scholar. He was a distant father who ate separately from his children and expected them to be in bed by 6:30 p.m. One can only speculate on the effect the war left on him. Thousands of returning soldiers, of course, suffered from what today we call post-traumatic stress syndrome. Richard Sr. apparently also suffered bouts of depression. At any rate, it seems clear that after the war Major Dyer-Bennet was primed for a change. Canada must have seemed a kind of adventure, an opportunity for a fresh start.

On her own after her husband's departure, Miriam Sr. moved with her five young children in 1925 to Berkeley, California. Such circumstances would have been daunting to any single mother, but Miriam was a strong and independent-minded woman. Like many of her generation, Miriam believed that an old or-der—as represented by pre–World War I Europe—was passing, and a new world was dawning. It seems clear that each of her children benefited from her wisdom and guidance throughout their lives. Miriam's working life was varied. She taught German at Taft Union High School in Taft, California, from 1936 to 1954, and Social Science at Taft Junior College in the same city before returning to Union High to serve as a guidance counselor.

Though Miriam's father, Edward Bull Clapp, had retired as a classicist from the university, her parents still called Berkeley home. Berkeley is a beautiful city in northern California, perched on the eastern shore of the San Francisco Bay. Thanks to the presence of the esteemed University of California at Berkeley, the city enjoys a wonderful reputation as one of the most cultured in the United States. At the time of the Dyer-Bennet family's move, the city of 56,000 was still recovering from a major fire that had devastated the area two years previously.

It seems safe to say that it was Miriam's mother, May Wolcott Clapp, who pro-vided Dyer-Bennet with his musical genes. Before meeting her husband May had attended Wellesley, a liberal arts college for women in Massachusetts. She played the piano expertly and particularly loved Chopin and the *lieder* of Schubert and Schumann. In his notes to *Richard Dyer-Bennet 3*, Dyer-Bennet mentions that his grandmother taught him "Dinah and Villikens," and dozens of other songs reached his ears from the same source. In Berkeley young Dick also had his first formal introduction to music as a member of Wheeler Becket's children's chorus. Though not able to read music at the time, he was offered the role of Hansel in a 1928 production of Humperdinck's *Hansel and Gretel*. Undaunted, he learned and sang the part by heart. Writing in 1960, Dyer-Bennet remembered: "My voice ranged upwards to the high 'C,' and I do not remember knowing what a vocal problem was. If my part went high, I sang high; if I went low, I sang low; if Mr. Becket called for a crescendo or decrescendo, I obliged. All vowel sounds seemed equally easy on any pitch within my range. Such is the suppleness and spontaneity of childhood."[38] In the same document, Dyer-Bennet described his voice at seventeen as "still essentially that of a boy soprano, beginning to merge into a lyric tenor. It never 'broke' in the usual way, but gradually became more tenor and less soprano in quality and dropped down the scale in range."

Sports also played a large part in Dyer-Bennet's Berkeley years and helped him fit in with his classmates. "My British speech and short trousers drew unwanted attention, but a natural proclivity for games and sports of all kinds balanced the ledger."[39] He loved to play tennis and handball and excelled as a goalkeeper in soccer. Lanky but well coordinated, Dyer-Bennet eventually would grow to a height of 5' 11". In 1935, while playing for the San Francisco soccer league's Olympic Club, he was spotted by a professional scout who offered him a chance to play professionally with Scotland's famed Glasgow Rangers. Due to his enthusiasm for singing, and a broken nose suffered in a soccer match, Dyer-Bennet declined the invitation to become a professional athlete. He kept himself in top physical shape throughout his life, however. Besides soccer and tennis, he also enjoyed rock climbing.

In 1929 Miriam Dyer-Bennet pursued an opportunity to study philosophy and psychology at the University of Göttingen, in central Germany, halfway between Bonn and Berlin. Her time in Germany, she hoped, would prepare her for eventual further study at Berkeley. Again all five children accompanied her. According to Miriam Jr. it was the first time in a number of years that all the children had been together. Dick, John, and Fred had been attending the Deane School in Santa Barbara, three hundred miles distant from Berkeley. In 1928–29 Dick ranked sixth in a class of sixteen, earning highest marks in English and history while struggling with Latin. He was chosen the best all-around junior.

Like Berkeley, Göttingen was dominated by its prestigious university, founded in 1734. Indeed, during the coming world war, the Allies agreed not to bomb Göttingen and Heidelberg as long as the Nazis would similarly spare Oxford and Cambridge. In Germany, Dick and John studied at the local gymnasium (the equivalent of U.S. high school). John was engrossed in his study of the violin, and Dick particularly enjoyed school outings where singing was an integral part of the hikes. "Jan Hinnerk," later recorded on *Richard Dyer-Bennet 2*, was one of the songs he was introduced to at this time. It was in Germany, too, on his seventeenth birthday, that his mother presented Dick with his first guitar. He received some rudimentary instruction on the instrument from a local cello player and then set about learning a few basic chords on his own.

Even though it would not be until 1933 that Hitler seized power as chancellor, Germany's emerging political climate was not lost on Dick, then 16. On August 2, 1929, for example, a Nazi rally in Nuremburg attracted a crowd of 150,000, five times as many as had attended a similar function just two years previous. In 1930 Hitler assumed the position of supreme SA (*Sturm Abteilung*, or stormtroopers) leader, and his party won 18 percent of the vote in the Reichstag election. Mrs. Dyer-Bennet was also keenly aware of the growing danger. She had entered into a relationship with Adam von Trott zu Solz (1909–1944), a graduate student at Göttingen who was studying Hegel. Opposed to and frightened by the effect the Nazis were having on his homeland, Solz would leave for Great Britain in 1931, to study there as a Rhodes scholar. Miriam's friendship with Solz furthered her understanding of National Socialism and must have informed her decision to return her family to America in 1931. In an essay written about Solz, Miriam is described as being "a woman of great emotional and intellectual strength who would serve for several years as an emotional rock for Trott to lean on."[40] Solz returned to Germany once the war began and lost his life due to his involvement with Claus von Stauffenberg's unsuccessful assassination attempt on Hitler in 1944. That Miriam could play such an important role in a talented young man's life speaks to her tremendous vitality and strength of character.

Back in California, Dick faced a difficult transitional period. While his experiences in Germany had largely been happy, he felt a bit left behind and that he had missed in those two years a part of life with his friends that could never be recovered. Friends were beginning to date, considering which college to attend, and what their careers might be. Just as sports had helped him socially at Deane, now "singing and playing the guitar helped him fit into the new social milieu."[41] His time in Germany had also awoken his sense of politics. Unlike his more sheltered American peers, he had in some ways been forced to consider and confront a growing menace. That he was now de facto male head of the household must have added to his burdens.

In the fall of 1932, Dyer-Bennet enrolled at the University of California at Berkeley. He joined the Psi Upsilon fraternity and intended to major in public speaking. Dyer-Bennet also took courses in English, philosophy, history, geology, Greek, physical education, and music. His grades were average, with highest marks coming in English and public speaking, and lowest in geology.

It was outside the classroom, however, that Dyer-Bennet had his moment of destiny. During his sophomore year, he informally sang a number of songs at a friend's Christmas party. "The main entertainment of the evening," he would later recall, "was two Beethoven quartets, played by a group that included my brother John, and it was thought that a few songs between quartets might be a desirable change of pace. So there I was, with my half-dozen chords and my light voice, its range now limited by misuse to hardly more than an octave. I seem to have had some feeling for song, however, because after my performance a tall and imposing middle-aged woman introduced herself to me as a singer and teacher of singing and urged me to consider making a career of my hobby."[42]

This woman was Gertrude Wheeler Beckman. Born in 1879, she had studied voice with Ida Auer-Herbeck. Like Auer-Herbeck, Beckman stressed a natural approach to singing. As she states in her book *Tools for Speaking and Singing* (1955), "the one thing we can do to help is to get in line with Nature and cooperate with her by becoming children again."[43] Beckman was a true enthusiast, and it is easy to see why she was so inspirational to the young Dyer-Bennet. "If music means much to you," she wrote in her book's introduction, "and if you have an urge to sing—you can! No one else can touch the instrument within you. You and you only are the *real teacher*, and there must be no doubt whatever about your way of procedure."[44]

Dyer-Bennet was continually praised by critics for his diction, and this asset can be traced to his years of study with Beckman. In *Tools for Speaking and Singing*, she devotes individual chapters to the practice of good diction in English, German, Italian, and French. Pure vowels and purity of pitch were essential to good singing, she argued, but she also stressed less technical aspects of singing. "People who sing really well are those who have found the magic combination of *hearing* and *feeling, resonance plus singing on the breath*, which together constitute the heart's desire, vocally."[45] Ever apparent in his singing is Dyer-Bennet's emotional take on the song, a lesson learned well from both Scholander and Beckman.

Sven Scholander had met Beckman in the early 1900s and, eager to preserve the art of the minstrel he had resurrected, asked her to keep an eye out for anyone who showed an inclination and talent for this kind of singing. In Dyer-Bennet, Beckman believed she had found such a performer. His voice, though small, was full of emotion and promise, his gift for musical storytelling already apparent. At the conclusion of his performance that day in Berkeley, Beckman approached Dyer-Bennet and told him about Scholander. With the proper teaching, she suggested, he might have a career along the same lines. "Feeling that he may have found his calling, Dyer-Bennet switched his major from English to music, began to study voice with Beckman, and built a repertoire of songs."[46] His daily lessons began almost immediately, and the results were gratifying.

Under Beckman's guidance Dyer-Bennet "gradually began to overcome the habits that had robbed my voice of its natural range, resonance, and flexibility."[47] Dyer-Bennet describes his lessons with Beckman as "the most demanding and meticulously painstaking work"[48] he had ever done. At that time, he notes, his voice was "breathy and without sufficient resonance to be heard in even a small auditorium."[49] It was not with folk songs that Dyer-Bennet began his lessons. "We started with Carissimi, Caldara, Lotti, Gluck, Pergolesi, Paisiello, Monteverdi, Caccini, and the Scarlattis; next came Handel, Purcell, and Mozart; finally, Schubert, Schumann, Brahms, and Wolf."[50] Beckman was a teacher of good singing, not of folk singing. She believed that a classical base was necessary if Dyer-Bennet were to follow in Scholander's footsteps, and that three to four years of study were required before a singer was ready for a public career. Whatever Dyer-Bennet learned in his lessons, it was the idea of a career like Scholander's that beckoned him on. "I was enthralled by the story of Scholander's life,"[51] Dyer-Bennet later wrote.

And so we return to Stockholm in 1935. During the two months Dyer-Bennet remained there, he saw Scholander half a dozen times. Suitably impressed with his young visitor's talent and sheer enthusiasm, Scholander made the grand gesture of presenting Dyer-Bennet with his songbook. From this source Dyer-Bennet learned nearly one hundred songs, and many of these later became staples of his own repertoire. Equally important as the songs themselves, however, was the feeling for folk music Dyer-Bennet absorbed in Scholander's presence. Years later he told Nat Hentoff that his credo remained that of Scholander: "the value lies inherent in the song, not in the regional mannerisms or colloquialisms."[52] Before leaving Sweden, Dyer-Bennet purchased a "lute-guitar" made by Alfred Brock, instrument maker to the King of Sweden, for the equivalent of seventy-five dollars. He also purchased a great number of songbooks, noting at one point in a letter to his mother that he was looking forward to returning to the United States via England, where "I can feel as I eat that I am not eating away the cost of a book of folk songs I very much want."[53]

In another letter to his mother Dyer-Bennet claimed: "Yes, it is proving a worthwhile trip, like so many of the things we Dyer-Bennets do which look, at the outset, to be great gambles. I am learning priceless things from Sven. Rather I should say he is having a priceless effect on me, for I am not learning 'things' in the ordinary sense between pupil and teacher. My heavens what an artist that man must have been, and still is for that matter."[54] Meeting Scholander confirmed Dyer-Bennet's decision to become a professional musician. "It was hearing that man in the summer of 1935 that really set my course for me,"[55] he said many years later.

On his journey homeward the young singer spent time in England and Wales. There he sang for assembled union members, parishioners, and even grocery store customers. "In the town of Pontyprid, I heard singing that rose above the squalor and gray misery of those damned coal towns. I heard two great choirs and one old harper who played and sang in Welsh and English with great beauty and power in a tradition he claimed had come down in his family from the ancient Welsh kings."[56] It must have been gratifying to young Dyer-Bennet that his audiences there were composed mainly of working folk, English mill workers and Welsh coal miners. Scholander, after all, had told him that "the only way to learn the art of minstrelsy is to sing to the people, feel their response, and make them believe in what you are singing."[57] At this point Dyer-Bennet was still considering England as a possible base for his career. In a letter to his mother he writes: "I am in good health and spending my time very usefully preparing the ground for a professional start here inside two years time."[58]

Buoyed by his time spent with Scholander and the successful appearances in his homeland, Dyer-Bennet made the momentous decision to drop out of Berkeley one year shy of graduation. "Now I could read Goethe for myself, you know,"[59] he later joked. That he was prepared to take such a step speaks volumes for his growing confidence in himself and his art. Upon his return to California he continued to study with Beckman, now concentrating on seventeenth- and eighteenth-century Italian songs, as well as pieces by Handel, Mozart, Schubert, Schumann, Franz, Brahms, and Wolf. "All this was good for my voice and general musical awareness. It also filled my mind with ideas for accompaniments."[60]

During this period Dyer-Bennet fell in love with Elizabeth (Bebe) Hoar Pepper, the daughter of a Berkeley philosophy professor. A fellow musician, Elizabeth played second violin in John Dyer-Bennet's string quartet. In a letter to his mother, Dyer-Bennet notes: "Glad you and Bebe get along well. I suppose she will join a sorority. I think she is a strong enough individual to hold out against the 'sheepmaking' influences of the only ones I know anything of."[61] Though members of both families advised against it—reasoning both parties were too young—the couple wed in 1936. The marriage produced two daughters, Ellen and Eunice, but both Elizabeth and Dick soon realized that they had, in fact, acted rashly. The couple would eventually divorce in 1945. Leaving his two daughters was very difficult for Dyer-Bennet. He knew all too well the hurt that could result from a father's decision to leave his family. Dyer-Bennet found some consolation in the fact that he was able to establish a relationship with Ellen in later years.

As his lessons with Beckman continued, Dyer-Bennet made a tentative beginning to his career. At first he sang mostly in California, at locations such as the International House at the University of California, San Francisco Junior College, and the Theater of the Golden Bough in Carmel. Dyer-Bennet's talent was spotted during a 1938 performance at a local women's association by noted *San Francisco Chronicle* critic Alfred Frankenstein. So impressed was Frankenstein by the young singer that he encouraged him to move to New York and find management. Later that same year Dyer-Bennet followed Frankenstein's advice and made the first of several long journeys east via Greyhound bus.

In New York, Dyer-Bennet auditioned for concert managers, radio stations, and record companies, all without success. Those who heard him were impressed but unsure what to make of him and his material. Dyer-Bennet's venture must have struck them as risky, unprecedented as his particular art was in the United States. He was told by one prospective agent that he was "too special" for concert audiences. Such remarks must have stung the young singer, believing as he did that the minstrel is essentially a people's artist. That Dyer-Bennet's art was not easily labeled proved a formidable hurdle for years to come. "It was not easy to explain to concert managers just what I did,"[62] Dyer-Bennet later wrote. Some thought his material "too corny." One booking agent went so far as to ask, "Yes, we've heard of Dyer-Bennet, but what does he do? Is he Gene Autry in evening clothes?"[63] The impresario Charles Wagner "told him that he had a lovely voice but that no one would come to hear folk songs."[64]

Still, some valuable contacts were made in these early sojourns. Redfern Mason, music critic for the *Boston Transcript*, gave Dyer-Bennet some encouraging words and even suggested the singer adapt "I Once Loved a Boy" for his own purposes, as he thought it suited his tenor. (The song, retitled "I Once Loved a Girl," was recorded in 1962 for *Richard Dyer-Bennet 10*.) Mason thought highly of Dyer-Bennet's lute playing, diction, and his taste. Edward Prime-Stevenson, former music critic for *Harper's*, was equally impressed.

> I have no hesitation in putting Mr. Dyer-Bennet in the first rank. When one encounters a young man, the happy possessor of a singing-voice of as superior virile quality throughout; of as perfect vocal technique; of as fluent a diction in half-a-dozen languages and dialects; of a vividly dramatic temperament for interpreting whatever in a program demands the dramatic; of as delightfully communicative a sense of humour for diverting his listeners; and of a platform personality as engaging, it is a pleasure indeed to lend one's ears and to praise.[65]

Stevenson resisted the temptation many subsequent peers would resort to, namely to style Dyer-Bennet as one who harkens back to a previous age. Folk music, he writes, "is not an intellectualized form of folk-art, nor a return to anything, but a constant expression of an inherent feeling for song and story."[66]

In a letter home, Dyer-Bennet describes his April 1939 trip as "invaluable—new songs, new friends, new connections, lots of experience, groundwork for future trips."[67] Later that spring he elaborates. "A season of concerts certainly solidifies good points and shows up bad ones. My singing is going very well. There are lots of little things to learn, but basically it is good and sound, as my trip proved to me. I found that my voice remained in good shape, though in use for lengthy periods of time night after night either in concert, rehearsal, audition, or just practice."[68] In the same letter he mentions how much he enjoyed being in North Carolina, even indicating it as a possible future home. "The ballad singer tradition is still alive in that region, and quite a group of progressive artists and educators seem to be gathering in the neighborhood of Greensborough and Burlington. The forming of a small experimental folk theater there is being considered by this group, and it's quite possible that Bebe and I may find ourselves living there within a few years." Still, it was New York that was very much on his mind. "The most encouraging thing was the response from professional music and theater people in New York. They seemed to feel that there is a definite place there for what I am doing—in fact, a need for the simplicity of the folksong."

Despite such optimism, his paid performances were infrequent enough that it seemed doubtful he would ever realize his dream. Then, in 1941, in the most unlikely of places, Dyer-Bennet found an audience and his first taste of professional success. That summer he wrote his mother: "This has been a most successful trip and I believe marks the beginning of a financially successful career. I have had a two weeks' night club engagement and am re-engaged for September. I am under contract to a reliable concert management and expect results in that field next season. Other irons are in the fire and it is not unlikely that recordings, radio, and the legitimate theatre are in store for the future."[69] The young minstrel was on his way.

Chapter 2

New York

Have you seen but a white lily grow?

In the early 1940s, New York was the place to be if you sang folk songs. The city was at that time enjoying a sort of golden age. It was home to three professional baseball teams, over six hundred theaters, and dozens of newspapers. Network radio had its base here, and Tin Pan Alley was pumping out songs by the hundreds. Folk musicians from all over the country were congregating there, enjoying the camaraderie, swapping songs, and performing whenever and wherever they could.

Foremost among this group was Woodrow Wilson Guthrie (1912–1967), known to one and all simply as Woody. In 1940 the self-styled Dust Bowl refugee accepted friend Will Geer's invitation to join him in New York. Born in Oklahoma, Guthrie had lived at various times in Texas and California. Really, though, the road was his home. Guthrie was the consummate wanderer, always looking for something new and something to believe in. He filled notebook after notebook with drawings, stories, and songs. One of the first songs Guthrie wrote in New York was a direct response to Irving Berlin's "God Bless America," then saturating the airwaves. In the decades to come "This Land Is Your Land" would come to be the nation's best-known folk song, but at the time Guthrie simply filed it away with his other material. Dyer-Bennet was once recruited to school

Guthrie so that he could more effectively play the part of a balladeer for Earl Robinson's production of *The Lonesome Train*. Dyer-Bennet's wife, Mel, recalls the lessons: "When they sent Woody to our house, he said, 'Just don't make me sound like opera.'"[1] Though Guthrie eventually warmed to both Dick and Mel, the part was eventually given to the more conventional Burl Ives.

Guthrie's protégé was Pete Seeger, a banjo player seven years his junior but filled with the same kind of energy and enthusiasm for social change. Born in 1919, he met Guthrie in March 1940 at the Grapes of Wrath benefit concert for California migrant workers, at which Dyer-Bennet also performed. Seeger's father was well-known musicologist Charles Seeger (1886–1979), and Pete recognized the novelty of his desire to play "mere" folk music. He was immediately struck by Guthrie's genuineness and inherent feel for the music. What he did not know was that Guthrie was himself from a middle-class family. Seeger and Guthrie would hook up later on a cross-country road trip that would cement their bond.

The third major figure in American folk music during this era was Huddie Ledbetter, known as Lead Belly (1885–1949). If Guthrie and Seeger were middle-class men playing the music of the folk, Lead Belly was the real thing. By the time he arrived in New York with musicologist and folk song collector John Lomax (1867–1948), Ledbetter had already served prison time for murder. He was a field hand who had mastered the intricacies of the twelve-string guitar. As such, Guthrie and Seeger revered him. While his folk singing peers dressed casually to show their solidarity with the working class, Lead Belly always performed in a suit. The Weavers, a polished folksong group Seeger would later found with Lee Hays, Ronnie Gilbert, and Fred Hellerman, scored a massive hit with Lead Belly's signature song, "Goodnight Irene," just months after his death.

Other important figures in the New York folk singing community of the time were Millard Lampell (1919–1997), John Lomax's daughter Bess (born 1921), Arthur Stern, and Sis Cunningham (1909–2004), who together joined Seeger and Guthrie to form the Almanac Singers. The Almanacs were quite political and composed topical songs to convey their disapproval of the state of the country. Cisco Houston (1918–1961), a polished performer with a beautiful baritone voice, was Guthrie's best friend and frequent performing partner. Some chided Houston for his voice, feeling it was too smooth for folk music. Similar charges would be made against Dyer-Bennet. Aunt Molly Jackson (1880–1960) was a transplant from the coal fields of Kentucky who had been brought north by eager union organizers to acquaint the public with the plight of the miners. Josh White (1914–1969) sang the blues with a powerful voice, and boasted both a distinctive guitar style and a notable stage presence. Sonny Terry (1911–1986) played the harmonica as no one had before him; his usual performing partner was guitarist and singer Brownie McGee (1915–1996).

Finally, there was Burl Ives (1909–1995). Ives was a large man from Illinois with a trained voice who embraced folk music after becoming disillusioned with college. He rambled around the country, a la Guthrie, before eventually landing in New York. There he began his own radio show, *The Wayfaring Stranger*, named after one of his favorite ballads. Unlike Guthrie, Seeger, and Lead Belly, Ives was a polished singer whose voice found great appeal with contemporary audiences. In the forties he was already known by many as "America's Balladeer." In the fifties he found great success as an actor, eventually winning an Academy Award in 1958 as best supporting actor in the film *The Big Country*. The same year he appeared as "Big Daddy," a role written for him by Tennessee Williams for his play *Cat on a Hot Tin Roof*.

Ives and Dyer-Bennet worked together on occasion. "Gilbert Seldes was running an experimental TV station in the Grand Central Building for CBS," Dyer-Bennet recalled. "He heard Burl, then heard me, and engaged us both for three programs, me singing English and Scottish ballads, and Burl singing the American descendants of these ballads. A nice musical idea. I did the 'Golden Vanitee' [*sic*]; Burl, the 'Turkish Reverie.' We did the English and American versions of 'Barbara Allen' and 'Lord Randall,' then 'Go Tell Aunt Rhody' together. I loved that program."[2]

Dyer-Bennet and Seeger knew each other as well. Seeger was notorious for singing wherever and whenever he could, and Dyer-Bennet tried to warn him about the damage this could do to his voice. Much later in his career Seeger realized that Dyer-Bennet had been right and asked the minstrel to teach him some voice exercises. "I could use your advice about my voice," Seeger wrote to Dyer-Bennet. "After mistreating it for 50 or more years, finally it told me that I'd better learn to use it correctly or quit singing completely. I can hit a note high or low on pitch, still, but if I try and hold it for more than a half second, it wobbles so outrageously that I've had to stop singing a number of my favorites songs."[3] A lunch was arranged to discuss the topic, but at the last moment Seeger was asked to give a concert for some schoolchildren, and the opportunity was missed.

Dyer-Bennet liked and admired Guthrie, good-humoredly tolerating the Oklahoman's flirtation with his wife, Melvene. "I like your wife's eyeballs,"[4] Guthrie once said to him with a smile. The proud Guthrie even once asked Dick to teach him how to sing a high A in preparation for a stage show audition. Some tension existed between Dyer-Bennet and the native-born American singers, however. They never fully considered Dyer-Bennet "American enough" to perform some of their nation's songs. Dyer-Bennet and Lead Belly, however, formed a mutual admiration society and often sang together. It is hard to imagine two more different men, though they did both prefer to perform in suits. Dick always let Lead Belly pick the tunes they would perform, one of his favorites being the children's song, "Three Crows." Dyer-Bennet, in turn, would include Lead Belly's "Green Corn" on his children's album many years later. Elaine Lambert Lewis, host of a weekly folksong show called *Folk Songs of the Seven Million*, recalls the two men performing together at the Village Vanguard. "I'll never forget a version of the 'Midnight Special' with Leadbelly leading, and in lieu of a chain gang, Dick and his Swedish lute supplying the chorus."[5]

Unlike many of the other singers in the community, Lead Belly was interested in learning more about singing methods from Dick. Mel Dyer-Bennet recalled the fun when the two men got together: "It was sweet and funny and unbelievable, those two voices together. And they were so fond of each other."[6] Years later, when Lead Belly began suffering from Lou Gehrig's disease and was no longer able to perform, Dyer-Bennet took his place for one concert. "It was 1949, I got a call one day in Aspen from a manager in Omaha, who booked Leadbelly for a series of concerts in the Texas Panhandle. Leadbelly was too sick to go on. Would I go down to Lubbock, Texas, and substitute for him?"[7] One can imagine the surprise in store for the audience. "So I sang some of his songs for them, songs we used to do at the Vanguard. I told them about Leadbelly—his power, his dignity, his courtliness, how in spite of everything he wasn't consumed with black anger."[8]

While his peers performed at hootenannies and various benefit concerts, Dyer-Bennet's big break came from an unexpected source. In 1941 he was hired to perform at a nightclub called Le Ruban Bleu (the blue ribbon). "To most of 1940s America, nightlife in New York City was synonymous with grandeur, audience participation, and—most of all—money."[9] Nightclubs there greatly increased in number in the 1940s, reflecting a growing need for city dwellers to escape from the cares of modern life. Herbert Jacoby, a tall, cold, rather ominous Frenchman, had opened the club in 1937. He frequently booked European acts, and Dyer-Bennet's passion for minstrelsy in the European tradition must have caught his ear. Jacoby sensed, no doubt, that Dyer-Bennet's art would likely be appreciated by the kind of sophisticated, cosmopolitan audiences his club attracted.

Le Ruban Bleu seated 125 and was housed in the upper level of Theodore's, an Italian restaurant on East 56th Street. Audience members were usually quite close to the performers, and no sound system was utilized. Lotte Lenya, star of Kurt Weill's adaptation of Brecht's famed *Three Penny Opera*, had performed there in 1938, and frequent clientele included such luminaries as Cole Porter, Noel Coward, and Marlene Dietrich. Other performers of note included the comedienne Paula Laurence, harpist Caspar Reardon, and jazz singer Maxine Sullivan (1911–1987). Dyer-Bennet had never dreamed he would work in such a place, and the pay was a modest fifty dollars a week. Still, the work was regular and the exposure vital to his prospects.

Meanwhile, Burl Ives had been performing at another New York nightclub, the Village Vanguard, along with Lead Belly, Pearl Bailey, and dozens of others. When he was drafted in 1942, Ives recommended Dyer-Bennet as a successor, and Vanguard owner Max Gordon agreed without even asking for an audition. It was a match made in heaven. Gordon was everything Jacoby was not. Born in Lithuania, Gordon came to New York in 1908. He had grown up in Portland, Oregon, and graduated from nearby Reed College as a literature major. Gordon's parents wanted him to become a lawyer, but young Max lasted only six weeks at Columbia Law School. Though he had no experience as a businessman or nightclub owner, Gordon opened the Village Fair in 1932, which soon went bust. In 1933 Gordon found a basement location on Charles Street that he and a plumber friend renovated. In February 1934 he paid fifty dollars as the first month's lease and set up shop as the Village Vanguard. A mural portraying a demonstration in Union Square dominated the small room; among the first artists to appear there were the poets John Rose Gildea and Joseph Ferdinand Gould (1889–1957).

Gordon was beloved by the performers he hired. In his introduction to Gordon's book, *Live at the Village Vanguard*, Nat Hentoff notes: "the thing is Max knows how to listen, and how to watch while he's listening."[10] Jazz was his favorite form of music, but he was able to sense the importance of any type of music and "why it needs a forum, why it needs the Vanguard."[11] Perhaps most importantly, he gave the entertainers he hired absolute freedom to perform how they liked. As Dyer-Bennet noted to Gordon, "you never once told me what songs to sing."[12] As at Le Ruban Bleu, Dyer-Bennet used no microphone at the Vanguard. "I could sing the bloodiest or the gentlest songs at the Vanguard. You let me alone. That's what was so good about the place."[13] Dyer-Bennet soon gained a regular following at the Vanguard. During one of Dyer-Bennet's rare absences, Gordon recalls, patrons would ask him, "Is that skinny, blond, beak-nosed Englishman with the lute still singing at your place?"[14] Other patrons would wait for an intermission and then offer to sing songs for Dyer-Bennet they thought would be good for his act—in fact, that is how he came to know "The Garden Where the Praties Grow," later recorded on *Richard Dyer-Bennet 2*.

While at the Vanguard, the minstrel was able to repay, in part, his debt to Sven Scholander. One night Scholander's son, Sten, was in the audience, and Dyer-Bennet sang for him a selection of his father's songs. Dyer-Bennet's performance moved Scholander to tears. After the show Scholander promised that on his next trip abroad he would bring Dyer-Bennet LPs his father had recorded. Sadly, young Scholander was not able to make good on his promise. In 1946, he was one of several passengers killed in a fire on board a Swedish ship bound for the United States.

Writing in 1961, Dyer-Bennet had fond recollections of both the Vanguard and its owner. "There I became a true professional, singing three shows a night, six nights a week. Max—may he prosper ever—did not urge me to rely only on my lighter, comic repertoire, but allowed me to experiment with all the songs I knew. This freedom was most important, for it allowed me to develop a repertoire worthy of the concert stage."[15] Dyer-Bennet became Gordon's favorite singer and would later serve as best man at Gordon's wedding. During the years Dyer-Bennet was blacklisted, Gordon often had the minstrel return for short engagements. Gordon ran the club until his death in 1989, and his wife still manages the establishment.

Gordon provided Dyer-Bennet plenty of work. For the next three years Dyer-Bennet gave three shows a night, six nights a week at the Vanguard, a strenuous work load that eventually led to his being rushed to Bellevue Hospital, suffering from a hemorrhaging ulcer. Besides this regular gig, Dyer-Bennet was also performing frequently at various benefits. This meant a frantic schedule where he would "rush off between shows, sing two or three songs, and rush back to the club."[16] In his first year of work at the Vanguard, Dick made $85 a week, a nice increase from Jacoby's wages. This figure was raised to $150 a year later, and eventually grew to $350 by the time his regular gig at the club was over. In the hustle and bustle of the club, Dyer-Bennet sometimes had trouble being heard. One New Year's Eve he was introduced, took his place on stage, and waited for the din to die down. "I stood there waiting for quiet, one minute, two minutes, three minutes," he recalled. "So, I turned around and walked off. If they didn't want to hear me, the hell with 'em."[17] At the second show that night Gordon took the stage with his singer and "emitted a 'shh' that shook the house. All service stopped, the waiters stood at attention. People stopped talking, glared down people who didn't, and before I knew it a dead silence spread over the place. I opened with the quietest song, Ben Jonson's 'Where the White Lily Grows,' at midnight on a New Year's Eve."[18] Another memorable night at the club occurred when some drunken sailors started picking a fight. Luckily, muscular Burl Ives, just mustered out of the Army, was present to lend a hand. "When that sailor punched me on the nose," Dyer-Bennet recalled, "I let go a backhand with my open palm across his Adam's apple. I used to play a pretty good game of tennis, you know."[19]

Besides putting bread on the table and allowing him to hone his craft, Dyer-Bennet's years at the Village Vanguard laid the groundwork for his concert career. Two regulars at the club were Mike Quill (1905–1966) and Ted Zittel. Quill was involved in the Transport Workers Union, and Zittel was his publicity man. Dyer-Bennet always included a few extra Irish ballads when he knew Quill was in the audience. Quill delighted in telling friends that he had been a dispatch rider for the Irish Republican Army. Though he had no experience in the concert business, Zittel arranged for Dyer-Bennet to sing for the transport union at Madison Square Garden, and following that success arranged for the minstrel to sing at one of New York's most prestigious concert venues, Town Hall.

Originally designed as a meeting space for suffragists (The League for Political Education), the building that became known as Town Hall, located on West 43rd Street between 6th Avenue and Broadway, opened in 1921. The architects designed the facility with democratic principles in mind. Unlike other performance halls of its kind, there were no box seats in Town Hall, and no seats with obstructed views. The acoustics were superb, and for so large a facility (more than fourteen hundred seats at the time) it offered an air of intimacy. Town Hall also became known as a forum for a free exchange of ideas. *America's Town Meetings of the Air*, a radio series on NBC, debuted there in 1935; its format consisted of four speakers discussing important issues of the day. Lecture series, boasting names such as Carl Sandburg and Orson Welles, also found a home there. True to its original mission, Town Hall was the first venue to present in concert African American opera singer Marian Anderson, hitherto a frequent victim of discrimination. Other artists of Dyer-Bennet's era who performed at the venue include Dizzy Gillespie, Charlie Parker, Aaron Copland, Billie Holiday, Andres Segovia, and Paul Robeson.

Dyer-Bennet's debut at Town Hall came on March 4, 1944. So great was the demand for tickets that police on horseback restrained the overflow crowd as it waited. Only two weeks earlier Dyer-Bennet had decided to switch from steel to gut guitar strings. "He preferred to take the chance," Mel recalled years later. "The feeling of taking a correct step musically meant more to him than the risk."[20] Dyer-Bennet chose the spirited Irish folk song "Come All Ye" as his first number in a set dominated by songs from the British Isles. It was followed by "The Spanish Lady," "The Golden Vanity," "Greensleeves," "Blow the Candles Out," "The Wee Cooper of Fife," and "Lord Rendal." Following an intermission, the young singer opened the second part of the program with the a cappella "Agincourt Song." Years later Mel Dyer-Bennet stated that he chose the unaccompanied "Agincourt Song" to prove that he could maintain its key throughout. "He wanted to prove it; and he did. He plucked a string before he started the song, sang it beautifully, with the guitar resting on the bench. And at the end of the song, he played the same note again to show he was in the same key. It was very brassy and as he did it he grinned."[21] "Have You Seen But a Whyte Lillie Grown," "Binnorie," "When Cockleshells Turn Silver Bells," "The Keeper," "Mo Mary," and "The Three Ravens" followed. The final portion of the program featured "Drill, Ye Tarriers, Drill," "The Foggy Dew," "Lolly-To-Dum-Day," "Three Fishers," "The Soldier and the Lady," "The Devil and the Farmer's Wife," and "The Sally Gardens," a Yeats

poem set to a traditional tune. Dyer-Bennet closed the show with that most famous of English ballads, "Barbara Allen." A number of encores were played to
satisfy the enthusiastic crowd.

In his Monday morning review of the show, Louis Biancolli of the *New York
World Telegram* wrote that Town Hall was "turned into a snug little campfire
setting by Richard Dyer-Bennet's cozy style of minstrelsy."[22] He continued in a
similarly enthusiastic manner: "In his scheme each song is treated like something
alive, long thought dead, but merely waiting for the art of fanning it back into
life." Dyer-Bennet must have been gratified to read that the reviewer noted that
the singer "never was in the way of his art. True minstrel, he always gave the song
right of way." A number of reviews praised Dyer-Bennet's diction, the sharp con-
trasts lent by his skillful use of pianissimo and fortissimo, and his skillful guitar
accompaniment. The *New York Times* reviewer went so far as to state that Dyer-
Bennet's guitar playing was "an art in itself."[23]

By the time of his Town Hall debut Dyer-Bennet had abandoned the lute in
favor of the guitar, because he found it gave him greater flexibility in accompaniment. He had begun by experimenting with steel-string guitars, but only embraced the instrument for good once he had heard a classic Spanish guitar. In 1943
he had begun studying with the famed Cuban-American guitarist José Rey de la
Torre (1917–1994). De la Torre had, in turn, been taught by the famed Miguel
Llobet (1878–1938), sometimes credited with teaching Segovia. Since de la Torre
made few recordings in his lifetime, and those on a small label that soon failed
(Philharmonia), he is not well-known today. If his name has faded, however, his
reputation as one of the finest proponents of his art has not. Contemporary reis-
sues on CD of his recordings of works by Isaac Albeniz (1860–1909) and Enrique
Granados (1867–1916) have sparked new interest in his work and generated enthusiastic reviews.

Dyer-Bennet acknowledged the debt he owed the guitarist. "His experience
with singers who 'just wanted to learn a couple chords' had made him wary, but,
after hearing me sing, he decided that my musical intentions were honorable, and
accepted me. He drilled me on hand positions, scales, arpeggios, and, in short,
started me off as though I hoped to become a virtuoso guitarist. Though I will
never gain such proficiency, it is thanks to him that I have become able to play the
accompaniments to the great lute songs of John Dowland and Thomas Campion
and the *vihuela* parts in Luis Milan's songs."[24] Dyer-Bennet continued to play the
lute on occasion, but the guitar became his instrument of choice.

So successful was his Town Hall debut that Dyer-Bennet was booked to play
there again in April and May. The following year brought three further appearances by the increasingly popular singer. In his review of the April 21, 1945, concert, the *New York Herald-Tribune* critic noted that Dyer-Bennet "has become

much smoother and more professional in the last year, and his diction, if possible, is even clearer than it was before."[25] That same year, critic Paul Bowles suggested one possible explanation for Dyer-Bennet's remarkable popularity. "One of the reasons for the success of this sort of music, aside from Mr. Dyer-Bennet's very evident ability to sing it, is the fact that the idiom retains a high degree of potential personality-projection in its performance. And the words of ballads such as these can still give the illusion that they are somehow directly identified with the individual who sings them, an element which has been largely lost in the development of the art song."[26] Another critic noted that "he never dresses up an old song in mawkish new clothes."[27]

Dyer-Bennet's Town Hall performances quickly became highly anticipated annual (or semi-annual) events that usually resulted in sellout crowds. These appearances continued with few interruptions until 1962. A 1954 concert celebrated the tenth anniversary of his Town Hall debut, and the program consisted entirely of requests from the audience.

While critical reaction to these concerts was generally very positive, a few dissenting opinions were voiced. One reviewer found Dyer-Bennet's approach too refined. "Mr. Dyer-Bennet's genteel artistry purifies and dignifies all it touches, sometimes past a desirable point. His art lacks guts; all soul and no bawdry."[28] Writing for the *Herald-Tribune* in 1948, well-known critic Virgil Thomson mixed praise with criticism.

> His work is expert, dignified, and thoroughly high class. It is almost too high class, indeed, for comfort. Whether folk music is at its best in so carefully performed a presentation remains always a worrisome question after hearing him. Certainly he gives us of the grandest in folk literature, and that is a pleasure. Certainly he offers it with full respect for its high musical and poetic value, and that also is a pleasure. He does not overdress it harmonically, and he does not style it for tears or cuteness. What he does do that your reporter finds a little oppressive is to manipulate with a showman's master hand that whole gamut of audience responses that are more a result of timed stimulation than of direct, of [sic] straightforward communication. His work and repertory are very beautiful, but one resents receiving each piece like a well-placed blow. After about twenty of these, one is punch-drunk, feels like standing up and waving the artist off with a handkerchief in old Chataqua style.[29]

Thomson also raises the issue of the singer's voice. "Actually Dyer-Bennett [sic] is not quite a satisfactory singer. His is a small voice, a tenorino of limited range; and he doesn't really sing. He only croons. The crooning technique is effective for patter songs and for airs of restricted range but thoroughly inadequate for soaring melody, as in 'Annie Laurie,' 'Drink to Me Only' or the 'Londonderry Air.'"[30]

A look at the program for the 1948 concert Thomson reviewed illustrates how Dyer-Bennet liked to group songs in his performances. Interestingly, he opened that night with "The Nightingale," a song from England that he never record-ed. Four Scottish songs follow: "The Piper of Dundee," "Annie Laurie," "Corn Rigs Are Bonnie," and "The Laird of Cockpen." A number of comic songs—for which he was becoming very well known--are then included: "The Wife Wrapt in Sheepskin," "Phyllis and Her Mother," "Jan Hinnerk," "The Beloved Kitten," "Woman, Go Home!" and "The Ghost of Basel." Seven songs of diverse origins complete the list: "Moonrise," "Drink to Me Only with Thine Eyes," "Gently, Johnny, My Jingalo," "My Gentle Harp" (identified by Thomson by its alternate title "Londonderry Air"), "As I Was Going to Ballynure," "John Riley," "The Roving Gambler," and the moving "Pull Off Your Old Coat." Dyer-Bennet gave much thought to the arrangements of his programs, both in concert, and, when he had control over such matters, in the studio. While usually grouped by country of origin, songs were also divided by tempo. Some critics noted a lagging of in-terest during the slower numbers from members of his audience, many of whom were in their twenties and thirties.

The brilliant acoustics of Town Hall were perfectly suited to Dyer-Bennet's light tenor and allowed him, as always, to work without a microphone. He fre-quently argued against the use of a microphone, believing that becoming reliant on it could eventually create bad habits and damage the voice. This is not to say that Dyer-Bennet did not realize the shortcomings of his voice. He called his voice "rather sweet but limited"[31] and repeatedly insisted that he succeeded in spite of his voice rather than because of it. Responding to attacks that his style of singing was too rarified for his material, he wrote, "No song is ever harmed by being articulated clearly, on pitch, with sufficient control of phrase and dynamics to make the most of the poetry and melody."[32]

Conrad Osborne wrote an essay on Dyer-Bennet's voice to accompany the 1997 Smithsonian-Folkways release of *Richard Dyer-Bennet 1*. There he states that Dyer-Bennet "generally sang in what amounted to high baritone keys— roughly from C below middle C to the G above it, about an octave and a fifth— where he could keep the words light and undistorted and the tone free from stress or stiffening."[33] Dyer-Bennet was also famous for his exactness of pitch, as demonstrated by the unaccompanied "Agincourt Song." But perhaps the most striking quality of Dyer-Bennet's singing was his ability to dramatize the actions of a song through changes in tempo and volume and thus hold the audience's interest. Writing for the *New York Post* in 1946, Harriet Johnson stated: "One of the extraordinary things to me about this 20th century minstrel was the un-divided attention which every person gave him. As he sang one ballad after the other and accompanied himself on the guitar, not a sound, not a whisper, could be heard in the auditorium. I've never seen such concentration anywhere before."[34] Scholander, of course, had displayed similar dramatic qualities, and the lesson was not lost on his protégé.

Nowhere is this flair for drama more evident than in Dyer-Bennet's interpretation of "The Lonesome Valley," a song describing man's transition from life to death. Soft but insistent guitar chords begin the performance and prepare the listener for something of ominous portent. Dyer-Bennet begins with the song's chorus, lingering on the word "cross" to signify the length and difficulty of the traveler's passage. He appropriately substitutes the informal "ya" for "you" at the end of the third line. During the transition between the chorus and the first verse, the guitar increases in both volume and tension, heightening the listener's sense of anticipation. Then, his voice suddenly full of immense power, Dyer-Bennet begins the first verse, stretching "river" taut before releasing it. The soft chorus/forceful verse pattern is maintained throughout the song, the listener's ear especially impressed with the contrast between the gentle "cross" and the ringing "river" (and succeeding "John") of the verse. The diminishing "soul" at the end of the first verse is a lovely example of Dyer-Bennet's use of pianissimo, signifying, perhaps, the ebbing of life and leading gently into the chorus. In the third line of the second verse, the word "natural" stretches Dyer-Bennet's voice to the limits of its range and power, as it suddenly jumps an octave. The startling effort lends true force to the life/death theme of the song, as if to say: Each man must face his death alone, a lonesome end to his journey. Such melancholy pieces provided the perfect setting for Dyer-Bennet's brand of dramatic singing. He believed that the eternal themes of nature, war, and death stir the human soul unlike anything else.

Dyer-Bennet's success at his three 1944 Town Hall concerts was sufficient to allow Zittel to book him at Carnegie Hall for November 18th of that year. He thus became one of the first solo performers of folk music to perform at this most prestigious of venues. For his opening number that night he chose "How Hell Busted Loose Up at Blue Mountain Lake," an American lumberjack song. This somewhat odd choice was made perhaps to establish the English-born minstrel as an American folk singer. It was followed by "Have You Seen But a Whyte Lillie Grow," a very quiet song with lyrics by Ben Jonson. "I knew that in this vast hall," Dyer-Bennet later recalled, "and with no amplification at all I had to get the audience used—right from the very beginning—of their having to sit absolutely silently without a single rustle of a program or sneeze or cough or footscrape. And if I couldn't get them to do that, I was lost . . . Then by contrast after that when I sang a good full bodied song my voice probably sounded quite large."[35] Next came the humorous "Kerry Recruit," followed by "Black Is the Color of My True Love's Hair," "Blow the Candles Out," and the pastoral "Two Maidens Went Milking One Day."

The second part of the program contained mostly American songs. "Lolly-Too-Dum-Day" was followed by "The Black Jack Gypsy," "The Swapping Song," "Fain Would I Wed a Fair Young Maid," "Bow Down," "The Foggy Dew," and the English navy song, "Willie Taylor." The final third of the program was equally divided between American and English songs. "Jennie Jenkins" kicked things off, followed by "Barbara Allen," "Drill, Ye Tarriers, Drill," "The Bailiff's Daughter of Islington," "The Charleston Merchant," "The Coasts of High Barbary," and John Jacob Niles's "Venezuela." For his finale, Dyer-Bennet chose one of America's most famous folk songs, "John Henry."

This was another interesting and daring selection. Dyer-Bennet was sometimes ridiculed for singing a song so linked to African American culture. He responded to such remarks by stating that "this is a universal, classic tragedy of one man against impossible odds. Secondly, the man singing the song is the narrator. He is not John Henry. I, therefore, do not have to affect the speech of a Negro railroad worker to communicate the story."[36] A soft but rhythmically insistent guitar introduction immediately establishes a railroad feel to the performance, and the accompaniment to the singing later rings like the folk hero's hammer. At the conclusion of the fourth verse, as John Henry's wife heads to the mountain to hear her husband's hammer ring, Dyer-Bennet inserts a guitar solo, halting his rolling accompaniment to accent the sound of hammer on iron and to set off the drama that will unfold in the following verses. Another, briefer solo follows John Henry's death in the seventh verse. The guitar this time sounds a more plaintive note. Dyer-Bennet sings the beginning of the final verse very quietly, further distinguishing the fortissimo conclusion to the song where both "steel" and "driving" are stretched to near breaking point.

Reviewing the Carnegie Hall concert for the *New York Times*, Walter Winchell, then the leading reviewer of Broadway productions, praised Dyer-Bennet's contemporary approach to his traditional material and highlighted the singer's approach to his less serious material. "Mr. Dyer-Bennet's art is essentially that of a ballad singer, a combination of music, declamation, and acting, yet done in his own distinctive style. The racy, tangy, pawky, and occasionally grisly humor would have delighted the Elizabethans, as it did last night's audience."[37] Another critic noted the progress Dyer-Bennet had made.

This art has developed notably since the singer gave his first recital in Town Hall. For one thing, the voice last night was much stronger, the tone was finer and the musical intent more obvious and effective. For another thing, the facial expression and dramatic [*sic*] were better done than heretofore, while the diction and the phrasing continued to be exceptional. All of these things made it possible for the singer to project his art even more effectively than he had done before.

Furthermore, Mr. Dyer-Bennet has become an excellent guitarist and this puts a finishing touch to the whole entertainment as a fine thing."[38]

Also in attendance that night in Carnegie Hall—as a guest of composer Sam Barlow—was Sol Hurok (1888–1974), the famous impresario. From humble immigrant roots, Hurok (born Solomon Izrailevich Gurkov) had quickly risen to the top of his profession. As the literature from his agency stated: "As a lad of sixteen Hurok arrived in this country with three dollars in his jeans, and not long after was spending his hard-earned pennies for standing-room at the opera. His love of music and theater, coupled with driving enterprise, soon led him to manage the entertainment programs for a community center in Brooklyn."[39] Hurok loved ballet even more than music and was responsible for bringing talents like Anna Pavlova (1881–1931) and Isadora Duncan (1877–1927) to American audiences.

One of the keys to Hurok's success was his ability to cater "to the whims of temperamental and talented performers and offering them up with unmatched gusto and panache to an impressionable American audience whose income and desire for high-class entertainment were shooting up as fast as the skyscrapers in Manhattan."[40] There was also a good deal of P. T. Barnum in Hurok. To say that he knew his way around advertising and public relations understates the case considerably. Such was his success that to be "the Hurok" came into the language to mean one who was the best at what he did. This was a man larger than life. "Almost never did he forget that he wasn't just Sol Hurok; he was an institution, he was 'S. Hurok presents.'"[41] To Hurok his clients were his children, and he looked after their wellbeing with fierce loyalty.

During an intermission at Dyer-Bennet's Carnegie Hall debut, Hurok asked to speak with the singer. Years later Dyer-Bennet described their meeting. "After the first group of songs, Hurok came backstage and offered to undertake my management. He said 'I've heard this sort of thing once before; in Riga, in about 1920, I heard a Swedish singer . . .' 'Sven Scholander?' I interrupted. 'Yes!' said Hurok, 'but you are too young to have heard him!' Then I told Hurok about my meeting with old Scholander in 1935. Two days later I signed a contract with Hurok, and my professional future was in the best of hands."[42] Far from being intimidated by Hurok, Dyer-Bennet declined the impresario's request to repeat "White Lily," stating that he never repeated a song during a concert. "You know your business!" Hurok is said to have replied.

If his professional future looked bright, Dyer-Bennet's personal life also held great prospects. Thanks to Melvene (Mel) Ipcar, Dyer-Bennet's heart was also now in safe hands. Born in New York City in 1916, Mel's life was changed forever when she saw the German dancer Mary Wigman perform. Wigman (1886–1973) is often credited as the founder of expressionist dance, and her performance left

Mel deeply moved and suddenly aware of new meanings in human motion and rhythms. Her path in life now clear, Mel decided to forego college in order to study dance with one of Wigman's students, Hanya Holm (1893–1992). When she met Dyer-Bennet in 1942 after one of his many Village Vanguard performances, Mel immediately fell deeply in love. An artist herself, Mel was immediately struck by Dyer-Bennet's posture, "the way he held his lute."[43] She also noticed immediately Dyer-Bennet's ability to connect with an audience. "I saw an expression on his face that really meant something to me. His intention about reaching those people, drunk or not. That really fascinated me. His whole bearing was so new to me as a performer."[44] At the time, however, Dyer-Bennet was married, the father of two daughters. Nor was Mel free, then engaged to a successful young psychiatrist. Difficult months followed before each party was emotionally free to embark on the new relationship. The couple eventually wed on May 11, 1945. A daughter, Bonnie, was born in 1943; a second child, Brooke, in 1946.

Mel was a talented dancer, working in the early 1940s with Hanya Holm's troupe. The German-born Holm later became a successful choreographer, working on shows such as *My Fair Lady* and *Camelot*. After an injury forced her to stop performing as a dancer, Mel began a second career as a therapist in what she termed "psychomotility." This approach emphasized the unity between mind and body; she used it to help treat a number of disorders, including schizophrenia. In the late 1940s Mel was offered a job teaching dance at the famous Austen Riggs Center in Stockbridge, Massachusetts, a psychiatric treatment facility. While there, however, she felt that some of her duties were inappropriate. Mel soon realized that attempting to teach dance to psychiatric patients was not a good use of her energy or theirs, and she began to develop her own approach to integrating motion and intention. One of the doctors whose work she admired, however, was the famous psychoanalyst Erik Erikson (1902–1994) who served as her supervisor and mentor. Erikson encouraged Mel to develop her own approach to treating postural and psychological problems. She would continue this work throughout her life.

Besides providing vital emotional support, Mel played a major role in Dyer-Bennet's artistic career. She was his sounding board for new ideas and possibilities, and Dyer-Bennet trusted her opinion above all others in matters of business, music, and life.

Dyer-Bennet had become an American citizen in 1934, but a chronic stomach ulcer kept him out of the armed forces during World War II. Instead Dyer-Bennet served his adopted country by working for the Office of War Information, or OWI. Formed in 1942, this organization was charged "with the responsibility of all propaganda, both foreign and domestic."[45] It consisted of fourteen branches and worked in all available media, though radio was perhaps its preferred vehicle.

The OWI was convinced that the home front was not doing all it could to help the United States win the war. In large part this attitude was the result of surveys the office conducted, asking citizens if they felt people were taking the war seriously enough. In July 1942 sixty-two percent of those surveyed had answered "no!" Since the power of song was well documented, the OWI held out great hope that another "Over There" might be written to improve domestic morale and provide a rallying cry for Americans at home and abroad. Though the notion seems quaint today, to that point every major war in American history, from "Yankee Doodle" onward, had some song associated with it. The trick, the office felt, was to find a radio-friendly song. Pete Seeger's Almanac Singers had earlier written dozens of songs about the war, but CBS had dropped them for their tendency to espouse pro-labor sentiments.

Dyer-Bennet specialized in writing OWI songs that illustrated the latest news from the war. Since many of these topical efforts were written in taxi rides to the studio, they were not all of high quality. Several recorded in 1943 still exist on tape. These include "Rommel the Fox," "Who Enters Russia by the Sword," "The Hood and the Bismarck," "MacArthur the Rattler," "Some People Think Hitler Is Dead," "The World's Too Small for Fascists," "Finland Rise Again," and "Passive Resistance," a humorous song about a farmer in Norway for which the singer later received a citation from that country's government.

> *This is the story of passive resistance*
> *Of a man who refused to give Nazis assistance.*
> *A farmer there lived in occupied Norway*
> *Who found a grim warning tacked onto his doorway.*
> *It read: "You have failed to come up to your quota*
> *Next week if you fail by a single iota*
> *Your farm will be taken and you will be killed.*
> *This is the law and it must be fulfilled."*

> *The farmer replied: "Sirs, the undersigned begs*
> *To inform you concerning my quota of eggs*
> *I posted the warning right where the hens live*
> *But the stubborn old bipeds still failed to give*
> *So I wrung all their necks, the foul saboteurs*
> *Delighted to serve you, sincerely yrs."*

Though the first to recognize such songs' ephemeral nature, Dyer-Bennet enjoyed the work, reflecting that such topical songs had traditionally been associated with minstrelsy.

Telegrams like the one below were often the source of Dyer-Bennet's compositions.

Please get this to Richard Dyer-Bennet, care Al Sherman, Hotel Cairo, Washington D.C. Tell Bennet for additional information to contact Mrs. Menefee, Foreign Broadcasting Information Service, Social Security Bulxxx [sic] Building. He is to tell Mrs. Menefee he was referred by Elizabeth Donney of the O.W.I. Also tell Bennet I will expect him Thursday in Studio 3B, NBC, at 4:30. Herewith follows the material. Hideki Tojo—His utterances and absurdities. Address to 84th Japanese Diet, Jan. 21, '44. "Viewing the war situation in greater East Asia, the brilliant success with which our forces are achieving in the Solomons area, in the Gilberts area, and in China are indeed without parallel in military history, and the only ones who do not know this are the peoples of the U.S. and Britain, whose eyes have been blinded by their leaders."

From this message came the following untitled song.

Premier Hideki Tojo is a twister of the truth
The result of eating corkscrews in his adolescent youth.
The spirals of his larynx give his words an eerie twist
And you have to unwind every word to understand the gist.

"Our aims are very laudable" said Tojo to the Diet
"Out of Asiatic chaos we're creating peace and quiet.
Our hearts are full of kindness for every one of you
We know you won't resist us; we'll kill you if you do.

"We have military genius and in China we can show it
But the Chinese are the only ones who do not seem to know it.
We have conquered the Pacific and there's only one thing lacking:
The British and Americans just won't accept the fact."

Thus speaks the Premier Tojo to the people of Japan
And the price they pay is heavy for believing to the man
So take caution from this tale if you wish to speak the truth
And refrain from eating corkscrews in your adolescent youth.

Between his work for the OWI and performances at the Village Vanguard and various war-related benefits, Dyer-Bennet's health began to suffer. In 1945 he was forced to spend two months in a hospital recuperating. Once fit again,

Dyer-Bennet traveled to the Philippines as part of the USO to sing to hospital-ized soldiers for $175 a week. V-J Day found him in Manila. The long war finally over, Dyer-Bennet was free to return to New York and begin his first national tour for Hurok. The so-called twentieth-century minstrel was now set to travel the nation, looking for his own court among the urban and campus audiences of postwar America.

CHAPTER 3

EARLY RECORDINGS

There was a wealthy merchant, in Charleston he did dwell . . .

Between 1941 and the founding of his own label in 1955, Dyer-Bennet recorded albums for Stinson, Vox, Decca, Continental, Mercury, Remington, and
Concert Hall. They vary greatly in recording quality, selection of material, and
performance. The fact that Dyer-Bennet later rerecorded nearly all of the songs
included on these albums indicates that he was not entirely satisfied with either his performances or their production. In a sense, these early recordings
serve as a sort of dress rehearsal for the self-produced albums and, unlike them,
probably will never be rereleased. Many of these early recording sessions were
rushed affairs. Sometimes Dyer-Bennet did not have final say as to which songs
would be recorded, or how they might be grouped on the album's final release.
Remuneration was also a concern. According to Mel Dyer-Bennet, Decca was
one of the only companies that gave her husband a fair share of the albums'
royalties.

The minstrel first appeared on record in 1941, thanks to Harvard professor
Dr. Frederick Packard who underwrote all recording and production costs for
an album titled *Ballads and Folksongs Sung by Richard Dyer-Bennet.* Privately issued on three 12" 78s, the album is a collector's item. Six of its selections ("Come

All Ye," "Cockle Shells," "Early One Morning," "Lord Rendal," "Brigg Fair," and "The Leprechaun") would eventually be rerecorded for inclusion on commercial releases. Its other three songs ("The Charleston Merchant," "The Golden Vanity," and "The Lincolnshire Poacher") were recorded later that same year for Dyer-Bennet's first commercial release, *Richard Dyer-Bennet: Lute Singer. Lute Singer* contains three 12" 78s, four sides with single songs, and two with paired selections. Dyer-Bennet is shown on the cover in full concert dress playing a lute, along with the subtitle *Ballads and Folk Songs*. A short booklet is included that, in addition to the songs' lyrics, contains a brief biographical sketch of the performer. The eight recordings from *Lute Singer* were released as side B of *Richard Dyer-Bennet and Tom Glazer Sings* [*sic*] *Olden Ballads*, and new versions would later be recorded by Dyer-Bennet on various albums for his own label.

As a debut recording, *Lute Singer* is quite admirable, flawed only by existing recording technology and slight vocal affectations. Appropriately enough, Dyer-Bennet begins with "The Golden Vanity," a song Scholander had sung to him on his visit to Sweden six years earlier. Dyer-Bennet is obviously at ease with the song, and it has a slightly more natural feel than some of the album's other recordings. It features a lovely and moving use of pianissimo for the word "lowland" in the chorus. Two humorous songs from the English Midlands, "The Lincolnshire Poacher" and "The Derby Ram," make up the other side of the record. The former sounds a bit brusque compared to the version Dyer-Bennet would record more than twenty years later for his own label. This early performance is fully twenty seconds shorter than the version on *Richard Dyer-Bennet 10*. One suspects its tempo might have been quickened in order to fit the two songs on a single side of the 78 r.p.m. recording. The final verse is Dyer-Bennet's own. "The Derby Ram" displays admirable diction in its rather crowded verses, which border on recitative. The singer takes great delight in his ability to sustain and vary the word "I" during the chorus following the third verse. "The Swagman," better known as "Waltzing Matilda," features a lovely rendition of the final chorus. On his notes to *Richard Dyer-Bennet 4*, for which the song was rerecorded, the minstrel writes that the idea to sing the chorus in waltz time was his own.

The remaining four songs on *Lute Singer* are all either set at sea or have a nautical theme. "The House Carpenter," a haunting tale from the American tradition, features varied vocal tones to convey the exchanges between the woman who has left home, husband, and baby behind and the lover who has tempted her away. Dyer-Bennet also effectively employs a change of key in the last verse to portray the woman's regret as the ship they are traveling on sinks to rise no more. Again, the last verse is the singer's own. A lively, if somewhat rushed, interpretation of "The Charleston Merchant" follows. Scholander's influence is shown by Dyer-Bennet's rapping of his fist on the body of his lute to simulate the merchant's knock on the door in the third verse. The young singer again affects a number of different voices to portray the song's cast of characters. Other characteristic Dyer-Bennet touches are the slowed tempo used to accent the sweat falling from the brow of the men carrying the tailor in the merchant's sea chest, and the dramatic pause employed after the chest, tailor and all, is thrown into the sea. Dyer-Bennet learned the song from the American folksong collector and scholar Fletcher Collins (1906–2005) but added the final verse himself. In a 1939 letter to his mother he describes his first meeting with Collins and the songs he learned from him. "I brought back about twenty new songs to learn, which also provides me with plenty to do. Some of these are American folk ballads and are unlike anything I have. I got them down in North Carolina from a young English professor who is collecting songs. My week in North Carolina was the most interesting part of the whole trip. The ballad tradition is still alive in that region."[1]

The two sea songs included on the flip side of the recording, "What Shall We Do with the Drunken Sailor?" and "Hullabaloo Belay," are spirited, if somewhat rushed in their delivery. Friend David Lloyd Garrison taught Dyer-Bennet both songs in Santa Barbara in 1929.

The album was not widely reviewed, but New York Times music critic Howard Taubman praised the album's selections, noting that Dyer-Bennet "sings them with refreshing feeling and musicianship. Like most folk singers, he tends to use more mezza voce than is needful, but he can sing out with a heartiness that the songs require."[2]

Dyer-Bennet recorded *Babes of the Zoo* in 1944. Produced to raise money for Russian war relief, it is a twelve-minute piece for children describing the adventures of various baby animals. Most of these episodes are sung, though some are spoken. Dyer-Bennet is accompanied by an orchestra (conducted by Charles Lichter) throughout. The *New York Times* called the piece "charming" and described Dyer-Bennet as a "gifted ballad singer," before noting that the "album is above reproach."[3]

Love Songs, Dyer-Bennet's second album for adults, was issued by the Disc Company of America label in 1946. Recorded at 78 r.p.m., the six songs are presented this time as single sides. Full lyrics are included, and a short essay by Dyer-Bennet's friend, musicologist John Ward, explains the significance of the album's title. "For the traditional singer, there are only two kinds of music," he writes, "religious songs and 'love songs.'"[4] The latter, Ward notes, is a designation used by traditionalists to describe "everything secular," though he defines such songs as those in which the singer "expresses himself in the first person singular and relates an amorous adventure." The album cover features the art of David Stone Martin (1913–1992), a painter who provided album art for more than 250 recordings, mostly for jazz labels.

"Going to Ballynure" is a lively song that employs a motif found often in Irish folk songs: the narrator relating a conversation he hears between courting lovers. Ward notes that the song was collected by Herbert Hughes in County Antrim, and that it is a fragment of a longer ballad. It is backed by "Blow the Candles Out," first printed, Ward notes, in Thomas D'Urfey's *Wit and Mirth: or Pills to Purge Melancholy*, published in 1682. Dyer-Bennet's performance here is nearly identical to that later included on *Richard Dyer-Bennet 2*. "Brigg Fair" is a lover's statement of constancy and features a lovely accompaniment. "Two Maidens Went Milking One Day" is sung somewhat less playfully than the version on *Richard Dyer-Bennet 2*, where Dyer-Bennet includes "la la las" at the end of every verse and omits the whistling found here at the song's conclusion. Burl Ives taught Dyer-Bennet the song in 1942. The hauntingly beautiful fragment, "Westryn Wind," provides another example of Dyer-Bennet's excellent use of pianissimo and fortissimo to convey the emotional power of the song. One can easily imagine a troubadour singing this song to his patrons at court.

John Jacob Niles (1892–1980) is the source of "Venezuela," though whether he penned the song himself or simply collected it from the singing of Barbados sailors remains a matter of debate. Eager to seem authentic to the folk singing community, Niles would sometimes claim that a song he had, in fact, composed himself was traditional. Niles performed in a most unusual way, seeming to embody his songs, rather than merely sing them. He sang in a high, sometimes eerie voice, and did not always consistently follow a song's melody. To an even greater degree than Scholander's, Niles's songs sometimes resembled short plays, with the singer moving about the stage with his dulcimer and using his entire body to dramatize the story's action and emotion. Niles gave American music such songs as "Black Is the Color of My True Love's Hair" (performed by Dyer-Bennet in concert) and "Go Away from My Window," later recorded by Joan Baez and rewritten by Bob Dylan as "It Ain't Me, Babe." Though Niles made much of the fact that he was merely a "Boone Creek Boy" from Kentucky, he was well-read and quite urbane. He listed Gertrude Stein among his friends. Dyer-Bennet certainly admired both the man and his art. "Venezuela" became a well-loved part of the minstrel's repertoire and later appeared on *Richard Dyer-Bennet 5* in very similar form.

In a review of *Love Songs*, an unidentified critic notes Dyer-Bennet's growth as an artist. "I have been hearing Dyer-Bennet since his night club debut before the war, and there is no question that he is a constantly improving singer. There is now more naturalness in his delivery than ever before, which, together with his suitable voice quality, his excellent diction and unostentatious musicianship, make for a thoroughly enjoyable performance."[5] Howard Taubman of the *New York Times* summarizes the album as containing "charming songs, charmingly done."[6]

Nineteen forty-six also saw the release of two albums of folk songs arranged by Beethoven, *Scottish Songs* and *Irish Songs*. While some classify much of Dyer-Bennet's repertoire as "art songs," it is the selections on these two albums that best fit that description. As to their relation to folk music, Philip Miller writes in his liner notes to *Irish Songs* that "it had not yet occurred to anyone that folk music was folk music precisely because it was a more or less primitive expression of the spirit and the life of the people; and that in order to retain its essential character it must not necessarily be brought to conform strictly to the established rules of art."[7] Both albums were released by Concert Hall, a label that had been formed that year with an expressed purpose to record unfamiliar music. The albums demonstrate both Dyer-Bennet's educated approach to folk music and his desire to broaden his listeners' musical horizons.

Indeed, these songs are little known and have often been dismissed as "hack work" for the great composer. Between 1809 and 1818 Beethoven wrote settings for 179 songs, most of them from Scotland, Ireland, and Wales. George Thomson (1757–1851), an enthusiast from Edinburgh, commissioned and subsequently published them. Thomson was the secretary of a Board of Trustees for the Encouragement of Arts and Manufacturers in Scotland and was "a man of culture, with influential acquaintances and an enthusiasm for the old airs and melodies in his country."[8] Neither poets nor composer worked under ideal conditions. "Each was sent a bare outline of the melody annotated with Italian musical terms. The poet might be supplied with the first stanza of the song but had no idea of the composer's treatment of the melody; for his part, the composer had no text at all from which to work."[9] Some of the songs are remarkably good given these constraints. It should also be noted that "partly because he wanted to cater to conventional tastes, Thomson bowdlerized both the texts and the tunes of the traditional folk songs."[10] Similarly, though Robert Burns was among those involved in the project, "this was a time when every pressure was being put on people in all walks of life in Scotland to repress their Scottishness and adopt English ways, speech and manners."[11]

In his liner notes to *Richard Dyer-Bennet 7*, the album on which Dyer-Bennet rerecorded the Beethoven songs, the singer gives his own opinion of the project's difficulties. "When Thompson [*sic*] felt the setting did not match the words, he commissioned new words to be written. In the case of the musical poet, this can be satisfactory; in several instances I fear the poets concerned were not very musical, for the prosody is awkward. Furthermore, the vocal line is sometimes doubled by violin or 'cello as well as by piano."[12] Dyer-Bennet concludes, however, by stating that "whatever they are, the songs have life, charm and even beauty, and in the instrumental interludes and codas you may hear now and again the unmistakable touch of the German master."

Dyer-Bennet's voice is well suited to these parlor pieces, and the ensemble that accompanies him (Ignace Strasvogel on piano, Stefan Frenkel on violin, and Jascha Bernstein on cello) performs excellently. *Irish Songs* was released as a 78 r.p.m. recording. The vocal tracks sound a bit muddy to the modern ear and sometimes fail to assert themselves over the accompaniment. While all the tracks are based on Irish melodies, writers from all around the British Isles provided their lyrics. William Smyth (1765–1849) wrote the lyrics of "Oh, Who My Dear Dermot." Smyth, a history professor at Cambridge and a poet, contributed forty poems for Beethoven, more than any other poet involved in the project. His verses here concern the treachery of Dermot MacMurrough, King of Leinster (Ireland), who, after being driven out of his lands in the twelfth century, sought the aid of Norman barons to help him win back his holdings. Three verses exist, but here Dyer-Bennet sings only the first and the third. This, and similar amendments to other songs, are probably due to the time constraints of the recording technology. When rerecorded on *Richard Dyer-Bennet 7*, all three verses are included. The song laments Dermot's decision to seek foreign aid, and the omitted second verse is not vital to its message.

"The Morning Air Plays on My Face," written by Scottish poetess and dramatist Joanna Baillie (1762–1851), is a celebration of nature's beauties. The original text runs to four verses, but Dyer-Bennet omits the last. "Morning A Cruel Turmoiler Is" features lyrics by Alexander Boswell (1706–1782). Its lively tune matches the playful banter of the lyrics, which celebrate pursuits best suited for nocturnal enjoyment. Dyer-Bennet's enjoyment of ornamenting the last word of each verse is evident. Thomson sometimes objected to phrases and words submitted by the poets and usually wound up convincing them to make revisions. Here Thomson objected to Boswell's use of the word "turmoiler" but, in this instance, the poet succeeded in convincing him that the word was "essential for the rhyme."[13] The great Scots poet Robert Burns penned the words to "Once More I Hail Thee" and eighteen other pieces used by Beethoven for Thomson's project. Like so many other Burns poems, this lyric describes the painful parting between lovers. The musical setting is beautiful, with Strasvogel's piano leading the way. On this recording the last verse is omitted, though it would be included on *Richard Dyer-Bennet 7*. Boswell again supplies the lyrics for "The Pulse of an Irishman," based on the lively tune "St. Patrick's Day." "The Return to Ulster" is the sad tale of the poet's return to the city of his youth, still haunted by the memory of the girl who turned him away there. Sir Walter Scott's verse originally ran to two stanzas, but here again the second is omitted.

Scottish Songs was released as a 33 r.p.m. LP, and its sound is much cleaner than *Irish Songs*. Dyer-Bennet is accompanied by the same trio as on *Irish Songs*. "Faithfu' Johnie" is a tender love song of commitment written by Mrs. Anne

Grant (1755–1838), a Scottish poetess. Dyer-Bennet sings four verses on this recording, while only three appear on the song as recorded on *Richard Dyer-Bennet
7.* "Oh, Sweet Were the Hours" is a lively drinking song that the minstrel would
not include on his rerecording of the Beethoven songs. Smyth is again the author,
changing the original text from "Oh, Can You Sew Cushions." "Oh, How Can
I Be Blithe and Glad" is a Robert Burns poem also known as "The Bonnie Lad
That's Far Awa." Dyer-Bennet sings only four of the original five verses, and substitutes "and all my tears be tears of joy / when he comes home that's far awa'" for
the original "and my sweet baby will be born / and he'll be hame that's far awa'"
in the final verse. This is, no doubt, a result of his using Thomson's bowdlerized
text. Thomson "intended his publication to be sung by young ladies, for whom
the bawdy texts found in some folksongs would clearly be unsuitable."[14] Though
set to a beautiful tune, "Oh, How Can I Be Blithe and Glad" would also be omitted from *Richard Dyer-Bennet 7.* "Could This Ill World Have Been Contrived"
is a lively tune that good-naturedly bemoans man's attraction to woman. It, too,
was omitted from *Richard Dyer-Bennet 7.*

The lyrics to "Sunset" were written by the famed Scottish author Sir Walter
Scott (1771–1832), who provided Beethoven with nine poems for musical setting.
The song, replete with romantic images of nature, is a mournful reflection on
aging. The setting to "Again My Lyre" provides Dyer-Bennet with a number of
vocal challenges, each of which he admirably meets. The text, by William Smyth,
concerns music's sometimes painful affinity for recalling the past and was one
of Thomson's favorite lyrics. Sir Walter Scott's "On the Massacre of Glencoe"
is a reflection on the notorious murder in 1692 of thirty-eight members of the
Macdonald clan. What made the crime especially heinous was that the killers,
English troops led by Captain Robert Campbell, had enjoyed the Macdonalds'
hospitality the evening before the massacre. "The British Light Dragoons," again
by Scott, casts English men of arms in a more favorable light. The spirited melody celebrates their bravery in England's Peninsula War (1807–1814) against
Napoleon. "O Mary at Thy Window Be" is a Robert Burns piece that asks the
song's namesake, "Canst thou break that heart of his / Whose only fault is loving
thee?" The song would not be included on *Richard Dyer-Bennet 7.* The album
closes with the catchy "Bonnie Laddie, Hieland Laddie." Scottish poet James
Hogg (1770–1835) wrote the lyric, which leaves unanswered its vital question—if
O'Donald's men fought or ran at the Battle of Waterloo (1815).

In his review of the album, Howard Taubman of *The New York Times* named
Dyer-Bennet "a happy choice for the Scottish songs," noting that his tenor is "not
the fat kind of voice one is accustomed to in concert hall and opera house."[15]

Dyer-Bennet's next recording was released in 1947. *Vox Presents Richard Dyer-
Bennet Singing Minstrel Songs of the U.S.A.* was issued as a 78 album and featured

eight songs, six from America and two from England. "Old Bangum" is the fanciful tale of a hero's slaughter of a wild boar. It is a sort of mock epic and would later appear in much the same form on *Richard Dyer-Bennet 6*, an album of songs for children. One of Dyer-Bennet's dogs was named Bangum in honor of the song's protagonist. Dyer-Bennet learned both this song and "The Quaker Lover" from Fletcher Collins. The latter song pokes fun at an earnest Quaker's attempt to woo a carefree Presbyterian maiden. It proved popular enough with audiences to later be included on *Richard Dyer-Bennet 5*, his album of requests. "Along the Colorado Trail" features a whistled introduction. Interestingly, Dyer-Bennet here pronounces "Colorado" with a long "a." The song was not included on any of the Dyer-Bennet label records, but does appear on a 1962 Stinson recording, *More Songs by the 20th-Century Minstrel*.

A lovely guitar figure introduces "When Cockleshells Turn Silverbells," learned by Dyer-Bennet from Dolly Abbott in 1939 in New York. In his 1971 *Richard Dyer-Bennet Folk Song Book*, Dyer-Bennet elaborates on the song's provenance. "She had heard it from an old cleaning woman whose singing had ascended the heating system in Dolly's building. Descending to the basement, Dolly found the source of the music and learned the song. The singer was Irish, but she said she had learned the song from her mother, who was a Cornishwoman."[16] Thematically it is a forerunner to the American song "Come All You Fair and Tender Maidens." "Cockleshells" would be rerecorded on *Richard Dyer-Bennet 2* nine years later.

John Jacob Niles is again the source of "The Lass from the Low Country." In his liner notes for *Richard Dyer-Bennet 3*, on which the song also appears, Dyer-Bennet notes "I have never known Niles to concern himself with a second rate song. This is one of his gems."[17] Dyer-Bennet thought enough of "The Racket Round Blue Mountain Lake" (also known as "How Hell Busted Loose Up at Blue Mountain Lake" and "Blue Mountain Lake") to include it as part of his Carnegie Hall appearance, and to record it again for Stinson in 1962. Here, however, the presentation sounds rather rushed. "The Turkish Reverie" is the American version of "The Golden Vanity." Dyer-Bennet learned it from Burl Ives in 1941 and later included it on *Richard Dyer-Bennet 2*. While the lyrical content of both songs is quite similar, their melodies differ greatly. The negro spiritual "Were You There" was recorded only for this album. Despite the fact that he was not a religious man, Dyer-Bennet sings it with real feeling and lends it his own special beauty.

Dyer-Bennet recorded an album titled simply *Ballads* for Stinson sometime in the 1940s. Stinson, located in Granada Hills, California, was a major name in the folk recording industry at the time, having previously issued records by Burl Ives, Josh White, Woody Guthrie, Pete Seeger, Lead Belly, and many others. *Ballads* is in some ways a forerunner to Dyer-Bennet's first album of children's songs on his own label, *Richard Dyer-Bennet 6*, in that five of its eight songs would later

appear on that album: "Come All Ye," "The Frog and the Mouse," "John Peel,"
"Little Pigs," and "Three Jolly Rogues of Lynn." Dyer-Bennet notes with humor
that "Come All Ye" is an Irish tune he learned in Nevada from a man of German
extraction. It features a bouncing guitar accompaniment and pitch-perfect whistling. "The Frog and the Mouse" is a variant of the song better known as "Frog
Went A-Courting." Dyer-Bennet's version features a happier ending than do most
of the others in that the frog is not gobbled up. Dyer-Bennet also adds a final verse
that describes the couple's offspring ("and they had long tails and webbed feet").
Richard Dyer-Bennet 6 has an American variant of the same song. "John Peel" is a
charming English song that honors the memory of a celebrated fox hunter. Dyer-
Bennet lends it an appropriately nostalgic feel and sings the song quite tenderly.
"Three Jolly Rogues of Lynn" rattles along at a breakneck pace, clocking in at just
over one minute. Dyer-Bennet identifies it in his 1946 songbook as "a descendant
of the English ballad, 'King Arthur's Sons.'"[18]

The Scottish tune "Little Pigs" was apparently a favorite of the singer; he included it in both of his songbooks. Certainly it is enjoyable to listen to, and must
have been fun to sing as well, featuring as it does various whistles and snorts.
Dyer-Bennet playfully notes in his 1971 songbook that "it sounds rather spirited
for a lullaby, but then the Scots are a hardy race, and perhaps: The Scots what hae
wi' Wallace bled / Like braw, strong tunes when off to bed."[19] "The Eddystone
Light" is a nautical fairy tale that would later appear on *Richard Dyer-Bennet 12*.
Its final verse was composed by Dyer-Bennet and quickly found its way into the
tradition. The Weavers, for example, later included it on their recording of the
song. "Molly Malone" was never recorded on his own label. Dyer-Bennet's change
to a minor key in the final verse indicates, however, that he gave the song some
thought, and it was included on a later Stinson release. "Oh, No, John" is a playful
courting song that was not included on any of the recordings Dyer-Bennet made
for his own label. Its humor lies in the framing of the man's questions and the
ambiguity of the woman's constant answer, "oh, no, John."

1949 saw Dyer-Bennet's first stereo release, Decca's *Richard Dyer-Bennett [sic]:
Twentieth-Century Minstrel*. Despite the egregious misspelling of the artist's name
on its cover, this was Dyer-Bennet's most accomplished release to date. Originally
a British company, Decca established an American branch in 1934. By the 1940s
the label boasted such names as the Andrews Sisters, Count Basie, Billie Holiday,
and Louie Armstrong. That Decca was interested in recording Dyer-Bennet is a
sign of his growing reputation within the industry.

The album's liner notes were written by Alan Lomax (1915–2002), son of
famed musicologist John Lomax (1867–1948) and an authority on folk music in
his own right. His notes attempt to place Dyer-Bennet in a context the modern
listener might understand.

Mr. Bennett [*sic*] sings with the pure "white" tone of the classical European tenor. He plays his guitar as if it were a lute or a harpsichord. The resulting combination is that of the courtly singer of ages gone by, the professional troubadour who entertained in the halls of princes, and who amused or moved the ladies of the court when their lords had ridden off to war or to the hunt. His songs are of olden times, in the purest tradition of English lyricism and balladry, reflecting in their antique severity the restraint and the high canons of taste that have always distinguished true folk song.[20]

The album opens with the humorous "The Devil and the Farmer's Wife," a song that argues that "The women are worse than the men / They went down to Hell and got kicked out again." The song's rhythm is quite tricky, and Dyer-Bennet would change it when he rerecorded it on *Richard Dyer-Bennet 13*. "Eggs and Marrowbone" continues the theme of the malevolent wife, in this instance a woman who "loved her husband dearly but another man twice as well" and thus wants to do away with her spouse. The song was rerecorded for *Richard Dyer-Bennet 2*, where Dyer-Bennet notes that he achieved a "certain ruthless continuity"[21] by practicing the minstrel's prerogative of piecing together several versions of the song and adding a final verse to more satisfactorily complete the story. In "The Willow Tree" the battle of the sexes continues as a maiden outwits her would-be murderer. That she accomplishes this by appealing to his good manners is amusing, making Dyer-Bennet's playful mock sentiment in his final verse entirely appropriate. He would later rerecord the song on *Richard Dyer-Bennet 12*. The melody of "Villikens and his Dinah" is familiar to American ears as "Sweet Betsy from Pike"; though the singer learned it from his American grandmother, the song is Cockney in origin. The message conveyed in the final verse—"'Tis better by far to die and grow cold / Than to marry a suitor for silver and gold"—is somewhat diluted by the comical tone employed earlier in the song. The dialog between mother and daughter in "Lolly Toodum" is once more comical. Dyer-Bennet must not have thought a great deal of the selection, though, as he would never record it again. That "Mo Mary," a beautiful tune from Scotland's Hebrides islands, suffered the same fate is more mysterious. Dyer-Bennet had included the piece in his 1946 songbook, and here he gives it a lovely reading, reaching the very limit of his range in its moving conclusion.

The LP's second side opens with "The Swapping Song," performed here in a slower tempo than employed on *Richard Dyer-Bennet 3*, on which it also appears. It is a comic tale of a man who continuously swaps property until he finally receives what he has needed all along to restore order to his household—a cat. That the feline is ultimately preferable to a wife recalls the message of "The Devil and the Farmer's Wife." "The Old Maid" continues to poke fun at the fairer sex. It is a mere fragment and, though included in the 1946 songbook, was never again re-corded by Dyer-Bennet. "Early One Morning" is ideally suited to Dyer-Bennet's gift for pianissimo and was later rerecorded for *Richard Dyer-Bennet 9*.

"Greensleeves" is one of the songs most often associated with the twentieth-century minstrel, appearing on no fewer than five of his recordings. In his 1971 songbook, Dyer-Bennet states that the tune was often performed as a solo piece for lute and serves as an excellent jig at a faster tempo.[22] Its fame is testified to by the fact that both Shakespeare (in *The Merry Wives of Windsor*) and the diarist Pepys mention it in their writing. The song's enduring popularity has led certain writers to assign it rather fanciful origins. Some believe that King Henry VIII wrote the song about his courtship with Anne Boleyn, but this is unlikely; oth-ers point out that the lyrics are ironic since the lady in the song may have been a prostitute. In Renaissance England, they argue, the color green was associated with the world's oldest profession. While some versions run to as many as eigh-teen verses, Dyer-Bennet includes only the first, followed by a chorus, explaining that it is not a narrative ballad and that its meaning is apparent from the single verse. Dyer-Bennet whistles one verse, lending the listener time to reflect on the narrator's quandary. His inclusion of only the single verse sharpens the song and focuses its power. This decision may also have been partly due to a disagreement Dyer-Bennet had with Pete Seeger about the song. "He really was hurt," Seeger recalls, "when I made fun of all the verses of 'Greensleeves.' It was a pop song, you know, not a folk song, of the sixteenth century. The rest of the verses kind of repeat themselves. 'I did this and I did that but thou wouldst not love me.' Dick was really hurt by that because he loved that song."[23]

"Oh Sally My Dear" signals a return to the lighthearted. Its chorus leads one to assume it is Irish, and the song shares some lyrics with the tune known al-ternately as "Blackbirds and Thrushes," "Hares on the Mountain," or "If All the Young Girls." This is Dyer-Bennet's only recording of the song. The album closes with "Fain Would I Wed," written by Thomas Campion (1567–1620) and learned by Dyer-Bennet from John Ward. Like "Greensleeves" the song dates from the sixteenth century; unlike that famous song, however, this piece about a fickle lover features complex syntax and can sound rather confusing to modern ears. In his notes to *Richard Dyer-Bennet 3*, the singer acknowledged another potential source of confusion. "I have altered the last two lines in order to avoid an ambi-guity. The original lines seemed to suggest that a woman is speaking, whereas the first two verses are clearly a man's statement."[24] Since Campion's text (*The Fourth Booke of Ayres*, XXIIII) seems to indicate quite clearly that a woman is, in fact, speaking, one can attribute the alterations—either by Ward or Dyer-Bennet—to the folk process.

Dyer-Bennet's second recording for Stinson shares the same title as his Decca release, *Richard Dyer-Bennet: The Twentieth Century Minstrel*. The exact date of the recording is unknown but probably was in the early 1950s. The album cover is once again by David Stone Martin and incorrectly shows Dyer-Bennet playing the guitar left-handed. The singer's name is also misspelled on the back of the album. Ken Goldstein provides short liner notes. The album is simply a combination of the tracks from the Disc release, *Love Songs*, and the first Stinson recording, *Ballads*.

Two other early Dyer-Bennet albums are duplicative. *Folk Songs* (Remington, 1951) contains the same songs included on the Continental Records release of the same name (date uncertain). "White Lily" and "Pull Off Your Old Coat" are listed on the Remington record but do not actually appear on the recording. One can only guess at the reason for the omissions. The album's cover is rather amateurish in execution and portrays a highlander, a town crier, and a rural couple, designed, no doubt, to match the range of characters that people its songs. *Folk Songs* is, nevertheless, a major release. A number of songs that were staples in Dyer-Bennet's repertoire appear here on record for the first time. The *New York Times* praised the album, its only reservation being that his "artistry has to make its way through quite a lot of surface noise."[25]

The album begins with "Lord Randall," a famous ballad from Scotland and northern England. The song details a conversation between a mother and her dying son, poisoned by his sweetheart. Dyer-Bennet included the song on *Richard Dyer-Bennet 5* with only slight variations. The son's wrath upon realizing his fate is an excellent example of the drama Dyer-Bennet could bring to a song. "Kitty My Love" is a very short courting song that ends with the suitor's proposal still unanswered. "The Rising of the Moon" is a traditional Irish tune given new lyrics by John Keegan Casey circa 1858. It celebrates the uprising of 1798 and, with a different melody, became a standard in the 1960s for the Clancy Brothers and Tommy Makem. Dyer-Bennet's version is based on that found in Colin O'Lochlainn's *More Irish Street Ballads* and, while perhaps less melodic than its successor, provides a higher sense of drama.

The next three songs on the Remington LP were rerecorded for *Richard Dyer-Bennet 10* in 1962. This fact seems to indicate that Remington gave Dyer-Bennet some say in determining the album's running order. "The Wife Wrapped in the Wether's Skin" is a song from America's Appalachian region. It tells the story of the taming of a shrew and betrays the sensibility of a bygone era. When rerecorded in 1962, "Jenny" is substituted for "Johnny" in the chorus. In the notes for that album Dyer-Bennet explains ("for the benefit of urbanites") that a wether is a castrated ram. "My Good Old Man" is an American song about a "hant," or ghost.

In his notes to *Richard Dyer-Bennet 10*, Dyer-Bennet writes that "I understand the implication to be that the interrogator (the old woman) is already a hant."[26] It is yet another conversation song and allows the singer to display his ability to create two distinct and believable personas in the same song. "Lowlands" is a beautiful piece—probably originally a sea shanty—about the loneliness of a sailor's life, and the power of his dreams. Its elegant guitar accompaniment is among Dyer-Bennet's best.

Side one closes with the masterful "John Henry." This is the first of four appearances on Dyer-Bennet recordings. In this version, John Henry's efforts "burst his heart" instead of breaking his back as in the setting used for *Richard Dyer-Bennet 5*. Another old favorite, "The Golden Vanity," opens side two. Dyer-Bennet varies the chorus beautifully to match the swiftly changing fortunes of the cabin boy who sinks "the Spanish enemy." It is followed by another Elizabethan song, "Greensleeves." The mood then changes with the boastful, triumphant "Bonnie Dundee." Written by Sir Walter Raleigh to a traditional tune, it was later included on *Richard Dyer-Bennet 4*, where the singer explains that John Graham, Viscount Dundee, was a royalist who opposed Scottish covenanters' efforts to block Charles I's introduction of the episcopacy. "Binnorie" ends a familiar story of sisterly conflict in a novel way. The older sister drowns the younger when she discovers that her lover prefers her sister. Later, at court, a harp made from bones and hair of the murder victim plays a tune that betrays the older sister's villainy. "Binnorie" is a variation of the Scottish song "The Twa Sisters" and was later included on *Richard Dyer-Bennet 9*. "Bow Down," recorded for his first children's album (*Richard Dyer-Bennet 6*), tells a similar story that ends more happily.

"The Laird of Cockpen" was originally the work of Carolina Oliphant, or Lady Nairne (1766–1845). Its seven verses tell the tale of a proud Scottish Laird who is rebuked by a penniless Mistress Jean. When recorded for *Richard Dyer-Bennet 9*, however, Dyer-Bennet includes two additional verses from the pen of Sir Alexander Boswell, father of Johnson biographer James Boswell. Apparently the lady's effrontery was too much for Mr. Boswell, who made her relent upon realizing her foolishness. "The Lonesome Dove" is a tender love song that expresses the narrator's constancy. Dyer-Bennet did not include it on any subsequent albums; perhaps he was not comfortable with the song's range. The delightful "Kerry Recruit" closes the album. It relates in humorous and poetic detail the adventures of a naïve young Irish soldier in the Crimean War (1853–56). Dyer-Bennet added the final verse about the Russian artillery during the latter stages of World War II, when, he notes, the Soviet army's strength was still appreciated by the American public. The final verse also provides a frame of sorts to the song and was preserved when rerecorded for *Richard Dyer-Bennet 4* in 1957, despite that later era's political tensions. In his 1971 songbook, Dyer-Bennet speculates that "The Kerry Recruit" is probably not a true rural Irish folk song but rather "an English city man's view of an Irish yokel."[27] Dyer-Bennet's father knew the song as performed by the Irish baritone Plunkett Greene (1865–1936). The Makem Brothers recorded the song for their 2004 album *Stand Together*, where they include Dyer-Bennet's final verse.

Of the eighty-four songs recorded on these early albums, Dyer-Bennet would eventually rerecord sixty-five (77 percent) of them when he established his own label in 1955. Thus these early recordings form an important foundation and allow us to compare his early style to that of his mature years. Though in many ways inferior to the Dyer-Bennet label albums, they are well worth exploring and will reward the listener for his perseverance in trying to obtain them.

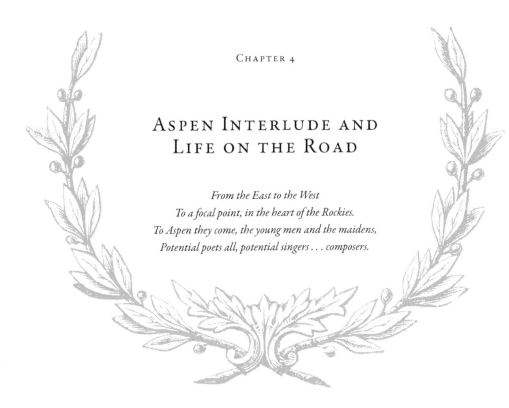

CHAPTER 4

ASPEN INTERLUDE AND
LIFE ON THE ROAD

From the East to the West
To a focal point, in the heart of the Rockies.
To Aspen they come, the young men and the maidens,
Potential poets all, potential singers . . . composers.

As the excitement of his first tours subsided, Dyer-Bennet began to feel the familiar burdens of life on the road. He missed Mel terribly and longed to be closer to daughters Bonnie and Brooke. Mel also hoped to free her husband from some of the rigors of nightclub life. The hours were long, and his health suffered. As he mused on the challenges of being husband, father, and touring artist, Dyer-Bennet was offered an opportunity he found he could not resist. Walter Paepcke (1896–1960), chairman of the Chicago-based Container Corporation of America, invited Dyer-Bennet to found a school of minstrelsy in Aspen, Colorado. Paepcke loved the area and had already opened the Aspen Skiing Corporation there in 1946. Dyer-Bennet knew Paepcke well, having performed at a concert organized by him in 1946, and was aware of the industrialist's ambition to transform Aspen into a cultural mecca.

Aspen was founded in 1879 as Ute City by H. B. Gillespie. Located two hundred miles southwest of Denver in the heart of the Rocky Mountains, Aspen is 7,908 feet above sea level. Miners discovered silver deposits nearby, and the settlement had grown to include three hundred residents by 1880, when it was given its current name by B. Clark Wheeler after the trees that grew plentifully in the area. A full-scale silver boom followed, and by 1893 Aspen's population had swelled to twelve thousand. That same year, however, silver was demonetized, and the boom was over. By 1930 the once bustling town claimed only seven hundred inhabitants. A renaissance of sorts began in 1936 when three investors established a ski area there, but the transformation of Aspen from a sleepy mountain village to an internationally known resort is due mostly to Paepcke.

The offer intrigued Dyer-Bennet. Ideally, he envisioned the school as a place where he and a hand-picked staff might train others to follow in his footsteps. Scholander and Beckman had done so much for him; now here was an opportunity for Dyer-Bennet to train others to carry on the tradition of minstrelsy. The desire and ability to teach ran throughout the Dyer-Bennet family: brother John became a professor of mathematics at Carleton College, brother Christopher taught sociology for the University of California system, and his mother, of course, was currently teaching in California. After consulting Mel, Dyer-Bennet decided to accept Paepcke's offer of a free home in Aspen where he might base his operations. The lure of rural Colorado as an ideal place to raise his daughters surely played a role in his decision as well. Hurok was against the idea, however, reminding Dyer-Bennet that New York was the entertainment capital of the world and warning him that relocating so far west would eliminate valuable opportunities to augment his position as one of the country's premier folk singers. With some trepidation, Dyer-Bennet chose to gamble.

By the summer of 1947, Dyer-Bennet had assembled a talented staff that would help students improve not only their musical abilities, but also their lives. Introductory work for all students, for example, included physical preparation, relaxation, individual posture correction, improvisational experience, body movement, primitive drumming, visual arts, and story telling. These introductory sessions were under Mel's supervision and would later include time with her brother-in-law, George Saslow (1906–2006), professor of psychiatry at Washington University in St. Louis. The school's brochure elaborated on its initial goals:

> The summer work is intended to introduce the student to an approach which is concerned equally with his growth as a human being and development of his technical proficiency. Our aim is to help him achieve a high degree of self-activity, to increase his capacity for both work and play, to encourage him to experiment with ideas and stimulate in him a compelling demand for the development of techniques. We are interested in working only with people who accept as an obligation to themselves and society the importance of achieving the fullest realization of their potentialities.[1]

During the three years the school existed, a number of well-known figures lent their talents as teachers or guest performers. Miriam Gideon (1906–1996) led classes in composition. Her composing career included more than fifty works, and in 1975 she became only the second woman elected to membership in the American Academy and Institute of Arts and Letters. Student Will Holt, who would later find fame as the composer of the hit song "Lemon Tree," found Gideon "extremely important. She was a 12 tone composer. She influenced me enormously, certainly in terms of the kind of music that one could hear that I had not heard before—Alban Berg, things like that."[2]

Sam Eskin (1898–1974), the legendary folk song collector, visited the school and served as a sort of living encyclopedia of song—especially those of a bawdy nature. Eskin's work—consisting of 15,795 manuscripts and 715 sound recordings—would eventually be included in the Library of Congress and run to 56.5 lineal feet. Eskin's presence was especially valuable because of one of Dyer-Bennet's hopes for the school: that it might become a research center for the collection of folk songs. Josef Marais (1905–1978) and Miranda Baruch de la Pardo (1912–1986) were a husband and wife duo who performed under the name Marais and Miranda. They sang songs of the African veldt and also many pieces from the European and American folk music tradition. The duo visited Aspen in both 1948 and 1949, performing a concert and introducing Dyer-Bennet's students to songs from another culture. Marais and Miranda had, like Dyer-Bennet, worked in the Office of War Information and performed at the Village Vanguard. John Ward, the Harvard musicologist who had helped Dyer-Bennet so greatly earlier in his career, was also on hand.

Musical training, of course, made up a large part of the school's curriculum, and most classes were taught by experts who had been instrumental in Dyer-Bennet's own development as a musician. Rey de la Torre, for example, taught classical Spanish guitar, and Dyer-Bennet's first voice teacher, Gertrude Wheeler Beckman, offered her services as well. Beckman arrived in July 1948. One of the first things she felt the school needed was an anthem. What she came up with was this:

From the East, to the West
To a focal point, in the heart of the Rockies.
To Aspen they come, the young men and the maidens,
Potential poets all, potential singers . . . composers.

Bring the lute, bring the guitar,
Bring the minstrels, gaily singing.
To Aspen they come, the young men and the maidens
Potential poets all, potential singers . . . composers.

Beckman was quite excited to be working with her star pupil again. She notes in a journal she kept chronicling her work in Aspen that "after being here three weeks yesterday I gave Dick his first singing lesson in seven years."[3] Her entries shed great light on Dyer-Bennet, Mel, and her own teaching methods. "Dick is a joy to work with," she notes, "more than ever now, because he has discovered so much for himself." During her time in Aspen, Beckman worked with Dick mostly on his vowels, and together they tackled a number of Italian arias and Mozart songs, including "Ridente la calma." Ever the teacher, she remarks that Dyer-Bennet's "muscles that flank the spinal column at the base of the neck do not work enough. They slump (as they were always prone to do) when he tilts his chin up and his head back too far." Later she mentions that he "has grown careless about mouth positions, probably due to his desire to let the ear do all the directing," concluding the entry with a declaration that "it's good to be needed!" Beckman is full of praise for Mel, stating that she "has Dick's number. She says he never moves until he feels he must have a certain thing. Then he goes after it, tooth and nail. He is greatly in need of the body work Mel gives these students for two hours each morning." She also observes that "Dick's rhythmic sense is his weak point, and I wish he had as good a sense of rhythm as Mel." She finds that on his early recordings he rather "chased through his songs."

Beckman delighted in meeting and working with Marais and Miranda. "They are a charming pair as they sit or stand together on the stage, he with his guitar flung over his shoulder, she in her long-sleeved evening frock of blue soft figured stuff, cut off the shoulders, her bronze-gold hair done in a beautiful, mysterious fashion, like an auriol framing her charming face." She later observes that "they are quite the most exciting thing that has ever come my way."

In her entry of August 3, Beckman describes a discussion about the academy's curriculum that sheds light on Dyer-Bennet's hopes for the school. "The other day there was a school discussion as to whether John Ward should continue his lectures on the growth of folk music, or whether he should talk on Mozart, Beethoven, Bach, Schubert, etc. Opinion was divided, and at one point it seemed as though the folksong devotees would have their way, when Dick sprang to his feet and said very forcefully: 'I want it clearly understood that this school is not a school where only folksongs are taught—it is a music school, where the classics as well as music history—including the music of the folk—are studied.' . . . I was so proud of him, for such words point to a Dick with a bigger vision by a universe from the lad who years ago had to be persuaded that learning to read a printed page of music was really essential if he ever expected to sing for his supper!"

Despite her obvious enthusiasm, Beckman's continuing presence became rather uncomfortable for the Dyer-Bennets. The students considered her rather old-fashioned, and Dyer-Bennet was beginning to question some of her methods.

Finally, her former pupil gently explained to her that such work must be too tiring, and Beckman was driven to the airport.

Dyer-Bennet led classes in voice, music history (with special attention to the guitar, lute and *vihuela* songs of the sixteenth, seventeenth, and eighteenth centuries), and analysis of folk music. "What he was trying to do was to get the singer to coordinate with the song," says Will Holt. "It was how do you sing, and how do you sing easily, how to keep from being inhibited by the sounds you make, forgetfulness, and the like. . . . He would let us know when he felt we weren't following the path of a song. I don't remember but maybe a few times that he would teach by illustration—in other words, by his singing. It was always: 'you do it.' Or perhaps he would offer advice like 'the jaw, it looks like jaw tension here.' He left you up to your own devices to find out how best to accomplish what he was suggesting."

Mel led various movement activities designed to assist students with their singing and presentation. Along with dance technique, these included improvisation, dealing with space problems, rhythmic and emotional themes, and qualities of movement. Will Holt had originally been lured by the prospect of working with Dyer-Bennet, but he soon realized that Mel was an important part of the school as well. "She did the whole thing about movement and coordinating the body and also the psychological stuff. We would dance and sing just any notes that we wanted to sing and listen to each other, to see how we could make concord out of just moving around. It was extremely new, and people sort of laughed at it down in the street. They'd wonder what we were doing."

Val Sigstedt also attended the school's first session in 1947. Burl Ives had been a favorite of his before he heard Dyer-Bennet for the first time and became a convert. After hearing a radio ad for Dyer-Bennet's school, Sigstedt headed west from Pennsylvania. Sigstedt describes Mel as "a very powerful person, extremely intelligent, intensely artistic. As unflappable and unshakable as a rock. She was like a goddess in a way to us kids."[4] He recalls how her strength of character saw the school through a difficult period. "Some of the folks in Aspen responded with hostility towards the school and its leftist leanings. There was even a period when we felt we were going to be beat up, that we were going to have a pitched battle with them. And I remember Mel saying 'just get ready for it; it can come anytime.'" Echoing sentiments of many whose lives were touched by Mel, Sigstedt believes she "provided an amazing template for my later life." This was precisely the kind of endorsement the Dyer-Bennets would have wanted for their school.

Ruthie Becker was a seventeen-year-old actress from Chicago who saw the school's brochure and became intrigued. She was familiar with Dyer-Bennet's recordings and traveled west, determined to become a folksinger. Becker recalls some of her classmates from her first summer in Aspen. "There was Burt from

New York whose heart I broke for a whole week; there was Lannie, who both comforted him and eventually married him; there was Sabrina from somewhere whose soprano caused eagles to abandon their eyries; and there was Rick Dehr, who went on to run a famous restaurant in Los Angeles; there was Jeppy from the Bronx who spent her free time reading *The People's World* to her cowboy lovers, in a dedicated but futile effort to convert them to Communism."[5]

Students lived together in a house the Dyer-Bennets had rented for the purpose. Tuition was $250 for each eight-week session, though scholarships were available. "We all had chores that we had to do. Those Aspen houses didn't really have much heat, so I had to bring the coal up for the stoves," recalls Holt.

During Dyer-Bennet's residence there, Aspen's reputation as a cultural center continued to grow. In 1948, for example, an opera house opened, hosting performances by Burl Ives and Dyer-Bennet among others. Then, in July 1949 Paepcke brought the world to Aspen. He had decided to sponsor an ambitious festival that would serve two purposes: to celebrate the 200th birthday of the German poet Goethe, and to establish Aspen as a symbol of international culture. Robert M. Hutchins, chancellor of the University of Chicago, had also been instrumental in the festival's planning stages. He thought Aspen an ideal location for the conference—even going so far as to dub it an "incipient Salzburg." In his mind, Aspen provided "an atmosphere free from big city distractions and in an environment conducive to informal discussion and thorough immersion in the subject."[6] Nearly two thousand people from all over the world attended. Albert Schweitzer, on his only trip to the United States, made a point of speaking there. The famous Finnish-American architect Eero Saarinen designed a huge tent to house the festival's musical performances. Despite all the expense and planning, however, Mother Nature had the last laugh. Dimitri Mitropoulos led an orchestral performance of the Minneapolis Symphony inside the tent that ended disastrously. Will Holt witnessed the spectacle. "There was a deluge when the symphony was playing. The water came rushing in. It was rising up to the ankles, then practically up to the calves of the Minneapolis Symphony. It was about half an hour before they could come back. We were always at the mercy of the elements. This was the most extraordinary meeting of Nature and Art that I've ever been associated with." Holt also recalls how Aspen's altitude took Dorothy Maynor, a soprano, by surprise. "She was used to being on flat land. She was singing 'Oh, Sleep, Why Dost Thou Leave Me,' which has lots of technical challenges. Well, the poor lady could not adjust. She finally finished, just barely. And after the last note there was this huge hhhhhhhhhhhhhhh of inhalation."

Though he had hoped to use Aspen as a base for his touring, Dyer-Bennet was under constant pressure from Sol Hurok to return to New York. Hurok felt that far too many opportunities were being lost due to Dyer-Bennet's western isolation.

Finally Dyer-Bennet relented. Thus, after only three years, the school for minstrelsy closed its doors. Finances had always been tight, and Dyer-Bennet had long
questioned the commitment of most of the students. Many of them, Dyer-Bennet
had come to realize, had simply wanted to meet him and be near him. They were
not willing to put in the amount of work both he and Mel expected of them.

The school had been a noble experiment, however, and left a great impression on many of those who had attended. "He had the ability to touch audiences
with an exactness," Sigstedt recalls, describing Dyer-Bennet. "He understood that
every part of the sound was a separate penetration into the listener's psyche."
On a more personal level, Sigstedt calls Dyer-Bennet "a big brother I desperately
needed at the time." Sigstedt also met his first wife at the school. He eventually
returned to Pennsylvania and became a successful artist, specializing in stained
glass.

After the Aspen school closed, Will Holt joined the air force. Following his
discharge Holt returned to New York, where he enjoyed a successful career as a
performer, often playing at the Village Vanguard for Dyer-Bennet's great friend,
Max Gordon. Holt remains best known, of course, as the writer of "Lemon Tree,"
a hit for both Peter, Paul, and Mary and Trini Lopez. Holt later wrote for the
theater, finding great success with *Over Here*, which starred the Andrews Sisters.

Ruthie Buell (née Becker) now lives in California where she performs under
the name Uncle Ruthie. She has a razor-sharp wit and has written a great many humorous songs. Buell also finds great satisfaction in teaching blind preschoolers.

In 1949 the Dyer-Bennets left Aspen for a new home in Wood's Hole,
Massachusetts. The school of minstrelsy had closed its doors, but it was not the
last time that Dyer-Bennet would appear in a classroom.

Though he had signed on with Hurok in 1944, Dyer-Bennet was not able to begin making concert tours until after the war ended. Writing in 1961, Dyer-Bennet
estimated that he "sang about a dozen concerts my first season, and for small fees.
The next year there were fifteen, then eighteen, then twenty, and the fees were
rising; but until 1956 it was necessary to supplement my concert earnings with
night-club engagements. In the last five years I have appeared only on the concert
stage, and now I sing about fifty recitals a year."[7] Hurok basically subsidized these
lean early years, fully aware that the agency had to grow the careers of its more
fledgling artists. In his liner notes to *Richard Dyer-Bennet 1* the minstrel estimates
that from 1940 to 1955 he sang 250 concerts. In that entire period he never cancelled an engagement due to vocal indisposition; whatever he now thought of
Beckman's vocal training, it had left him with a sturdy, dependable instrument.

Dyer-Bennet toured all over the United States and Canada from 1945 until
1972. Concerts were generally held in small halls and auditoriums, or on college

campuses, where Dyer-Bennet felt most comfortable. "These audiences are not only interested in my kind of music, but also in its origins and background."[8] Larger venues, of course, were also booked. In 1962, for example, Dyer-Bennet sang at the World's Fair in Seattle, and the Town Hall concerts in New York continued on an annual basis from 1944 until 1962.

While it had been his practice early in his career to list his intended selections in concert programs, in later years Dyer-Bennet allowed his feeling for the audience to dictate his set list for the night. "There is a feeling which comes from the people sitting there. I get the feel of the audience, and try about four songs. Then from the response I know what a group will like and I sing this for it."[9] Dyer-Bennet felt no compunction, however, to simply cater to an audience's whims. "I always put in one or two really fine songs. There is some very fine material which is never going to 'reach' most people."[10] In the late 1960s Dyer-Bennet would sometimes list more than 160 songs in a concert program, numbering them and instructing the audience to give the number of their requests to the ushers during intermission. These songs would then make up the second part of the evening's program.

The tour itinerary for 1950 gives us a glimpse of the destinations and frequency of Dyer-Bennet's travels. The first dollar figure represents Dyer-Bennet's fee, the second Hurok's commission (generally 20 percent), if any.

1/10	Boston	$57	$0
2/8	Brooklyn	$400	$80
2/16	Columbia, MO	$500	$100
2/23	St. Louis	$500	$100
2/27	Hopkinsville, KY	$250	$37.50
3/2	Talladega, FL	$250	$37.50
3/5	New York	$515	$103
3/9	Williamstown, MA	$400	$80
3/19	Mt. Vernon, NY	$250	$37.50
3/20	St. Louis	$150	$22.50
3/21	Blytheville, AR	$250	$37.50
3/22	Philadelphia	No Fee	$0
3/24	Thomasville, NC	$250	$37.50
3/30	Boston	$200	$40
5/9	White Plains, NY	$400	$80

5/17	Cambridge, MA	$200	$40
9/3	Cambridge, MA	$300	$60
10/6	Greensboro, NC	$500	$100
11/9	Washington, DC	No Fee	$0
11/11	Town Hall, NY	$1,763	$150
11/15	Danbury, CT	$450	$90
11/16	Framingham, MA	$300	$45
12/4	Winnetka, IL	$250	$50
12/5	Chicago	$450	$90
12/12	Arkansas City, AR	$250	$37.50
12/15	St. Louis	$400	$80
12/18	Fairhope, AL	$250	$37.50
Totals		$9,485	$1,533

On the debit side, printing and publicity expenses totaled $1,820, transportation another $349.

As the years passed, Dyer-Bennet enjoyed an increasing number of bookings. "From 1945 to 1957 the number of concerts rose from 12 to 45. I found 45 too many and cut back to 35."[11] Dyer-Bennet's concert fees were increasing, too, of course. In the 1961–62 season, for example, his earnings were $7,000 greater than for the 1956–57 season, even though he sang ten fewer concerts. By the mid-1960s, Dyer-Bennet's appearance fee had risen to $1,250.

Dyer-Bennet did what he could to stay in good physical shape while on the road. He followed a regular exercise regimen and always traveled with his tennis racket in hope of finding someone with whom he could play a few sets. Still, it was not an easy life. "Each year," he wrote Mel in 1952 from a hotel in Abilene, Texas,

the touring strikes me a little differently. This time I am aware of it as a lonely business. Periods of complete silence are followed by periods of meeting many people. But these are people you see only once and under "social" conditions. Then follows another train trip and the cycle begins again. You don't see the same faces two days in a row and you remain a stranger. I can see the reason for the "entourages" of performers who can afford it. In a sense, the way to enjoy touring is to live promiscuously—I don't mean sexually—to live only in the moment without much thought for tomorrow and without measuring things by established habits of taste and standards. To do this you must be able to enjoy the day to day business of eating and drinking, whether the food and drink is good or not—you must simply settle for the best you can get at the moment. It seems not to be in my nature to live lightly and promiscuously as loosely defined above. Unless some compromise with my nature is possible—or it changes—I suppose I must learn to reconcile myself to periods which are in many ways unsatisfactory.[12]

According to his daughter Brooke, touring exhausted Dyer-Bennet. "When he was touring—much of it before flight was possible, so he was often going by long slow bus rides or trains—he often got into the next city late enough that it was hard to find even a diner open for some hot food. So on tour he often ate poorly and had to keep crazy hours. As a result, when he was home he was often recuperating from the effort."[13] Brooke Dyer-Bennet offers us further glimpses of her father's home life. "I remember him practicing guitar quite a bit when I was a teenager. And he did some singing at home, often when he was out walking, actually. And now the neighbors always mention how much they miss hearing him sing as he strode past their houses."

Bonnie Dyer-Bennet recalls her father's delight in telling stories and jokes, many of which he would pick up on his travels. "He also loved reading aloud, to us as kids, and to whoever was around if he came across something interesting or amusing in something he was reading to himself. I remember before he recorded *1601*, for example, he read it aloud more than once—needing to pause frequently because he was laughing so hard he couldn't continue."[14] Dyer-Bennet spent hours reading at home. His tastes were extensive and varied, ranging from Einstein to Pepys. He liked nothing more than to sit before the fire with a cup of tea and read for hour upon hour. Gastronomically, breakfast was his favorite meal, and he enjoyed roast beef and Yorkshire pudding. Dyer-Bennet also habitually smoked cigarettes and a pipe, and was known to enjoy a good cigar.

In October 1960 Dyer-Bennet made an extensive tour of Alaska, his second trip there in three years. In a letter home he told Mel that he had heard from a booking agent that "many musicians do not like the Alaskan tour enough to want to repeat it."[15] His 1957 tour there, though, was so well received that he had now a sort of open invitation to travel there anytime his schedule permitted. In 1961 Dyer-Bennet wrote an account of his Alaskan tour that offers valuable insight into both the place and the man.

I spent last October touring the far northwest, singing fifteen concerts in thirty days, and covering some five thousand miles. This was my second trip up there, the first having been in the Spring of 1957. . . . My itinerary began on the British Columbia coast, and went as follows: Kitimat, B.C.; Prince Rupert, B.C.; then into the Alaska towns of Ketchikan, Wrangell, Petersburg, Sitka, Juneau, Anchorage, Fairbanks; then to Whitehorse in the Canadian Yukon; then to Grande Prairie Prince George, B.C., and back to Vancouver.[16]

Dyer-Bennet notes that flying is often the only travel option in Alaska.

> A great deal of freight is delivered by boat, and passenger boat excursions are available in summer; but for the traveler who wishes to cover such distances in a month or so, flying is essential. The smaller coastal towns have no landing strips, and travel between these points is by small seaplane or amphibian. I particularly enjoyed the eight-passenger seaplanes. They fly at low altitude, high enough to afford a vista, but not so high as to preclude a detailed view. . . . A passenger has the delightful sense of doing something pleasantly dangerous, and at the same time unusually safe. After all, a seaplane over the Pacific can land at anytime. . . . The eye is constantly pleased and often startled by the juxtaposition of gem-like islands in calm waters, and the towering land mass, rising abruptly from the sea.

Dyer-Bennet describes his first stop, Kitimat, as a town of 10,000 full of contemporary buildings where the settlers are described as "new Canadians." Another port of call, Prince Rupert, he describes as full of "halibut, salmon, lumber, and pulp." Ketchikan, his first Alaskan stop, is notable for "the bustle and pace of American life after the two quiet Canadian towns." Sitka he describes as "a mixture of Indian, Russian, and American influences." The town is "a paradise for the hunter, fisherman, woodsman, mountaineer, and boatmen of all kinds."

The singer enjoyed Juneau, especially its museums. Of Alaska in general, he notes that "the old cultures are fast disappearing, and in a decade or so only the museums will retain evidence of how the native people once lived and what skills they had." He describes the famed Mendenhall Glacier as an "enormous, imperceptibly flowing river of ice" that "threatens to destroy every vestige of life within hundreds of miles." Anchorage has "an active summer music festival—orchestra, chorus, soloists. It also has neon lights, billboard advertisements, and slums. In short, most of the credits and debits of large cities anywhere in the world." Despite its fearsome reputation, the state is not as cold as he had expected: "I was at all times more comfortable than I have been on occasion in Winnipeg, Chicago, or even New York."

In conclusion, Dyer-Bennet writes that "Alaska is a vast, varied, wildly beautiful place, inhabited by small groups of friendly, hospitable, unusually individual people. It stands today, in relation to the other west coast states, as California once stood in relation to New England. In spite of a long and colorful history she is barely out of swaddling clothes. Her future is wide open. In point of space, resources, and geographic location—considering jet flight and eventual rocket transport—she may well become a key state."

Most of Dyer-Bennet's tours were limited to North America, but the minstrel did tour Europe on a number of occasions. In 1953 he returned to his native England, hoping to find receptive audiences for both his English and American songs. The concerts were not well publicized, however, and attendance was disappointing. In a letter to Mel, Dyer-Bennet explains: "I've been here 5 days and have not yet met with the Hurok representative. I don't believe he or the Holt office give a damn about my Wigmore Hall recital. No publicity seems to have been arranged—no radio, no interviews, nothing. I am very angry about it. However I am going after things on my own and will succeed in the long run with or without them."[17] Sadly, a similar 1961 attempt to expand his audience in England failed for much the same reason. "No interviews have been arranged. They have no press books, no pictures, no records—only the little concert fliers. . . . Someone in New York is at fault—or, rather, no one has competently handled me New York end [sic]."[18] If not financially successful, the visit proved pleasant in other ways. "London is as interesting as ever. Spring is here, and the grass and trees are green in all the little parks. It is good to see it all again, and I feel quite at home in some ways."

In 1966 Dyer-Bennet's long association with Hurok ended. He signed with Ann Summers Management, also of New York. The firm managed a large stable of singers, and ensembles such as the Eastman Brass Quintet, the Philadelphia Quartet, and the New York Jazz Sextet had also signed with them. Summers's promotional packet on Dyer-Bennet notes that, besides concerts, the singer is also available for "informal off-stage sessions." These included: "The Current Folksong Renaissance—Reasons and Directions"; "The English Ballad Transplanted in America"; "Songs from Shakespeare's Plays"; "The Historical Value of the Oral Tradition"; "The Fate of the Oral Tradition in an Industrial Society"; and "The Folksong as an Expression of Man's View of the Cosmos."

In 1968 Summers arranged for Dyer-Bennet to travel to Rome to sing at a concert in celebration of the 401st birth year of Claudio Monteverdi. The first half of his recital consisted entirely of songs from the sixteenth and seventeenth centuries and included Monteverdi's own "Lasciatemi Morire." In 1973 Dyer-Bennet left Summers and engaged friend Warren Syer (1923–2007) as his agent. Syer had already enjoyed a long career in media, rising to vice-president of consumer publications for *Billboard* and, in 1972, founding High Fidelity Cable Television, a multi-channel cable system for four Berkshire towns. Together Dyer-Bennet and Syer founded Associated Artists, Ltd. After his stroke in 1972, however, Dyer-Bennet's public performances became increasingly rare. Not until he became enchanted with the idea of performing Schubert's *Die schöne Müllerin* song cycle in the mid-1970s did he resume any kind of regular touring.

CHAPTER 5

THE BLACKLIST

I am very sorry I have to bring up names in this matter . . .
—BURL IVES

Richard Amour, the American poet, once observed that politics has too long been concerned with right or left instead of right or wrong. In the case of Richard Dyer-Bennet, this statement is sadly germane. During and after World War II, Dyer-Bennet took part in a number of activities for all the right reasons—compassion and concern for others—but in support of causes and organizations that attracted the attention of members of the United States government. Dyer-Bennet's actions would harm and alter his career irrevocably. Pete Seeger, himself a target of such attacks, sums up this period in Dyer-Bennet's life: "it was a great tragedy that the black list cut him down."[1]

American folk music has long been associated with leftist politics. "Though it is absurd to speak of a 'communist takeover' of American folk music, as the blacklisters of the 1950s did, it is also a distortion not to recognize the impact left-wing social movements in the past few generations had on the popularization of folk song in the United States."[2] As folk music spread to the cities of the United States it often was embraced by those with a leftist agenda. The power of music as a tool for social change was already well known. Any serious folk singer knew of *The Little Red Song Book*, originally published by the International Workers of the World, or Wobblies, in 1909. Within fourteen years this songbook had already gone through nineteen editions and contained songs—many written by immigrant Joe Hill and labor activist Ralph Chaplin—with new words set to old melodies designed to spread the organization's message of "one big union." Hill and Chaplin understood that a good song was worth a thousand speeches.

In the early 1940s the Almanac Singers were the best-known proponents of political songs. Led by Pete Seeger, Woody Guthrie, Millard Lampell, and Lee Hays, the Almanacs performed both traditional and topical songs. "Their content and style drew upon an eclectic musical heritage, including the nineteenth-century protest songs of England's Chartist movement and the crusade movement in the United States."[3] Their first album, titled *Songs for John Doe*, was released in March 1941 on Keynote Records, for whom Dyer-Bennet was also to record. Because they were written during the Nazi-Soviet non-aggression pact, nearly all of the early Almanac songs warned against American participation in World War II. When Germany invaded the Soviet Union, the Almanacs changed their stance accordingly. They even had a hit of sorts with "Round and Round Hitler's Grave."

As group members entered various branches of the armed forces, the original Almanacs began to dissolve. At a meeting held on May 12, 1942, Dyer-Bennet was mentioned as a possible member of the Headline Singers, a group that would carry on the legacy of the Almanacs. Nothing came of these plans, however, partially due to the fact that among his folksinger peers Dyer-Bennet was sometimes considered "too English." According to Pete Seeger, for example, Dyer-Bennet was "definitely English. He wasn't American."[4] It is certainly true that Dyer-Bennet never gained full acceptance from American singers. "There was probably a prejudice against people who spoke classical Oxford English," claims Seeger. "There was an attitude that 'you can't be a folk singer if you speak that kind of way.'"[5]

When Pete Seeger was discharged from the army in 1945, he returned to New York and organized a "home-from-the-war" party. Dyer-Bennet attended, as well as Lead Belly, Oscar Brand, John Jacob Niles, Woody Guthrie, and others. Seeger's idea was to establish an organization that would collect and disseminate music that could be used by any organization, but especially by unions. Thus *People's Songs* was born. Fred Hellerman, later a member of the Weavers, characterizes the times as one of "great social dislocation in this country. You had millions of servicemen coming back. Black soldiers coming back to Jim Crow after leaving Mississippi and going all over the world and finding that that's not the way it had to be, and coming back not willing to settle for that. Jobs, housing, price controls. A great social dislocation that needed attention. And that's partly what *People's Songs* was about, trying to address these sorts of things."[6] *People's Songs'* credo was boldly stated in its first monthly issue in February 1946: "The people are on the march and must have songs to sing. Now, in 1946, the truth must assert itself in many singing voices . . . It is clear that there must be an organization to make and send songs of labor to the American people through the land."[7]

Helping organize labor unions had become central to Pete Seeger's career, but he was by no means the only performer who entertained at union functions. "Musically speaking, left activists preferred the smoother voices and polished performance styles of Burl Ives and Josh White, which were aesthetically more pleasing to urban audiences familiar with fine art performances."[8] Dyer-Bennet, of course, was also in demand. "In 1949, the American Labor Party of Brooklyn called *People's Songs* and requested Irwin Silber to secure the services of Richard Dyer-Bennet for a fundraising event. Silber agreed but suggested the organization accept Pete Seeger if the first artist was not available. 'Oh, we know Pete,' the replay came. 'He's sung on our soundtrucks and [at] our parties for years. But we need someone who can bring in a mass audience. We need to raise money.'"[9] Seeger later defined this perceived slight as a turning point in his career. "When Irwin . . . told me [about] the conversation, I started doing some rethinking about my own work. Here I'd been knocking myself [out] all these years, congratulating myself on not 'going commercial' and the result was that I was not as much use to the Brooklyn ALP as was my friend [Dyer-Bennet], a highly conscientious and hardworking artist, but one who also set out in a more conventional fashion to build a career."[10]

Seeger redoubled his efforts to disseminate folk songs and, thanks partially to his tremendous success as a member of the Weavers, would soon become the best-known performer in the industry. Dyer-Bennet's fortunes, on the other hand, were about to take a decided turn for the worse. "It was a screwy period," remembers Seeger. "Americans had been told that if we don't purify our nation of traitors we will be taken over by the Communists."[11] In 1950 three former FBI agents, under the company name American Business Consultants, published a directory called *Red Channels*. It contained a list of 151 men and women in the entertainment industry who, they believed, were exerting Communist influence in that sphere. In the book's introduction, the authors quote from FBI Director J. Edgar Hoover's 1947 testimony before Congress. The Communist party, he claimed, "has departed from depending upon the printed word as its medium of propaganda and has taken to the air. Its members and sympathizers have not only infiltrated the airways but they are now persistently seeking radio channels."[12] To help prove their point the editors quoted Stalin, who had written in *Problems of Leninism* that "the dictatorship cannot be effectively realized without 'belts' to transmit power from the vanguard [the Communist Party] to the mass of the advanced class [the 'progressive' writers, actors, directors, etc.], and from this to the mass of those who labor [the public]."[13]

Red Channels was published for the edification of executives in the motion picture, radio, television, and recording industries so that they might silence the voices of those named in its pages. Some of the most famous artists listed were Leonard Bernstein, Aaron Copland, Dashiell Hammett, Lillian Hellman, Langston Hughes, Arthur Miller, Dorothy Parker, Burl Ives, Pete Seeger, Alan Lomax, Zero Mostel, Edward G. Robinson, Orson Welles, and even the striptease artist Gypsy Rose Lee. Dyer-Bennet, too, was named. His five offenses were that he 1.) sang at a Madison Square Garden rally on September 28, 1944, to celebrate twenty-five years of the Communist Party in America; 2.) was a sponsor of the Scientific and Cultural Conference for World Peace, held in 1949; 3.) sang at a party for Alexander Trachtenberg on December 3, 1944; 4.) entertained at a birthday party in honor of William Gropper on December 4, 1944; and 5.) was given a farewell concert by *People's Songs* in 1947 when he left New York for Aspen.

Most of the charges, such as they were, were true. Dyer-Bennet had sung that night in Madison Square Garden, and he had attended the Scientific and Cultural Conference for World Peace, held at the Waldorf-Astoria Hotel in March 1949. The conference was organized as a forum to generate ideas to counter the Marshall Plan, NATO, and Truman's policies in general. As for the other charges, Alexander Trachtenberg (1884–1966) had edited *The Collected Works of V. I. Lenin* (1927) and was thus an obvious target of American intelligence. William Gropper (1897–1977) was an American artist who had traveled to Russia in 1927 and whose work was later deemed "subversive" by Senator McCarthy. The final charge simply testifies to the editors' growing suspicion that *People's Songs* might, in fact, be growing as powerful as Seeger had hoped it might.

At nearly the same time, Dyer-Bennet's brother, John, also came under attack from the government. In 1954 he was cited as a security risk by the U.S. Army. A captain in the army at the time, John Dyer-Bennet was charged with contributing to the National Sharecropper's Organization. He was also taken to task for listing as character references in his defense persons who were members of suspicious organizations such as the Civil Rights Congress, the Labor Youth League, the Independent Progressive Party, and others. John also listed his older brother Richard as someone who might speak to his character. The Army was quite thorough in cataloging Richard's offenses, namely that he had been involved in one way or another with organizations cited by the United States Attorney General as subversive: the Joint Anti-Fascist Refugee Committee, American Youth for Democracy, the Congress of American-Soviet Friendship, and the American-Russian Institute.

Richard was not the only Dyer-Bennet family member John had listed as a character reference, nor was he the only one whose actions the army questioned. Both their mother Miriam and sister Miriam Jr. were cited due to suspected membership in the Young Communist League. Brother Fred Dyer-Bennet was cited as being a member of the American Student Union, an organization the army claimed was a Communist front. In a July 28, 1955, letter protesting his innocence, John Dyer-Bennet refutes the charges against his family. His sister, Miriam, he claims, attended a few meetings of the Young Communist League but never joined it. He admits that Fred was a member of the American Student Union, but previous to the years listed by the army, and at a time when the organization enjoyed the support of President Roosevelt. Regarding Richard's activities, he writes that "in general his policy was to sing benefits when he approved of the immediate cause being sided, without asking about the politics of the sponsoring organization."[14] John then reminds the army that Richard also sang at bond rallies, in V.A. wards, and for the USO. The charges against John Dyer-Bennet were eventually thrown out and, instead of being made to tender his resignation, he was offered an honorable discharge from the army.

In a letter written to John in 1954, Richard Dyer-Bennet discusses his past at some length and clearly states his political views.

> To begin with, I have twice been associated with clearly Communist groups.[15] The first association was in 1935 or 1937, when I attended three (possibly four) meetings of a group in Berkeley. I think it was a Young Communist League group. I went because I was interested and curious about Kenny May's zeal. [Note: May was a friend of the family and would eventually marry Miriam Jr.]. . . . The three (or four) meetings I attended in '36 or '37 were not very interesting to me. My memory is that the group was concerned with a mimeographed newsletter dealing with labor and political questions in the Bay Area. It seems rather childish now, but no doubt seemed to have some point then. At any rate, I was bored and did not continue to participate. Whether or not I was considered a member of the group I am not sure. . . . Again, in 1943 and 1944, I attended four meetings of a musicians' group sponsored by the Communist Political Association. I was certainly considered a member of this group—paid dues and was given a card which I threw away as it served no purpose. The meetings were open and one could bring anyone to them. I myself was taken to the first meeting as a non-member and attended at least one other meeting with non-members. The purpose of the meetings seemed to be to discuss the social and political functions of artists in our society. Nothing of real interest and value to me came from the four meetings and I ceased to attend, ceased to pay dues, and ceased to be considered a member. A member of the group came to see me in 1947 and discussed with me my reasons for dropping out. I discussed my thoughts freely on that occasion and no further attempt was made to re-engage my interest.

In the last ten years I have done a lot of reading, thinking, talking and arguing about social and political problems and methods of [illegible]. I believe there is a relationship between economic problems and general social wellbeing; and I believe that man must and will learn to plan and control his raw materials and devise a more equitable distribution of material goods. This makes me some kind of socialist, I presume.

I have come to distrust forms of government which accumulate great power in the hands of a group which cannot be voted out of office. I am in this regard anti-Soviet. It is possible that social and economic reform in Russia was only possible by a political revolt which inevitably put power into the hands of a dedicated, fanatical, well-meaning but ruthless group of men. Maybe Russia had to go through all this to burst out of a feudal, agrarian condition into an industrial 20th-century nation.

. . . I believe the Western world is faced with different problems than faced Russia in 1918, and we come to these problems with a background of very different traditions. We must therefore find our own solutions. What will happen in Italy and France I don't know, but in England and America our solutions will not be communism. I think, however, we will move toward some kind of democratic socialism—by which I mean that we will have a planned economy run by elected representatives whom we will vote in and out of office as we desire.

. . . I think you can see in the above pages the record of a slowly-maturing attitude towards life, our problems, and approaches to progress. Now, as to my singing activities, they were not related, consciously, to my political associates. I cannot give you a complete record of the groups for whom I did benefits, nor do I know how many are or have been listed by the Attorney General as subversive. From the rise of Hitler in Germany, through the Spanish Civil War, and the Second World War, I became increasingly aware of fascism. I would judge that ninety-odd percent of all the benefits I have sung since 1935 have been to raise money for groups which were avowedly anti-fascist and trying to help victims of fascism. Hence I sang for the Medical Bureau to aid Spanish Democracy, and the joint anti-fascist Refugee Committee. These groups were raising money to help the victims of fascism. Whether the groups were controlled by communists or not I do not know, and is beside the point. A decent piece of work is a decent piece of work, whoever does it. I would not refuse to help a communist save another human being's life even today. Did we not fight with the communists against Germany? I also sang for "China Aid" in '43 or '44 (not listed as subversive so far as I know), "Bundles for Britain" (surely not listed), "Soviet-American Friendship Committee" (I don't know if it is listed). All benefits for the above were to raise money for what I considered worthy causes—I received no payment of course.

. . . I sang once, in 1944, at a public rally in Madison Square Garden, sponsored by the Communist Party and commemorating the founding of the Red Army. There were a number of non-communist political big wigs present and speaking. This was not a benefit. I was engaged professionally ($400) to sing at a public rally honoring the founding of an Allied army. My managers at this time were "Music Corporation of America." When I asked them, "do you think it is wrong for me to sing at a Communist-sponsored meeting?" the answer was "For $400? Hell no!"

. . . In 1945 the F.B.I. cleared me for a three months U.S.O. tour in the Philippines. In 1953, the State Department cleared me for England. The authorized U.S. government people know damned well that I have never been engaged in any illegal or traitorous activities, that I am not a subversive. Only the professional anti-liberals, such as the editors of "Red Channels", have tried to damage me, and those birds consider Eisenhower dangerously liberal.

In a letter written early in 1955, Dyer-Bennet expresses no regret about his actions. "The fact that some of the organizations for whom I sang have since been listed by the Attorney General as subversive does not make me regret the little help I was able to give them. No man has much time to question the morals, politics or intentions of his allies during an emergency, nor is that an important issue in view of the immediate necessity."[16] Later in the same letter, he elaborates.

In the light of later events it may seem that I lent my aid to groups whose general purpose I could not agree with. If so, I would regret whatever part of my help went not to specific and worthy causes, but to general and unworthy ones. This regret, however, is distinct from any sense of shame. I regret many errors in my life, but I am fortunately able to say that I have no reason to feel shame for any of my activities or connections as a professional singer and as a man. I have never found myself involved with an activity which violated my own ethics and sense of decency. I believe in democratic procedure in government, majority rule in politics, and change by growth and education. I also believe the American tradition is firmly rooted enough to allow the inclusion in our society of all those degrees and shades of opinion which seek for the best path into the future.

In 1951 Dyer-Bennet's old friend Burl Ives had a top ten hit with his rendition of "On Top of Old Smoky." Ives's inclusion in *Red Channels*, however, had resulted in several terminated appearances. Ives felt threatened enough to voluntarily appear before a Senate sub-committee that dealt with the Subversive Infiltration of Radio, Television, and the Entertainment Industry. This group was part of a larger body, The House Committee on Un-American Activities, usually called the House Un-American Committee, or HUAC. Though usually associated with Senator Joseph McCarthy and the communist witch hunts of the 1950s, the committee was established in 1938 as the Dies Committee and continued to exist until 1975. The committee's original intention was to investigate individuals or groups who were suspected of threatening the American form of government. There had, of course, been numerous precedents of such hysteria in American history—the Alien and Sedition Acts (1798), the Know-Nothing Movement (1850s), and the Espionage Act of 1917.

On May 20, 1952, Ives gave his testimony. After summarizing his personal history for the committee, Ives explained in some detail why he was there. "I should like to say the reason I appear here this morning is the fact that my recent experience overseas has clarified my own mind in regard to my position in this case; not my position in regard to my thoughts on communism—that was settled a good many years ago, but in regard to appearing here and presenting my particular case. I should like to state that I made a decision a good many years ago in regard to communism. I realized I was not a Communist and did not believe in the Communist philosophy. But having been, for many years, around New York and in what they call the general labor movement, and at the time of the New Deal, I was in the middle of all of these artistic things that were happening. As a matter of fact, my first audience as a singer was various unions and so-called progressive organizations. At this time I sang for various groups wherever I could get an audience, because nobody would listen to me before, and to have an audience to sing my songs to made me very happy. My first premise was that I was a missionary, was and still am, for American folk songs. It was my ambition to bring these songs before the whole population of the United States, and that has been my prime aim in life. However, as I said, I made the decision many years ago in regard to the Communist philosophy. I did not participate in any of those organizations. I believe that most of these organizations at the time sounded like very positive and good things to do. They were known as good causes, so I sang for many of these things, with the sole purpose of doing good, not evil."[17]

Eventually Ives returns to his overseas experience. "That brings me up to the point . . . that while in Europe at this time I got my mind clarified, not in regard to any political things, because as I said before, that was clear, but my mind is clarified in regard to, well, let us say, my position in regard to this committee. I realized that it was my duty to come here and to tell you my position. I got to that point in this way: I was very fortunate to be able to go to Europe and sing. I was in Great Britain, France, and Italy. I happened to be, on the morning of May Day, in Rome. In the afternoon I was in Naples. There was a great deal of resentment of the United States that you could feel as well as see, and this annoyed me very much. And it was through my experience there with this feeling against my country that I began to realize that there is not this space where anybody who has been a liberal can escape to, and say, 'I will have no part of this thing.' There are only two positions, and there has never been any thought in my mind of being for anybody at any time who is an enemy of my country."[18]

At this point the committee asks Ives a quick question for clarification before allowing him to continue. "I have come here because I am a public figure, and because many people enjoy my singing. And I have come here to make my position clear for them, as well as for my own self. Before, when I felt put upon a little bit, I did not feel like coming down. I felt resentful that I should be cancelled off of a program because of this, because in my mind I knew that I was straight and clear."[19] Ives then confirms or denies for the committee his presence at several events. A remark that applies to many such appearances is "I may have appeared someplace, because I was running around singing any place I could in those days, but, in my mind, I have no recollection of any definite thing about the organization in regard to myself."[20] He then denies that he had anything to do with the Scientific and Cultural Conference for World Peace. When asked about his knowledge of the Communist Political Association, Ives replies: "I did not go as a communist, I went to find out what I could about communism, to see if it made any sense to me."[21]

Committee member Senator Connors then asks Ives for specifics: "Let me say that presumably the allegation you mentioned just prior to your recitation of the facts arose out of the meetings of the Communist Political Association which you attended, and I think it is incumbent upon us to find out if you can recall how many such meetings you did attend, and where the meetings were held, and specifically and importantly, who solicited your participation in these meetings."[22] It is in response to this request that Ives makes his damning statement about Dyer-Bennet. "Yes, I will be very happy to tell you all that I can about it. I first talked to an old friend of mine. I am very sorry that I have to bring up names in this matter, because I would like to be able to not mention other names, but I can't. I will have to do it, because these people will have to do as I have done, and many others. They will have to make up their minds on this matter. So, in my heart, I have to mention these names, although a couple of them are very good friends of mine. It was through a talk that I had with Mr. Richard Dyer-Bennett [sic]. He had just started into these lectures himself, and it was through him that I went there. I can also say that I had a conversation with him a few years back, and we had both come to the same conclusion, and he had also rejected it and didn't go back any more after, I think he told me it was 1945 or 1944, something like that. He went at the same time that I did, and we were really going to find out what this was about. From what I could gather on it, I didn't like it. After a time I went no more and rejected the idea, and that is that."[23]

The folk music community's reaction to Ives's testimony was predictably hostile. Pete Seeger portrayed his disgust in a review of Ives's book of sea songs (*Sea Songs of Sailing, Whaling, and Fishing*, 1956). "Burl Ives went to Washington, D.C. a few years ago, to the House Un-American Committee, and fingered, like any common stool-pigeon, some of his radical associates of the early 1940s. He did this not because he wanted to but because he felt it was the only way to preserve his lucrative contracts; and that makes his action all the more despicable."[24] Irwin Silber, editor of *Sing Out!* wrote: "The well known folksinger, who once joined in singing 'Solidarity Forever,' has a different tune today. It might be called 'Ballad for Stoolpigeons' or the 'Strange Case of the Wayfaring Stranger.'... The future of Burl Ives should be interesting. We've never seen anyone sing while crawling on his belly before."[25]

In his book *Naming Names*, Victor Navasky points out that Ives's behavior was far from typical. Only approximately "one-third of the witnesses who actually testified about subversion in the entertainment community chose to name names, to 'crawl through the mud,' to collaborate with the Committee and, at least as it looked from the outside, to betray their friends."[26] Among the majority was Pete Seeger. When called to testify before HUAC in 1955, Seeger took the high road. "I decline to discuss, under compulsion, where I have sung, and who has sung my songs, and who else has sung with me, and the people I have known. I love my country very dearly, and I greatly resent this implication that some of the places that I have sung and some of the people that I have known, and some of my opinions, whether they are religious or philosophical, or I might be a vegetarian, make me any less of an American."[27]

Others are less quick to judge Ives, citing what has been called the "dupe" hypothesis. "They suggest that numerous folk entrepreneurs associated with and performed for the Communist party and other groups because these fronts were the only ones interested in their type of music at the time. They argue that the Stalinists provided audiences and employment for 'folk' singers. When other opportunities appeared, these artists turned to more respectable audiences and other media of communication."[28]

There was never any question of Dyer-Bennet appearing before HUAC. Mel Dyer-Bennet recalls that a government lawyer once came to interview him about the matter. They had compiled a dossier on Dyer-Bennet that was full of untruths. Dyer-Bennet then offered to testify, saying that he would have attorney Telford Taylor (1908–1998), one of the lawyers from the Nuremberg Trials and a fan of the singer, represent him. The cowed government lawyer beat a hasty retreat. Unfortunately, however, the damage had already been done.

The recording industry took the blacklist quite seriously. "Faced with a choice between profit and principle, the business concerns did not hesitate.

CBS appointed a vice-president solely to ensure that no one upon whom suspicion had fallen was employed by the system; at NBC a legal department took care of the same operation."[29] Ronnie Gilbert of the Weavers remembers the sudden impact of the blacklist. One moment her group was on the top of the hit parade with their rendition of Lead Belly's "Goodnight, Irene." Then Seeger was listed in *Red Channels*. "The moment that we were headlined with 'Weavers Called Reds' that was the end of that. Bookings got cancelled, the State Fair got cancelled, all the major dates got cancelled."[30] Once booked for the largest auditoriums, the Weavers were now reduced to singing anywhere they could. Gilbert elaborates. "In 1953 we were singing in Daffy's Bar and Grill on the outskirts of Cleveland, and it became clear that there really wasn't much sense in trying to go on."[31]

Harold Leventhal, the Weavers' manager, outlined how the blacklist operated. "The record company, through record stores, was getting protests, why are you carrying the Weavers, and all that. So the stores dropped the records. What did they need trouble for? So they took the records off the shelves. When that happened, Decca literally dropped the Weavers. Without being official or otherwise, didn't make an issue about it, just, boom."[32] Some musicians tried to join together to fight the blacklist, but these efforts were poorly organized and unsuccessful. Speaking about the Weavers, Leventhal notes, "nobody in the music business came out in their defense. Nobody. Either from the record companies, or other artists. Nobody. There weren't many that could have, who understood the situation. There were a few, very few individuals that understood this, who held some high positions, but they never spoke out."[33]

Some artists did attempt to redress the wrongs done by the blacklist, however. Theodore Bikel (born 1924), both an accomplished actor and a folk singer of distinction, took up his pen. Writing on behalf of the arts chapter of the American Jewish Congress, Bikel claimed: "We, as artists, must protest an act that seeks to compel the performer to bargain for his livelihood with other values than his talent."[34] Playwright Elmer Rice (1892–1967) compared the blacklist to Soviet censorship. "I have repeatedly denounced the men who sit in the Kremlin for judging artists by political standards; I do not intend to acquiesce when the same procedure is followed by political commissars who sit in the offices of advertising agencies or business corporations."[35] Sadly, none of these noble efforts had much of an impact.

In another letter to his brother John, Dyer-Bennet writes that the editors of *Red Channels* had "told me that I can be removed from their blacklist by publicly recanting some former views, and by naming names and implicating as many other people as possible. In as much as I have never known any traitors, spies or saboteurs, I have no one on whom to inform except a few perfectly decent and well-meaning musicians who, I suspect, were motivated as I was. I am therefore considered 'uncooperative' and will remain blacklisted by a few fanatics. I am not concerned over this and hope it is not the basis for concern in your career."[36]

On January 27, 1955, Dyer-Bennet wrote his brother again, enclosing a notarized statement John could use in his own defense. In this letter he elaborates on his meeting with those responsible for blacklisting him.

> Concerning "Red Channels," in the summer of 1953 I met with Vincent K. Hartnett, one of the publishers of that blacklist. He read me the "charges" listed against me. Some of the information was accurate, some was partly accurate, and some was entirely inaccurate. I was, for instance, listed as singing for some organization on a date at which time I was 2,000 miles away. I was also mentioned in connection with events with which I had had no connection. Hartnett informed me they "had nothing on me" later than 1944, and that I had clearly had a "change of heart." He suggested I write an article for the *Saturday Evening Post*, or *Colliers*, confessing my sins and naming as many people as I could possibly involve. He said I would [sic] no more trouble from "Red Channels" if I would do this.[37]

Needless to say, Dyer-Bennet declined this offer. "Of course if he'd been willing to say: 'Senator McCarthy, I was once a member of the Communist Party,' he could have avoided a lot of trouble trying to get jobs,"[38] recalls Pete Seeger. "But he would have known that in the long run he would not only have been ashamed of himself, but the other people he might have named would have been ashamed of him. That's what happened to poor Burl Ives." Dyer-Bennet's business partner Harvey Cort believes that "Pete Seeger used the fact that he was blacklisted almost as good publicity. Dick couldn't do that. He wasn't singing left-wing or pro-labor stuff in the first place. When Dick got bombed with the Red Channels thing it interrupted his career. And when you interrupt a performer's career, it's very hard to get back the momentum. Your audience gets dispersed."[39]

It is, of course, impossible to accurately measure the impact the blacklist had on Dyer-Bennet's career. Certainly he received fewer bookings, and the fact that he decided in 1955 to found his own recording company indicates that other avenues might not have been available to him. Perhaps Oscar Brand puts it best. "He was doing very well until the blacklist. Hurok got him into places that ordinarily folk singers never would have. People who saw him wanted to hear the voice, the musicianship. He was flying and they shot him down."[40]

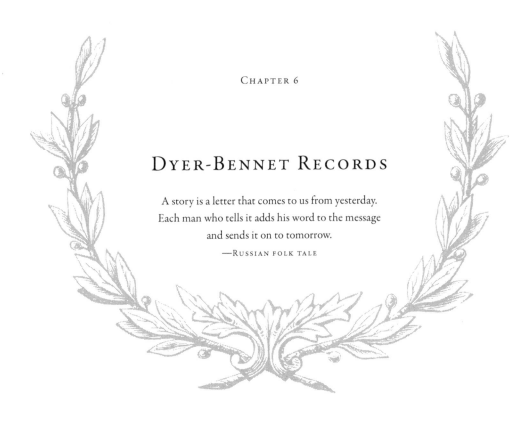

CHAPTER 6

DYER-BENNET RECORDS

A story is a letter that comes to us from yesterday.
Each man who tells it adds his word to the message
and sends it on to tomorrow.
—RUSSIAN FOLK TALE

In 1951 Dyer-Bennet and his family moved to the Berkshires in western Massachusetts. Again, the primary impetus behind the move was the welfare of the family. Bonnie was now seven and Brooke four, and Dyer-Bennet saw the rustic area as an ideal place for them to grow up. The territory is an extension of the Green Mountains and is quite beautiful, consisting mostly of wooded hills and small villages. Mount Greylock stands as the range's highest peak at 3,491 feet above sea level.

In 1954, the Dyer-Bennets bought land and had a cabin built in Monterey, 134 miles west of Boston, 140 miles north of New York. Originally known as South Tyringham, Monterey was settled in 1739 but was not incorporated as a separate town until 1847. In the 1950s the village was home to approximately eight hundred inhabitants. The family lived in the cabin until 1958, when they could finally afford to build a more substantial home on the property not far from the original dwelling. The new house was a one-story contemporary resting on the banks of a pond. Altogether the property ran to 37 acres. Ever the sportsman, Dyer-Bennet had an artificial grass tennis court constructed near the house in 1980 and often entertained opponents there. He took full advantage of the court's low bounce, frequently frustrating his opponents with his sliced ground strokes. One of the central design points of the new house was an area where Dyer-Bennet could make his own recordings. While the ideal of recording in his own house was never fully achieved (only some of the spoken pieces included on later albums were recorded there), Dyer-Bennet and his family grew to love the house and the beauty of its natural surroundings. After a lifetime of frequent resettling, the minstrel had at last found a real home.

Dyer-Bennet had long been dissatisfied with the standard of his commercially produced recordings, stating in a letter to his mother that though the most recent ones are "are a good deal better than my old ones, they are still disappointing to me."[1] Dyer-Bennet had also not been happy with the time constraints placed upon him by the various companies for whom he had recorded, some of which required him to complete an album in a single day. "In addition, the standard use of echo chambers and over-dependence on cutting, splicing, and dubbing to produce recordings was an esthetic anathema to him."[2] Issues such as cover design and program content were also important to the singer.

If Dyer-Bennet knew his preferences, he also knew his technical limitations. He set about finding a recording engineer and soon discovered a willing business partner in Harvey Cort, a television director and producer from New York. Together they founded Dyer-Bennet Records. "Their original intent was quite modest; Dyer-Bennet would use their first record for concert promotion purposes, while Cort intended to use it for personal gifts."[3] They had never heard of such single-artist labels gaining much popularity or wide distribution.

In 1955 Dyer-Bennet recorded *Richard Dyer-Bennet 1*, with Rudy van Gelder serving as recording engineer. "Rudy had a boutique sound recording studio where he did mostly top jazz musicians,"[4] Cort recalled. "He was a great recording engineer. I told him what I was trying to do, and he said he was willing to try it. I wanted to get a full frequency recording or dynamic recording—to get it sounding exactly as it did in a concert." Dyer-Bennet's dynamic range proved difficult to record. "A song like 'Lonesome Valley' had some very high stuff and some very low stuff in terms of dynamics of frequency. The grooves would create a pre-echo if you had too much of a booming sound. We tried to push the envelope and Rudy was the guy to do it. He actually stood there in making the master disc and widened the groove as it came up so that it wouldn't cause pre-echo."[5]

The album cover, featuring a black and white photo of Dyer-Bennet's head by Clemens Kalischer, was simple and elegant. Kalischer's photography would also feature on the covers of *Richard Dyer-Bennet 4, 6, 7, 8*, and *10*. Lyrics for all songs were included as an insert. The album is undoubtedly the highlight of Dyer-Bennet's recording career. Its sixteen tracks, divided into three thematic groups, include many of his signature songs and fan favorites. Nine of the songs would appear in his 1971 songbook; only one of them ("Phyllis and Her Mother") had appeared on any previous album. It is clear that with this album the artist intended to make a fresh start.

The recording sessions typically ran two to four hours. "We went until he got tired,"[6] Cort remembers. "He would be the determinant. We made no cutting. He didn't want any tape patching. It would be accurate to describe him as a perfectionist, but in some areas he was less so. For example, he felt the important thing was the interpretation. If his voice broke he didn't care that much—I cared a lot! He was looking to do the best performance. If there were slight things that were wrong, if it wasn't quite perfect he could live with that."[7] Still, the sessions proved quite demanding on the singer. "They were very stressful for him. He was trying to do *the* performance each time. He could excuse a less than perfect performance in a concert, but not on a record."[8]

Richard Dyer-Bennet 1 begins with the hauntingly beautiful "Oft in the Stilly Night." The tune is traditional, the lyrics by Thomas Moore (1779–1852). Moore was an Irish patriot whose songs found favor both in Ireland and England. Many of his compositions, including "The Minstrel Boy," "The Last Rose of Summer," and "Believe Me If All Those Endearing Young Charms" are still familiar to contemporary folk music fans. Among Moore songs, "Oft in the Stilly Night" is not widely known, but in Dyer-Bennet's hands it becomes a masterpiece. His delicate singing perfectly reflects the fragile sentiments of Moore's lyric. The song must be performed by a mature singer, one who has experienced the highs and lows of life. It is a fitting introduction to an album whose songs will span life's spectrum.

While the exact origin of "Molly Brannigan" was unknown to him, Dyer-Bennet believed it was a nineteenth-century Irish music hall song. The tune was originally called "Cossey's Jig" and was composed by Walker "Piper" Jackson. Dyer-Bennet brings great drama to the song, but his understanding of the lyric—taken from a John McCormack recording—is faulty. In the fifth verse, instead of "If I only had a blundergun / I'd go and fight a duel ma'am," he sings "If I only had a blundergun / I'd go and fight the Immelman!" This mondegreen does not detract from the power of the song, however. His guitar accompaniment is precise and beautiful and matches the changing pace of his vocal delivery. Dyer-Bennet's mastery of pianissimo and fortissimo is shown in the opening lines of the fourth and sixth verses, while the final line—so full of self-pity on paper—is sung with quiet power and genuine anguish.

Dyer-Bennet's accompaniment to "Down by the Sally Gardens" sounds almost harplike. This is appropriate, given that the tune is Irish. Its words were written by the greatest Irish poet of the twentieth century, W. B. Yeats (1865–1939). Yeats reconstructed the lyric after hearing a variation of it sung by an old woman in Sligo. The tune is also known as "The Maids of the Mourne Shore." The singer notes that his addition of *All* at the beginning of the first line is his error. This simple lyric of the transience of young love is perfectly suited to Dyer-Bennet's tenor.

"The Bold Fenian Men" (sometimes called "Down by the Glenside") stems from the 1916 Easter Rebellion in Dublin. Peadar Kearney (1883–1942), composer of the Irish national anthem "The Soldier's Song," took part in the rebellion and later wrote this song to honor his fellow fenians, or Irish patriots. ("Fenian" is derived from the Irish *Na Fianna* or *Na Fianna Éireann*, ancient warriors sworn to protect Ireland.) Kearney died in poverty, but he has achieved fame through his music. Dyer-Bennet's deliberate pace lends import to his subject and arrests the listener's attention. We are drawn in and listen raptly, just as the song's narrator listens to the old woman. Dyer-Bennet's operatic conclusion to the song is chilling in its intensity. The fact that the opening four songs on the album are Irish shows Dyer-Bennet's love of the cadences and rhythms of Irish music, as well as the influence of John McCormack.

Of "Three Fishers" Dyer-Bennet wrote: "When I was a small boy in England, I was occasionally taken to the seaside. I can remember seeing grey silhouettes of ships out on the water, and being told they were trawlers. This was the name given to the boats used by commercial fishermen. It seemed to me then a dangerous and exciting life, and I know now that it was also grim and not very rewarding. Before the days of steam it must have often been as Charles Kingsley tells us in this poem, set to music by John Hullah."[9] Dyer-Bennet's treatment of the chorus is particularly affecting, and his guitar chords sound appropriately ominous.

"The Bonnie Earl of Morey" is a famous ballad concerning the murder of a sixteenth-century Scottish nobleman. Edward Ives was so moved by Dyer-Bennet's interpretation of the ballad that he dedicated to him his book-length study of "the man, the murder, the ballad." In the prologue to his book, Ives describes hearing Dyer-Bennet sing the ballad for the first time.

> Now here I was in Town Hall again, center orchestra, third row back, just about the best seats in the house. . . . House lights down, stage lights up, and Dyer-Bennet walked out on the stage, impeccable as always in full soup-and-fish. . . . Then about halfway toward intermission came "The Bonnie Earl of Murray", a piece I knew I'd read over quickly as a child at some point but had never heard sung or even imagined still *could* be sung. I was stunned—there is no better word for it—by this angry lament that a fine young man, the Queen's love, should die so, perhaps by treachery ("Now wae be to thee, Huntly!"), all this to a powerful accompaniment that made it into something between a dead march and a war cry. For that moment I was not in Town Hall but somewhere on what might have been a moor before a swart tower from whose battlement a lone lady forever looked into the distance.[10]

While Dyer-Bennet's singing is characteristically dramatic, it is his guitar playing that leaves an even longer-lasting impression. The guitar, in fact, is heard alone for more than half of the recording. Its insistent call brings to mind the narrator's indignation; it also suggests the canter of horse hooves—both Morey's as he "sounds through the toon" and the messenger's as he rides to the castle to deliver the news of Morey's death to his wife.

"Fine Flowers in the Valley" is a Scottish song of the supernatural related in theme to the Child ballad "The Cruel Mother." Robert Burns composed a version of the song as well. Dyer-Bennet's performance again features expressive guitar accompaniment. His voice is restrained but capably renders the eerie atmosphere the song's theme requires.

Dyer-Bennet ends his first grouping of songs (and side one of the original LP) with the entertaining "Vicar of Bray." Indeed, the listener appreciates the lively tune after the solemnity rendered by its predecessors. In his album notes Dyer-Bennet points out that the song is not—as one Canadian music critic claimed—a satire on organized religion, but rather one on political opportunism. Its six verses cover a turbulent fifty-four-year period in English history that saw great religious changes in the reigns of Kings Charles II (1660–85), James II (1685–88), William III (1689–1702), Queen Anne (1702–14), and King George I (1714–27). That the clever vicar is able to adapt to each succeeding ecclesiastical twist is both his genius and the song's charm. Numerous historical models for the vicar have been proposed, including Simon Simonds, an independent under Cromwell, a Church of England cleric under Charles II, a catholic under James II, and a moderate Anglican under William III. Bray is shorthand for Bray-on-Thames, Berkshire. An English comic opera bearing the same name as the song was written by Sydney Grundy and debuted in 1882.

The second group of songs opens with Lord Byron's "So We'll Go No More A-Roving," a short lyric written in 1817. Dyer-Bennet composed its beautiful guitar accompaniment one night in a hotel room, a poetry anthology open before him. Joan Baez would use the same accompaniment when she included the song on her 1964 album, *Joan Baez 5*. Dyer-Bennet employs numerous tempo changes and well-placed rests to heighten the beauty of Byron's words.

"Phyllis and Her Mother" was learned from Sven Scholander. Dyer-Bennet's liner notes tell us that the song "was published in Germany in 1799, and both poet and composer were given as anonymous."[11] The translation from the German is the minstrel's own, one he characterizes as "more free than literal." It is a delightful story of youthful love's ultimate triumph and provides a nice change of pace to an album that deals mainly with more serious concerns. Again, the singer's reading is masterful, with varying tempos and vocal alterations that cleverly lead the song to its humorous conclusion.

Dyer-Bennet translated "The Joys of Love" from the French "Plaisir d'amour," though the minstrel notes that the original text may have been written by a German named Schwarzendorf. Dyer-Bennet displays wonderful control of his lower register in the piece before effortlessly soaring to his more accustomed heights. A tricky change of key is employed for the second verse, and his breath control is shown to good display, both in the transition to the final verse and in the song's last lines.

The final group of songs on the album is from the United States. Dyer-Bennet describes his "I'm a Poor Boy" as a composite of several versions he had heard. The singer's ability to sustain notes is on great display in this piece, and the guitar accompaniment is wonderfully vibrant. In typical fashion he sings the third verse in plaintive, subdued tones before belting out the final verse, his voice at its most powerful. "In singing this," Dyer-Bennet noted, "I sustain the high notes as long as possible, since it is one of those rare songs that are enhanced by as much soaring power as the singer can manage."[12]

Dyer-Bennet learned "Pull off Your Old Coat" from Sam Eskin. According to Eskin, this song originated in the United States and was taken to England before finding its way back home. In his 1971 songbook Dyer-Bennet notes that the song should be performed "sadly, with an underpinning of anger."[13] It is a protest song of sorts about the whims of fortune and the inequalities that color so much of life in both the new and the old world. Thematically it is related to the album's final song, in that both illustrate a dogged approach to life's difficult journey.

Dyer-Bennet describes "Down in the Valley" as "a much better song than is generally acknowledged—perhaps because we all know it so well; perhaps because there are many inferior variants of words and tune; perhaps because it can sound maudlinly sentimental when whined and in a way typical of some very popular country singers."[14] Mindful of this tendency, Dyer-Bennet's reading is quite simple; he allows the song to speak for itself while maintaining its gentle power. An uncharacteristic guitar error (in the first line of the third verse) was allowed to stand. Together with the mondegreen in "Molly Brannigan," it is proof that Dyer-Bennet did not allow his perfectionism to scuttle an otherwise beautiful performance. The penultimate verse ("Into the past, love, wanders my mind / Sad recollections are all that I find") is Dyer-Bennet's own and shows his ability not only to assimilate his words with the original but also to augment the song's meaning.

"Pedro" is an original Dyer-Bennet composition, his first (besides the OWI recordings) to appear on record. This inclusion is another indication of the new freedom the minstrel felt in having established his own label. Written in 1940, it includes a lively guitar accompaniment and celebrates the art of another minstrel, able with his guitar and voice to "steal all hearts away." Again, Dyer-Bennet admits a mistake—that he used *pueblo* as if it meant house instead of village—but allows it to stand "by invoking a poet's traditional privilege."[15] The final verse is lyrically the strongest, especially the description of the minstrel "setting a tune to the age-old mysteries."

The album, already so powerful in its themes and scope, closes with a number that will long be associated with Dyer-Bennet. "The Lonesome Valley" would be used from 1955 to 1996 by Chicago radio station WFMT as the closing number of *The Midnight Special*. Named after Lead Belly's famous song, the show began in 1953, broadcasting at 11 p.m. on Saturday nights, and hosted by Mike Nichols. Hearing "The Lonesome Valley" broadcast on WFMT was the introduction to Dyer-Bennet for hundreds of listeners. Norman Pellegrini, program director at WFMT from 1953 until 1996, recalls hearing a Studs Terkel interview with Dyer-Bennet that included a performance of the song. "We all fell in love with it from then on," observed Pellegrini. "It always reminded me of what it meant to think about one's own humanity, but at the same time it was comforting—as though Dyer-Bennet was saying he knew he and I were in this life thing together, and he understood."[16] Dyer-Bennet called it "the most powerful and moving American song I have yet encountered."[17] In his 1971 songbook he calls it his favorite "among truly indigenous American songs."[18] There he adds that "For years I did not perform the song because I could not find a suitable accompaniment. Finally I hit upon a slightly syncopated drumming on the guitar strings, and though it is unlike what the folk musician, black or white, would be apt to do, it is somehow thoroughly appropriate to both text and tune." Indeed, it is the unusual sound of this "drumming"—persistent as a heartbeat—that first gains the listener's attention. The song immediately addresses each of us, holds us spellbound. We are reminded of our journey's common end; how will we cross that valley when our turn comes? The guitar ceases its beat before the beginning of the first verse before springing back to life, heralding news of great import. Dyer-Bennet's voice sounds more powerful than we have ever heard it as he reminds us first of the difficulty of life's journey and then of the ultimate salvation that is available to any good man. The chorus brings us back down to earth, but only to prepare us for the next resounding declamation, even more commanding than the first due to Dyer-Bennet's going up a third of an interval to hit the A on the word *natural*. Like parishioners reminded of the horrors of hell, we now need soothing release, and it is provided in a final repetition of the haunting chorus.

Richard Dyer-Bennet 1 sold well (approximately four thousand copies) and was met with great critical praise. Writing in the *Record Changer*, Kenneth Goldstein claimed: "We can now appreciate his complaints about previous recordings. The first release under his own label is the finest album he has yet recorded. The singing is tops, the engineering is superb, the production job is excellent. Without a doubt this is a masterpiece of its kind."[19] John Conly reviewed many of Dyer-Bennet's releases for *Atlantic*. While probably not the most impartial critic—some of Dyer-Bennet's albums were recorded in his living room—he provided honest assessments of the records. About the first he wrote: "What I like is that he really can bring out the story-content of songs like 'The Vicar of Bray', 'The Bonny Earl of Morey', and 'Down in the Valley', as if there were joy for him in the telling. These songs were not fashioned to be heard as something quaint and bygone; they need no antique vestments."[20] He did note, however, that "the recording is almost too realistic; one can hear the singer inhale occasionally." Max de Schaunsee of the *Philadelphia Bulletin* called the album "the best recording he has done to date. I hope there will be more."[21] Elinor Hugh of the *Boston Herald* wrote "I cannot recommend it too highly."[22]

The album sold better than either Dyer-Bennet or Cort could have imagined. Cort "persuaded the manager of the Record Hunter, one of New York's best record stores, to take the records on consignment. The Record Hunter ran a newspaper ad announcing that Dyer-Bennet would be in the store signing copies of his album. . . . One of those who admired the album was Jac Holzman, the head of Electra Records. Holzman ran an ad in the monthly Schwann catalog for Dyer-Bennet's record, which he praised very highly. This remarkable act of generosity, which took Dyer-Bennet and Cort completely by surprise, opened up national distribution."[23] "We have never heard Mr. Dyer-Bennet sing better," the ad ran, "or be more perfectly recorded. Each enthralling moment is pure pleasure. Our guitars are doffed in his direction."[24]

Upon the reissue of *Richard Dyer-Bennet 1* by Smithsonian Folkways in 1997, Studs Terkel wrote: "My life has been enriched by Richard Dyer-Bennet's artistry; his tapes are still highlights among my programs. His wondrous lyric tenor and marvelously singular accompaniments—whether in classic ballads, raffish songs, or music from the centuries—must never be forgotten. With this reintroduction to Dyer-Bennet's music, Smithsonian Folkways Recordings offers the current generation of listeners an untapped treasure."[25]

Richard Dyer-Bennet 2 followed in 1956 with songs again divided into three groups. Dyer-Bennet writes that "Some songs previously recorded are offered again here because my audiences and I are fond of them, and because we believe they deserve the new home provided by superior recording techniques and better performances."[26] The previously recorded songs, as discussed in chapter 3, are "When Cockleshells Turn Silverbells," "Two Maidens Went Milking One Day," "Blow the Candles Out," "Eggs and Marrowbone," and "The Turkish Reverie."

Among the songs making their debut on this album, "Corns Rigs Are Bonnie" is a Robert Burns composition. The simple lyric describes the poet's roll in the hay—or, in this case, barley—with young Anne Rankine and aptly illustrates the poet's credo: "But all the pleasures e'er I saw / Tho' three times doubled fairly / That happy night was worth them all / Among the rigs o' barley." "The Garden Where the Praties Grow" is a lively nineteenth-century Irish tune. "Praties" are potatoes, and the "Grecian bend" referred to in the song "is that then-considered-elegant forward inclination of the torso above the tightly corseted waist and flaring bustle so fashionable in the late 19th-century."[27] Dyer-Bennet's singing matches the mischievous nature of the tune as he conspiratorially acquaints the listener with the virtues of his love. "The Bailiff's Daughter of Islington" stems from the seventeenth century. Islington is a borough of London. Dyer-Bennet learned the song as a boy and adds a last verse of his own. The song is an interesting variation on the more usual theme of the male cruelly teasing the patient female before ultimately revealing his true identity as her lover.

"Who Killed Cock Robin," usually simply titled "Cock Robin," is generally regarded as a children's song. Dyer-Bennet, however, writes, "In its present form the rhyme goes back to the 18th-century and may refer to intrigues surrounding the downfall of the Walpole ministry in 1742."[28] The minstrel changed the tune to suit the "mournful and sinister meaning" he wished his interpretation to have. Dyer-Bennet's achingly tender singing in the last verse is especially moving.

Three songs from Europe make up the second group. Dyer-Bennet learned the French folk song "Veillée de Noël" from his mentor, Sven Scholander. It is a gentle song about a gathering on Christmas Eve. "Jan Hinnerk" was learned in 1930 while Dyer-Bennet lived in Germany. The text is his own translation of a song originally written in the early nineteenth century, a fantastic story of a fiddle maker who can also make men of various nationalities. Dyer-Bennet obviously delights in singing the stereotypical tag lines of Dutchman ("Gottsverdori, Gottsverdori"), Englishman ("damn your eyes"), German ("Hoch der Kaiser!"), and Frenchman ("vive l'amour"). "Woman! Go Home!" is an Austrian song learned from Scholander about a woman who shows scant concern for her dying husband. Only when his will is read does she regain interest. Again the translation is Dyer-Bennet's own, and it wonderfully captures the mood of the song. Dyer-Bennet's ability to inhabit two different characters in a song is once more on display, and his guitar accompaniment is lively and inventive.

"The Beggar Man" is the lone tune in group three that Dyer-Bennet had not previously recorded. He first heard the song from a friend, Dolly Abbott, who, in turn, had learned it from the singing of an old woman of Cornish descent. It is part of the great Irish tradition of songs about beggars, joining tunes like "The Little Beggarman" and "The Jolly Beggar." Listening to the performance, one recalls Gertrude Wheeler Beckman's admonishment that Dyer-Bennet sometimes rushed a song.

Reviews of *Richard Dyer-Bennet 2* were glowing. Writing for *Atlantic*, Conly deemed the album "marvelous" and added, "I shall never tire of it and neither will you."[29] Howard La Fey was equally effusive in his praise. "All the qualities that shape his preeminence are present. In summation, a superb release by a superb artist. Miss it at your peril."[30] The *Chicago Heights Star* called the album "remarkably appealing because he sings without affectation and with a directness and intimacy that makes you dwell on the words of the song, savoring its mood."[31] *Billboard* described both Dyer-Bennet's performances and the album's engineering as "outstanding."[32]

Dyer-Bennet had now established a schedule of releasing one LP per year. Thus *Richard Dyer-Bennet 3* followed in 1957. Five of its thirteen songs had been recorded previously: "Dinah and Villikens," "Fain Would I Wed," "The Lass from the Low Country," "The Swapping Song," and "The House Carpenter." The album is again divided into three groups of songs. Group one begins with "The Lady's Policy," a song Dyer-Bennet's friend, John Ward, had brought to his attention. The famous English song collector Cecil Sharp (1859–1924) bowdlerized the lyrics before publishing them. While Dyer-Bennet notes that such editing often destroys a song, he indicates that this song actually benefits from Sharp's pruning. The last verse is Dyer-Bennet's own and sets up the whistled interlude near the song's conclusion.

Dyer-Bennet learned "Willie Taylor" from a friend while living in Berkeley. He describes the song as a burlesque of the often sentimental songs written about press gangs, groups of sailors who forcefully recruited young men into the navy. He notes, too, the melody's resemblance to "Reuben, Reuben I've Been Thinking" and the fact that in the last verse he injects a phrase from "Rule, Britannia" into his accompaniment.

"Charlie Is My Darling" is, of course, a Jacobite tune that honors Bonnie Prince Charlie of Scotland (1720–1788), who led the Scottish uprising of 1745 in an attempt to win the crown of England. Dyer-Bennet follows this song with "Lilli Bulero," a song published in 1687 by Lord Wharton that is decidedly anti-Jacobite in nature. In his 1971 songbook, Dyer-Bennet provides a scorecard of the players noted in the lyrics. "The Catholic James II appointed General Richard Talbot, newly created Earl of Tyrconnel, Lord Lieutenant of Ireland in 1686. Talbot was a furious papist and treated the Protestants with arbitrary violence. According to Percy's *Reliques* this song 'contributed not a little towards the great revolution in 1688.' The words 'lilli bulero' and 'bullen a la' are thought to be used as identification by the Irish Catholics during their massacre of the Protestants in 1641."[33]

The second group consists of two German songs. "The Beloved Kitten" is an Austrian folk song that Dyer-Bennet translated and augmented with a second

verse. "Spottlied auf Napoleons Rückzug Aus Russland 1812" mocks Napoleon as
he retreats from his disastrous invasion of Russia. Dyer-Bennet perfectly captures
the song's jubilant tone, and its tempo complements the speed of the Corsican's
flight to safety. Scholander's influence is most apparent when Dyer-Bennet al-
ters his voice to impersonate Napoleon. "The Warlike Lads of Russia," sung by
Englishman Nic Jones and others, treats the topic in much the same manner.

The album closes with "The Lady Who Loved a Swine" and "Go Down
Moses." Dyer-Bennet learned the former, a comic fragment, in 1942. The latter
is a famous spiritual whose chorus of "Let my people go" held sad significance
to enslaved American field hands. An agnostic, Dyer-Bennet found himself ill-
suited to perform many such songs, but "in rare cases the idiom is not too extreme
and the broad human statement is powerful enough to override my hesitation."[34]
In his album notes, Dyer-Bennet playfully spars with those who might question
why he would include a spiritual in his program. "The implication is that because
I am not a Negro I cannot possibly do justice to the song. May I point out that
I am also not an Elizabethan, Englishman, nor a Napoleonic European, or an
18th-century sailor—nor even a pig, though I represent one momentarily on this
record."[35]

The *Christian Science Monitor* hailed *Richard Dyer-Bennet 3* as "a decisive suc-
cess. The sound is excellent, the repertoire is chosen with discernment."[36] The
New York Folklore Quarterly deemed it "an essential part of any group of folk
recordings."[37] Conly described it as "faultless in sound and taste" and singled out
"Lilli Bulero," "Spottlied," and "Go Down Moses" as especially commendable.[38]
Edward Randal of *High Fidelity* wrote: "Dyer-Bennet is in top form; warmth, understanding, and a pervasive attention to nuance distinguish his performances."[39]
Writing for *Hi Fi Music at Home*, Robert Sherman noted that "once again his
performances sparkle with that rare blending of deep sincerity and supreme musicianship which is his hallmark."[40]

Dyer-Bennet customarily wrote short introductions to the albums appearing
on his label. His musings on *Richard Dyer-Bennet 4* provide a good example of
the singer's wit and insight into his recording methods.

> During this summer of 1957 I intended to record enough material for two 12 inch
> discs. Indeed, Gordon Holt and I spent our customary hours experimenting with
> microphone heights and distances and finally managed to capture 28 songs on tape.
> However, we were constantly contending with frogs, crickets, thunderstorms, and
> audible arrival of the Berkshire Branch of the N.Y., N.H., and Hartford Railway's
> night train in Great Barrington. You may ask why we did not seek the sound-
> proofed seclusion of a New York studio. The reasons are numerous and include:
> New York is 140 miles from my home and Great Barrington is 4; the private living

room of a friend was made available at almost any time and proved to have good acoustics; our hosts refreshed us with gin and tonic at intervals, a custom not yet established so far as I know by rival studios. To come to the point, upon close listening to the tapes we found 4 of the 28 songs marred by extraneous sounds. We also found that 14 of the songs, unmarred by the night sounds of the Berkshires, made an interesting record. In fact, my partner, Harvey Cort, believes that the selection thus pressed upon us is stronger than might otherwise have been the case. So here is our fourth release, and I trust Mr. Cort is right.[41]

In a separate "Concluding Note" Dyer-Bennet provides a good summation not only of the songs on this particular album, but on his entire recorded oeuvre.

I would like to call your attention to the scope and variety of material on this re-cord. There is music from England, Ireland, Scotland, Sweden, Germany, Australia, and America; and the time span is 13th to 20th century. What do these songs have in common? I do not have an answer, yet I feel a certain unity. Perhaps the unity exists only in the singer's mind, to be given a fleeting but recurring reality during the act of singing. Songs lie dormant in book, manuscript and memory until they are sung. A recording can capture these moments of life and prolong them indefi-nitely. This is the chief satisfaction for me in making records.[42]

Four selections on the album had been previously recorded: "The Rising of the Moon," "The Kerry Recruit," "The Bonnets of Bonnie Dundee," and "The Swagman," more popularly known as "Waltzing Matilda."

Dyer-Bennet learned "The May Day Carol" from his maternal grandmother. Though we now associate carols only with Christmas, they were formerly sung to celebrate other holidays. The song features a particularly beautiful accompani-ment, played on the minstrel's newly purchased Velazquez guitar. Though written in 5/4 time, "Searching for Lambs" includes one measure in 3/4. It is from Cecil Sharp's large collection of English folk songs. The origin of "The Spanish Lady in Dublin City" was unknown to Dyer-Bennet, but he speculates that "perhaps the lady, or her father, floated ashore on a spar from the wreck of the Spanish Armada."[43] The tune has since found its way into the repertoire of many Irish folk singers, who usually perform it at a faster tempo. "The Three Ra'ens" first appeared in print in 1611, but it originates from an even earlier date. One of the singer's friends dubbed it "a requiem for chivalry."[44] In the first verse, Dyer-Bennet's notes inform us, "make" is a variant of "mate," and the word "leman" in the final verse is old English for friend or companion. "Song of Reproach" is attributed to the famous German Minnesinger, Hermann von Damen (1255–1307). Dyer-Bennet sings his own translation of the text. "Jag Vill Ga Vall" is a Swedish shepherd song that Dyer-Bennet learned from Gertrude Wheeler Beckman in 1935. In his liner notes, the minstrel adds that "the whistling was not a part of the song as I learned it, though surely it is not an incongruous addition."[45]

Scholander is again the source for "The Three Tailors," a German folk song. Dyer-Bennet sings his own translation of the humorous song. "The Foggy, Foggy Dew" is a sad tale of illicit love. Dyer-Bennet writes: "In my college days, we used to think it a rather humorous and slightly bawdy song. . . . I now consider I have done the song justice only when my audience listens in absolute silence and no one so much as smiles, unless wistfully."[46] Given his mournful interpretation it is difficult to imagine any reaction other than the one he desires. Interestingly, Dyer-Bennet omits the verse that details the maiden's death. "The Fox," also known as "The Fox and the Geese," is an American variant of an English song. While the fox is usually portrayed as a sly villain of sorts, in this song he is seen merely as a good father. "Drill, Ye Tarriers, Drill" is a railroad work song. "Tarrier" is probably meant to indicate one who tarried while on the job. Dyer-Bennet's flamenco-like flourishes on the guitar between verses lend appropriate accompaniment.

In his review of *Richard Dyer-Bennet 4* for the *American Record Guide*, Robert Sherman wrote: "Once again the minstrel lives up to the high standards he has set for himself, and once again the superb engineering captures every nuance of his singing with flawless clarity and lifelike presence. Needless to say, all the songs are stamped with Dyer-Bennet's exceptional artistic and musical integrity. Belongs in every serious collection."[47] Conly joked in what was fast becoming an annual review for *Atlantic* that "yes, it gets monotonous, writing 'Richard Dyer-Bennet' over and over, but the record must be announced, and it must be said once again that this engaging bard is back at work."[48] After listing some of his favorite selections, he closes by writing "So, you see, you cannot afford to pass the record up. It's as simple as that."

Richard Dyer-Bennet 5 includes ten songs previously recorded for other labels that listeners had requested the minstrel to record on his own label. They are divided by album side as songs from the Old World and those from the New World. Though not requested like the others, "I Ride an Old Paint" and "Edward" were included on the album as songs with which Dyer-Bennet wished to become identified. The singer found "I Ride an Old Paint" in Carl Sandburg's collection *The American Songbag*, first published in 1927. In his 1971 songbook Dyer-Bennet describes it as a night-herding song.[49] Though it appears at first glance as a strange choice for the English-born minstrel, the song is well suited to his voice and effectively evokes the lonesome life of the cowboy. "Edward" is, of course, an old border ballad, but Dyer-Bennet's version originated in the southern Appalachian Mountains. Though the details vary, the basic story is sadly universal: a young man must flee his home after murdering a family member. In his 1971 songbook

Dyer-Bennet finds "in the words a rare suggestion of incest. Edward has killed his brother-in-law, who must be either his wife's brother or his sister's husband. And why has he killed? In a jealous rage over 'a little bit of bush that soon would have made a tree,' and that, I think, represents either a young woman or the child she carries within her. Therefore, either Edward's wife was her brother's mistress, or Edward was his own sister's lover."[50] In either case, Dyer-Bennet's musical interpretation gains ominous momentum with each verse before finally erupting with passion in the concluding stanza.

In his review for the *Reporter*, Nat Hentoff claimed that Dyer-Bennet's latest collection "can be recommended unreservedly."[51] Don Noel of the *Hartford Times* singled out the minstrel's guitar work, "ranging from the most intricate classic Spanish style to near-hillbilly, each suited to the song at hand."[52] He adds that "a better 'John Henry' than the one here would be hard to find." Paul Little praised the album's versatility. "We find the powerful Scottish-English ballad 'Edward,' Sandburg's 'I Ride an Old Paint,' the magnificent 'John Henry,' the grimly mordant 'Lord Rendal,' the classic 'Barbara Allen,' and his own fine version of 'Venezuela.'"[53]

Richard Dyer-Bennet 6 is an album of children's songs, or, rather songs "with young people in mind." In his liner notes Dyer-Bennet admits that he has "never learned a repertoire expressly for children, and therefore the best I can do was to choose from my regular repertoire those songs which seem to me to have a wide age appeal."[54] Appropriately, Dyer-Bennet's daughters, Bonnie and Brooke, appear on horseback on the sepia-tinted cover photograph; the family dog, Hopper, stands in the foreground.

Five of the album's sixteen tracks had appeared on previous releases: "Old Bangum," "Three Jolly Rogues of Lynn," "John Peel," "Frog Went A-Courting," and "Little Pigs." "Come All Ye" is an appropriate start to the album. Dyer-Bennet's jolly whistling sets the right tone, and his lively guitar playing serves as an invitation to accompany the minstrel on his musical journey. Burl Ives taught Dyer-Bennet "Aunt Rhody," and the idea to sing two verses in a minor key originated with Ives as well. David Flaherty, a friend of Dyer-Bennet, was the source for "The Leprechaun." The singer's otherworldly laugh at the song's conclusion is truly elfin. "The Piper of Dundee" begins side two with much the same gusto as "Come All Ye." "Bow Down," an American variant on "Binnorie," features an infectious chorus. "The Tailor and the Mouse" is delightfully silly. "I Went Out One Morning in May" and "Buckeye Jim" were both learned from Fletcher Collins, and are justly described as "poetic nonsense." Lead Belly is the source of "Green Corn," which shows off Dyer-Bennet's guitar playing prowess. The cockeyed logic of "Three Crows" is sure to appeal to any child within earshot and was apparently a great favorite of Lead Belly's. Dyer-Bennet learned "The Hole in the

Bottom of the Sea" from the singing of NYU students in 1939. Singing the song might be described as an act of sustained concentration.

Reviewing the album for *Parents Magazine*, Emma Dickson Sheehy wrote: "Probably we have no greater balladeer in America than Richard Dyer-Bennet. . . . No musically inclined family can afford to miss it."[55] Upon the album's 2000 release on compact disc, Richard Perry wrote: "Making no concession on length or complexity of language, Dyer-Bennet refuses to dumb down to young people; consequently this disc can be fully enjoyed by any adult who admires truly fine singing."[56]

On *Richard Dyer-Bennet 7* the singer returns to the Beethoven songs he had recorded in 1946 for Concert Hall. Omitted from the new recording were "Could This Ill World Have Been Contrived," "O Mary, At Thy Window Be," "Oh How Can I Be Blithe and Glad," and "Oh Sweet Were the Hours," all from *Scottish Songs*. For his accompanying trio he chose Natasha Magg, a Viennese pianist, the violinist Urico Rossi, and Fritz Magg on cello, late of the Metropolitan Opera. The record's sound is a great improvement on the Concert Hall albums, and Dyer-Bennet works well with his chosen musicians. In the *San Francisco Chronicle*, longtime fan Alfred Frankenstein wrote: "It is amply apparent that the songs recorded by Dyer-Bennet are the work of Beethoven in the full tide of his career. They stand up with the best of Beethoven's chamber music. Such, at least, is their effect when they are so well performed as they are in this instance."[57] Conly finds the recording "much better" than the Concert Hall releases, and writes that "only a slight echoic quality prevents all-out recommendation."[58] Carolyn Sanford of the *Orange County Daily News* described the performances as "characteristic of his greatly-admired artistic, but understated style" and singles out the cover photo of a held score as "both original and pleasing."[59]

Richard Dyer-Bennet 8 is subtitled *European Gems of Minstrelsy from the 15th to the 19th Centuries*. For the first time on any of Dyer-Bennet's folk song recordings, no American selections are included. Side one consists of English songs, mostly from famous poets, while side two is made up of selections from Germany and France. None of the pieces had previously been recorded by Dyer-Bennet.

The unaccompanied "Agincourt Song" celebrates England's 1415 victory over the French. As noted earlier, Dyer-Bennet was justly proud of his ability to maintain a perfect pitch throughout his performance of this piece. In "Come Live with Me" Dyer-Bennet knits together two poems and sets them to an original guitar accompaniment: Christopher Marlowe's (1564–1593) "The Passionate Shepherd to His Love" and "The Nymph's Reply" by Sir Walter Raleigh (1552–1618). "Come Away Death," from Shakespeare's *Twelfth Night*, was first set to music by Dr. Thomas Arne (1710–1778). The melody is not particularly distinguished. "I Care Not for These Ladies" is the work of Renaissance poet and composer Thomas

Campion. "Flow My Tears" comes from the pen of John Dowland. Dyer-Bennet writes in his liner notes that Dowland "did not attempt as much as did Byrd and Purcell, but his best songs have a flawless combination of lyric freshness and meticulous craftsmanship." In this performance Dyer-Bennet includes varied rests between verses. Friend John Ward is once more the source of "All in a Garden Green," an anonymous Elizabethan song.

The minstrel adds two final verses to "Henry Martin," a song taught to him backstage one night after a 1942 performance. These additions find the protagonist pirate brought to justice. Dyer-Bennet's guitar accompaniment is quite active and inventive throughout the piece. Joan Baez would record a very similar arrangement—though without Dyer-Bennet's added verses—on her first album, recorded in 1960, one year after *Richard Dyer-Bennet 8*. In a review of Baez's recording debut, a critic notes: "A comparison suggests itself between Miss Baez and Tenor Balladeer Richard Dyer-Bennett [*sic*], one of this listener's favorites. Playing through their renditions of 'Henry Martin,' one finds Miss Baez doing vocally the job of interpretation which Dyer-Bennett does with his magically fluent guitar."[60]

Indeed, more than any other contemporary performer, Baez can be said to have carried on the tradition of minstrelsy. Born in 1941 the daughter of a Mexican father and a Scottish mother, Baez rose to fame in the late 1950s singing traditional American and English songs. Her beautiful untrained voice had a three-octave range and, in the beginning of her career, her astute guitar provided her only accompaniment. Songs from Dyer-Bennet's repertoire that Baez sang included "Barbara Allen," "I Once Loved a Boy," "John Riley," "Cherry Tree Carol," and "Lonesome Valley." As the 1960s progressed, however, Baez moved away from traditional material in favor of contemporary compositions—some her own but most from the pens of Bob Dylan and other singer/songwriters. This was a transition Dyer-Bennet chose never to make.

The tender, unaccompanied fifteenth-century *Minnelied* "All mein Gedanken" (All My Thoughts) begins *Richard Dyer-Bennet 8*'s second side. Ever considerate of his listeners, Dyer-Bennet provides prose translations for each of the LP's seven foreign-language tracks. Goethe wrote the words to "Die Bekehrte Schäferin" (The Shepherdess Persuaded), while Friedrich Heinrich Himmel supplied its sprightly melody. Like many poets, Goethe collected folk songs and based this piece on one he heard in Alsace. "The song," Dyer-Bennet writes in his liner notes, "is an example of what a supremely gifted poet can do in traditional ballad form; let us admit that many of our prized traditional ballads are good in spite of, and not because of, quite inferior poetry."[61] In the song, the young shepherdess scorns the advances of two suitors before succumbing to the charms of a third. Dyer-Bennet's whistling echoes the flute played by the successful young man.

"Kränzelkraut" (Bridal Wreath), a folk song from Silesia, in east-central Europe, is a conversation between two would-be lovers. The man gains the woman only when he has decided he no longer likes her. "Jagabenteur" (Hunting Adventure) is attributed to Anton Wilhelm von Zuccalmaglio (1803–1869). Dyer-Bennet hints at Scholander's influence when he notes that "Unfortunately, there is no way, on this recording, of imitating the little hare in the last verse—a liberty I permit myself on the stage."[62] The hunter in the song lets his imagination run away with him, mistaking the rustling in the grass for a dangerous creature. In fact, the sounds have been made by a little hare. "Warnung" (Warning) is a traditional melody with words by Ernst Anschütz (1780–1861). The warning is directed to a fox who has stolen a goose. "Le Brave Marin" (The Brave Sailor) is a traditional ballad from Brittany, learned from Scholander. A sailor returns from the war to discover that his wife, thinking him dead, has remarried and borne three additional children. "Aminte" (a female name) is an anonymous eighteenth-century song, also learned from Scholander. It is an entreaty from a young man to his lover. If the young man is as appealing as the song's melody, then his efforts will surely succeed.

In his review of *Richard Dyer-Bennet 8*, Conly briefly notes that the songs are "all from ages we sometimes wish, briefly, we could be back in."[63] Alfred Frankenstein writes that "the performances are, as always, superbly finished both as to the singing and the guitar playing, and the recording is beautiful."[64] The *New York Times* noted: "All the restraint, good taste and scholarship associated with this performer are here in good measure."[65]

Richard Dyer-Bennet 9 ushered in the new decade. Five of its twelve songs had been previously recorded: "The Laird o' Cockpen," "The Two Sisters of Binnorie," "Early One Morning," and "Gently Johnny My Jingalo." "The British Light Dragoons" had appeared previously on the Concert Hall *Scottish Songs* LP, but on this release Dyer-Bennet preferred his guitar accompaniment over Beethoven's setting for piano, violin, and cello. Dyer-Bennet learned "The Pride of Petravore" in 1946 from Ralph Cullinan, a cast member of *The Second Best Bed*, a comedy by N. Richard Nash (1913–2000) about Shakespeare and his wife, Anne Hathaway.[66]

The album's second group of songs was all learned from Scholander. "Schneiders Höllenfahrt" (The Tailor's Journey to Hell) tells the tale of a clever tailor who, whisked down to Hell to outfit the clientele, turns the tables on his hosts. Dyer-Bennet's joyous "ha, ha" before the final verse was part of Scholander's own performance. "Der Tod von Basel" is a comic song about a young man who convinces Death to carry off his wife so that he can wed another. Sadly, he finds the new wife no better than the first. Scholander's influence is clear again in Dyer-Bennet's treatment of each verse's repetitive third line. "Le Joli Tambour" (The Handsome Drummer) is a playful conversation between a king and a drummer, who ultimately refuses the hand of the king's daughter because he knows of prettier women than she.

The album's final group consists of three American songs. "The Buffalo Skinners" is a well-known cowboy song from Sandburg's *American Songbag*. In the hands of Woody Guthrie and Cisco Houston, this song was deadly serious, but Dyer-Bennet's interpretation is almost gay in comparison. "John Riley" treats the common folk song theme of a lover who, before revealing his true identity to his beloved after a long absence, tests her fidelity. Joan Baez would record the song on her first LP. "The Cherry Tree Carol" is the American version of an English carol. Baez included the song on her 1961 release *Joan Baez 2*, though she does not include Dyer-Bennet's final verse.

Richard Dyer-Bennet 10 was recorded in Pittsfield, Massachusetts, in 1962. Dyer-Bennet Records partner Harvey Cort's influence on the minstrel's choice of material becomes clear when one reads a letter he wrote to Dyer-Bennet in 1961. There Cort lists twenty-six as yet unrecorded songs from the minstrel's repertoire that he feels should be included on future albums. "He certainly listened to what I had to say," Cort recalls. "But he would try to balance the material, and my own suggestions were not in any way meant to balance. I was just telling him songs I wanted to hear."[67]

Six songs listed in Cort's letter would appear on *Richard Dyer-Bennet 10*. Its red album cover evokes the blood red sun from one of its selections, "The Reaper's Ghost." Five of its fourteen songs had been recorded previously: "The Lincolnshire Poacher," "Lowlands," "I Once Loved a Girl," "The Wife Wrapped in the Wether's Skin," and "My Good Old Man."

Dyer-Bennet was familiar with John McCormack's piano arrangement of "She Moved Through the Fair," but found it unsuited to guitar accompaniment. Thus he contented himself with "a simple alteration of D major and E major chords," he states in the liner notes. The song is ideally suited to Dyer-Bennet's voice, and he gives a wonderful performance. "The Seven Little Pigs" is a short, comic song that Dyer-Bennet considered a "skillful imitation" of a folk song. "O Speak Then My Love" dates from sixteenth-century Spain. The original text by Luis Milan was in Portuguese; Dyer-Bennet here sings his own translation. John Ward is again the source of the piece, composed for vihuela, a lutelike instrument. Scholander taught Dyer-Bennet the beautiful "Le Veritable Amour" (True Love) in 1935. It was introduced to Scholander by a member of the author's (Loisa Puget [1810–1889]) family around the turn of the century. Dyer-Bennet's delicate transition into the last chorus is wonderfully controlled.

The minstrel opens the album's second side with two original compositions. Both are lyrically interesting and suitably melodic. "The Unfortunate Troubadour" was written in 1940 and is not, Dyer-Bennet playfully notes, based on personal experience. Dyer-Bennet's guitar beautifully echoes the "tra la las" of the chorus. The fact that the courted maiden sleeps while the troubadour sings his heart out to her adds a humorous touch to the piece. "The Reaper's Ghost" was inspired by a conversation Dyer-Bennet overheard in England in 1935 concerning the mysterious disappearance of a local farmhand. He succeeds in making the song sound appropriately haunting. The repetitive structure of the song lends it an insistent eeriness. "Two Comments" consists of two short Greek poems, translated by William Cowper (1731–1800) and set to music by Dyer-Bennet. Their tempo and tone stand in marked contrast, making the pairing all the more effective. "Go 'Way Old Man" was learned in California in 1936 from Barnard Wells, who had, in turn, become acquainted with the song in Kentucky. Who else but Dyer-Bennet could follow a piece based on classical poetry with a gentle mountain song and make both sound as natural as an evening breeze? "No Hiding Place" provides a rousing, humorous conclusion to the album. David Lloyd Garrison taught Dyer-Bennet the song in Santa Barbara in 1929. The minstrel's playful insertion of "hallelujah" in the final chorus indicates that he approaches the song with valuable objectivity.

The *Hartford Times* described *Richard Dyer-Bennet 10* as a "feast of balladry. He gives each piece its particular character of pain, passion, joy, love, humor, and even an eeriness to those ballads steeped in the lore of the supernatural. His voice and guitar transcend time and space to breathe life into notes and verses."[68]

In 1947, *San Francisco Chronicle* music critic Alfred Frankenstein suggested that Dyer-Bennet's voice might be well suited to the songs of American composer Stephen Foster (1826–1864). In 1962 Dyer-Bennet would act on Frankenstein's recommendation: *Richard Dyer-Bennet 11* consists entirely of Foster songs. The Temple of Music in Pittsfield, Massachusetts (also known as South Mountain), was again the recording venue. Harry Rubenstein provides piano accompaniment. Rubenstein had previously worked with Martha Graham and other modern dance groups, as well as founding the Berkshire Children's Choir and serving as music director at Windsor Mountain School in Lenox, Massachusetts. In 1971 he would transcribe piano accompaniments for Dyer-Bennet's songbook.

In preparation for the album, Dyer-Bennet and Rubenstein examined Foster's entire body of work (188 songs) before settling on the twelve pieces recorded. Discarding the offensive dialect songs, as well as the maudlin Civil War pieces, the duo found themselves "drawn to the languorous airs of nostalgia, sad remembrance and idyllic love. . . . These songs, while not towering works of art, have at least the charm and distinction of small works of art, and sound gracious and pleasant in these noisy times."[69]

Dyer-Bennet sounds perfectly at ease with "Linger in Blissful Repose" (1858). "Gentle Annie" (1856), a quiet song of mourning, was inspired by Foster's grandmother, Annie Pratt McGinnis Hart. "Come with Thy Sweet Voice Again" (1854), one of Foster's more obscure songs, begs that the addressed lover might "Come with the music that wells / From thy soul, from thy soul." The comic lyrics of "If You've Only Got a Moustache" (1864), written by Foster's friend and frequent collaborator George Cooper (1838–1927), lend a moment of levity to an otherwise solemn collection of songs. "Jeanie with the Light Brown Hair" (1854) is, of course, one of Foster's most famous songs. The composer's wife, Jane, served as his inspiration for this and many other songs. Dyer-Bennet sings this beautiful piece with appropriate tenderness. Foster revised William H. McCarthy's original words to "For Thee, Love, for Thee" and set it to music in 1859. The melody has considerable range, and the chorus is particularly earnest. "Ah, May the Red Rose Bloom Alway!" (1850) expresses a typical Foster concern: "Why should the beautiful ever weep / Why should the beautiful die?"

"Beautiful Dreamer" was one of the last songs Foster wrote and was published only after his death in 1864. Rubenstein's accompaniment is beautiful throughout but never more so than on this famous song. The lyrics of "Sweetly She Sleeps, My Alice Fair" (1851) were written by American poet Charles G. Eastman (1816–1860). George Cooper again supplied the lighthearted words to "There Are Plenty of Fish in the Sea" (1862). "Open Thy Lattice, Love," with words by George P. Morris (1802–1864), was Foster's first published song (1844). Dyer-Bennet decided to delete the published coda to the album's final number, "Come Where My Love Lies Dreaming" (1855). There had previously been speculation that the coda "was not Foster's idea but was suggested by Henry Kleber, a musician friend of Foster."[70] For the only time on the album, Dyer-Bennet's voice sounds uncomfortably stretched in this song's conclusion.

Frankenstein was well pleased with the outcome of his original suggestion. In the past, Frankenstein claimed, "chauvinistic phonies" had recorded Foster's songs "according to the commercial needs of the whims of the moment."[71] Reviewing Dyer-Bennet's album he writes that the minstrel is "the first person in history to record songs by Stephen Foster precisely as Foster wrote them, using Josiah Lilly's famous facsimile edition of the original sheet music."[72]

In 1969 Dyer-Bennet was touched when Evelyn Foster Morneweck, Stephen Foster's niece, wrote him, describing how happy she was with the album. "You included in your album several songs I never heard outside our own home."[73]

She was also full of praise for Rubenstein's accompaniments. "Please thank Mr. Rubenstein for his graceful, and lovely accompaniments to your singing. His touch is so gentle, yet so clear."

Dyer-Bennet's other 1962 release was titled *1601*, after the Mark Twain piece formally titled "Date, 1601. Conversation, as it was by the Social Fireside, in the Time of the Tudors." The conversation includes such notables as Ben Jonson, Shakespeare, Sir Walter Raleigh, Sir Francis Bacon, and Queen Elizabeth herself. "The first and chief matter of discussion is the occurrence amid this company of a phenomenon to which we may refer by the medical term 'crepitus' in lieu of the four-letter word beloved of Chaucer and Clemens which the dictionaries say is 'not now in decent use.'"[74] In short, these luminaries discuss who among them has farted.

Twain wrote *1601* during the summer of 1876 when he was otherwise composing his masterpiece, *Huckleberry Finn*. He was also researching material for what would later become *The Prince and the Pauper*. His research led him to Samuel Pepys's famous diary. Thus inspired, Twain wrote a sketch for a friend of his, the Reverend Joseph Hopkins Twichell, including it in a letter. Both found it highly amusing, as do most contemporary readers. The sketch, however, is generally not included in complete editions of Twain's works. Once Twichell began to share the piece, though, the cat was out of the bag. Numerous private editions of the sketch began to appear.

In his extensive liner notes, Dyer-Bennet warns: "If there are any words in the English language which you can under no circumstances tolerate, this record will prove intolerable to you."[75] He goes on to say that while he has no wish to offend, he does not consider Twain's piece offensive. He delights in the richness of the English language and believes "appropriate use can be found for any word ever coined." In "1601," he claims, Twain "wished to amuse, to instruct, and to puncture hypocrisy. Here his use of language is in turn elegant and coarse. Both qualities are true to life and, by contrast, wonderfully comic."

Earlier in his career Dyer-Bennet had defined his artistic philosophy.

> Here I wish to make a point central to my whole career. It is my own musical feeling, my own poetic sense, my own taste and morality which form the only ground on which I can firmly stand. If I step from this ground I am lost in a sea of conflicting opinions as to what the public wants of me, and I no longer know what I want of myself. Therefore, I do not set out to offend anyone, it is particularly myself I must not offend, and if, while adhering to my own ground and my own standards, I chance to affront someone else, it must be accepted on both sides as an unfortunate but unavoidable result of sound operational procedure.[76]

Dyer-Bennet with his mother.
Leicester, England, 1913.

Dyer-Bennet with his father and
grandfather, ca. 1915.

Dyer-Bennet as goalkeeper,
The Deane School. 1929.

En route from Germany, 1931. Rear, left to right: Richard, Miriam Sr., John. Front left to right: Christopher, Miriam, Fred.

At the beach on the Baltic. 1930. Left to right: Fred, Miriam Sr., Richard (standing), Miriam, Christopher.

Rock climbing. Richard Dyer-Bennet on left. Early 1930s.

Sven Scholander. Courtesy Nordiska museet, Stockholm, Sweden.

Early publicity shot with lute.
Early 1940s.

As the minstrel in Chatterton's play,
Second Best Bed, 1946. (Lucas and
Monroe, Inc., New York.)

Performing with Lead Belly
at the Village Vanguard.
Early 1940s.

Publicity shot, late 1940s.
(Joe Covello from Black
Star, Graybar Building,
New York.)

Mel Dyer-Bennet with students in Aspen:
Ruth Becker, Will Holt, ca. 1947.

With students in
Aspen, ca. 1947.
From left: Bert
Lasky, Will Holt,
two unknown
students.

With Studs Terkel at WFMT, mid-1950s. (Archie Lieberman.)

At work on a setting for
a song. Stockbridge, MA,
mid-1950s.

Playing tennis. 1960s.

With accompanist Nancy Garniez after a performance of *The Lovely Milleress* at Simon's Rock Early College, Great Barrington, MA. 1974.

With Garniez and producer Warren Syer at a recording session for *The Lovely Milleress*. South Mountain, Pittsfield, MA. 1977 or 1978. (Brooke Dyer-Bennet.)

Practicing on his harp at home in Monterey, 1980s.

Recording the *Odyssey* at home in Monterey, 1980. (Susan Fanshel.)

On side two of the album Dyer-Bennet sings six bawdy songs. "Old Joe Clark," learned from Fletcher Collins, kicks things off in rousing fashion. Though sung in innumerable variations, this is a piece most every folksinger has in his or her repertoire. Dyer-Bennet's guitar accompaniment is quite sprightly. "The Old Crab" is a Connecticut fisherman's song. Sam Eskin taught the singer some additional verses, and Dyer-Bennet adds his own as a finale. "The Tailor's Boy" dates from the seventeenth century. Dyer-Bennet sang the song in performances of *Second Best Bed* in 1946. The euphemistic rapping on the guitar body is the song's most memorable feature. Dyer-Bennet first heard "The Eer-i-e Canal" in Maine. When sung with less coarse lyrics the song was popular with the Weavers and a number of other performers in the 1950s. In 1946 *Boston Globe* critic Cyrus W. Durgin taught Dyer-Bennet "There Was a Friar in Our Town." Durgin also taught the minstrel how to "produce the startling sound effect by the sudden removal of an empty hollow-bottomed bottle from a wet table top."[77] The mock solemnity of the singing adds to the song's humor. Dyer-Bennet reports that "The Gathering of the Clan" may have been written by Robert Burns. In any case he chose to record "only such verses as Burns might have written."[78] The song is in many ways similar to "The Ball of Kerrimuir."

Dyer-Bennet and Cort realized that by releasing such a bawdy album they were taking a chance. "We thought we might be brought up on obscenity charges,"[79] says Cort. "At the time nobody had done anything like it. And no one from the Clemens family was going to admit—at least at that time—that it was Twain." Cort was not familiar with the fact that Canadian folksinger Ed McCurdy (1919–2000) had in 1956 released the first volume (of three) of bawdy songs entitled *When Dalliance Was in Flower*. McCurdy is now best remembered for composing the anti-war song "Last Night I Had the Strangest Dream." In his heyday he was quite popular and, like Dyer-Bennet, possessed a strong and beautiful voice. McCurdy's bawdy albums were well received and popular. As was *1601*; it sold well, and the reviews were quite positive. "Dyer-Bennet has produced a masterpiece—a reading of Mark Twain's irreverent Elizabethan sketch and a group of ribald American and British songs and ballads,"[80] wrote Henrietta Yurchenko in the *American Record Guide*. "Only a seasoned performer should dare such a disc; only a master of nuance could do it justice. Dyer-Bennet far exceeds the qualifications for such a task. It is the work of a mature artist. . . . The result is excruciatingly funny as well as aesthetically right. The songs admirably complement the reading. . . . As hilarious and uninhibited a collection as ever was recorded. Praise to Mr. Dyer-Bennet for his gentlemanly delivery, bold honesty, and uncompromising language withal! Caveat emptor. Not for the squeamish!" Other critics chimed in. "A delightfully bawdy disc,"[81] Everett Helm claimed in

Musical America. Stephanie Gervis, writing for the *Village Voice*, thought it "could not be better."[82] O. B. Brummel in *High Fidelity* praised its "uncompromising honesty" and "high artistry."[83]

In addition to releasing two recordings and performing at the Seattle World's Fair, Dyer-Bennet found time in 1962 to record eight songs for the WCBS-TV show *Camera Three* (broadcast on May 13) in New York. A videotape of the session has survived. The program runs to twenty-six minutes and begins with Dyer-Bennet singing "So We'll Go No More A-Roving." During this first number he appears uncharacteristically nervous, and the stark lighting does not do justice to his handsome face. A fine performance of "Waltzing Matilda" follows, complete with explanation of the Australian vocabulary vital to understanding the song. On the splendid guitar introduction to "The Bonnie Earl of Morey," the camera appropriately focuses on Dyer-Bennet's hands. A sprightly performance of "Aminte" is next, followed by "The Laird of Cockpen." At this point Dyer-Bennet describes Thomson's Beethoven project and is joined by unidentified musicians who accompany him on the piano, violin, and cello on "Bonnie Laddie, Hieland Laddie" and "On the Massacre of Glencoe." Dyer-Bennet closes the program by singing "The Lonesome Valley."

Richard Dyer-Bennet 12, subtitled *Songs of Ships, Seafaring Men, Watery Graves, Card Sharpers, a Giant Ram, an Indian Scalping, and One Edible Rat*, was released in 1964. The cover art by Martin Rosenzweig is colorful and creative. The album is a lighthearted collection, and Dyer-Bennet must have greatly enjoyed the recording process. Six of its selections appeared on previous albums: "The Drunken Sailor," "The Eddystone Light," "Hullabaloo Belay," "The Willow Tree," "The Charleston Merchant," and "The Derby Ram."

"Shallow Brown" is a capstan sea chanty, sung to a very basic guitar accompaniment. Dyer-Bennet categorizes "The Mermaid" as a faux sailor's song, more likely sung by glee clubs and the like. "Peter Gray" is a mock-serious piece about a young man who finds himself on the wrong end of an Indian tomahawk. Dyer-Bennet notes that his grandmother remembered hearing it in Illinois before the turn of the century. "The Roving Gambler" found great popularity with performers as diverse as the Everly Brothers, Burl Ives, and Simon and Garfunkel. Here Dyer-Bennet adds some distinctive guitar touches and vocal flourishes to the song. "Billy Barlow" includes the edible rat of the album's subtitle and is a comic delight. Dyer-Bennet has just as much fun with "Australian Girls," learned from David Garrison. Scholander would have been proud of the "rump pump pumps" Dyer-Bennet includes in its chorus. "Hanging Johnny" is a chanty learned from a British mariner, Cubit-Smith, with whom Dyer-Bennet used to enjoy drinking rum in his nightclub days. "Plain Language from Truthful James" is Dyer-Bennet's setting of a whimsical Bret Harte poem. Lest any Chinaman take offense from the song, Dyer-Bennet is quick to point out "that in Harte's poem all the participants are rascals."[84]

While conceding that most of the album's songs are familiar, Nat Hentoff adds that "Dyer-Bennet transmutes them into his own conception of contemporary minstrelsy. He does not try for ethnic authenticity, but functions instead as a refreshingly unpretentious and highly astute 'art singer' of folk material. . . . He uses his voice with such control and sensitivity that he achieves a more subtle spectrum of dynamics and a more flexible melodic flow than do many of his contemporaries in the folk field."[85]

The other recording Dyer-Bennet released in 1964 would prove to be the last of his numbered albums. *Stories and Songs for Children and Their Parents* is the subtitle of *Richard Dyer-Bennet 13*. The cover photo by Betty Rosenzweig was previously used on the back cover of *Richard Dyer-Bennet 2*. Only four songs appear on the record. Two had appeared previously, "The Devil and the Farmer's Wife" and "The Fox and the Geese." Fletcher Collins is again the source for "The Soldier and the Lady." Dyer-Bennet provides appropriate whistling and drumlike thrumming on the guitar to complement a tale about a soldier who deceives a girl into buying him a new wardrobe. Indeed, the theme of deception runs throughout nearly all of the album's stories and songs. "The Old Gray Goose" was learned from Lead Belly during Dyer-Bennet's nightclub days. Though straightforward enough literally, the song is sometimes interpreted as a kind of protest song, the indefatigable goose suggesting the resilience and ultimate triumph of the downtrodden African American.

While completely different in tone, of course, from *1601*, this album also features spoken recitations. Four Georgian (Russian) folk tales comprise the bulk of the recording. All four stem from *Yes and No Stories* by George (1898–1978) and Helen Papashvily (1906–1996), originally published in 1946. A Russian immigrant, George Papashvily was an accomplished sculptor and published a number of books with his wife. In his liner notes, Dyer-Bennet writes that the songs and stories "are meant to cause a mixture of laughter and that slight, delicious tingling along the spine."[86]

Each story begins with the curious phrase "There was, there was, and yet there was not . . ." In the first story, "The Tale of the Tales," the phrase is explained as meaning "that what comes after is true and true but then again not so true." A sentence from the tale serves as an apt description of Dyer-Bennet's career. "A story is a letter that comes to us from yesterday. Each man who tells it adds his word to the message and sends it on to tomorrow."[87] "The Man Who Was Full of Fun" concerns the crafty Vanno, who fools his neighbors into believing that a rabbit can talk, a guitar can resurrect the dead, and a farm exists at the bottom of a lake. In "The King of the Noise" a sly fox fools a king into believing a miller (who has earlier spared the animal's life) controls all sounds in the world and is a worthy son-in-law. "The Wolf Who Knew How to be a Friend" is a tale in which a wolf helps the youngest of three sons triumph over his two treacherous brothers and win the love of a girl.

High Fidelity gave the album a glowing review. "Beset by the endless flood of folk combos belting out their frenetic counterfeits, one turns with gratitude to the pure freshet of these releases. Richard Dyer-Bennet, a veteran balladeer of superlative gifts and solid integrity, subtly transmutes traditional songs into art songs; in each case, he illuminates the song's emotional soul."[88]

Dyer-Bennet apparently wanted to continue recording stories for children. A 1966 letter from E. B. White indicates that Dyer-Bennet had contacted him asking permission to record some of his work. White responds by pointing out that *Stuart Little* has already been recorded, and that he is not entirely sure he wants *Charlotte's Web* to be recorded. "I suggest that, if you are willing, you send me a couple of records—Number 5 and Number 13. I would like very much to hear them. At this time, though, I can't give you any indication of whether I shall let the book go onto records."[89] Sadly, nothing tangible came of this correspondence.

Though he had established Dyer-Bennet Records to record his own repertoire, in 1960 the singer expressed his admiration for the Danish mezzo tenor Aksel Schiøtz (1906–1975) by inviting him to record for the label. Dyer-Bennet had first heard Schiøtz sing on a recording in 1947 and immediately recognized a kindred spirit. "Since that time," Dyer-Bennet writes in his liner notes, "there has been no other singer for me."[90] Schiøtz faced medical problems throughout his career. In 1946 the right side of his face was left partially paralyzed due to an operation that removed a tumor on the acoustic nerve. In 1950 a brain tumor impaired Schiøtz's speech. At the time of his recording for Dyer-Bennet, Schiøtz was teaching at the Royal Conservatory of Music in Toronto. His voice was now a baritone. On the Dyer-Bennet recording, titled *Aksel Schiøtz, baritone, singing Schubert, Bellman, Wolf, Brahms* the Dane sings four groups of songs by these composers. He is accompanied by Dyer-Bennet on the guitar and Paul Ulanowsky on piano. *High Fidelity* praised the album, adding that "Fortunately we need not fall back on our admiration for his courage and determination as justification for this release, for the essentials of Schiøtz's art are intact."[91] In 1963, Dyer-Bennet and Schiøtz collaborated again on stage in Boulder, Colorado, and remained close friends until Schiøtz's death.

After completing *Richard Dyer-Bennet 13* in 1964, the minstrel abandoned the recording studio for more than a decade. The process had never been enjoyable for him, and his mind was turning to other projects, most notably his translation of Schubert's song cycle, *Die schöne Müllerin*. Dyer-Bennet was also growing increasingly dissatisfied with his voice. What he perceived as its limitations would eventually lead him to seek the assistance of Cornelius Reid in 1968.

While the exact origin of every song recorded by Dyer-Bennet for his own label is not clear, it is possible to establish approximate percentages. Fully one-third are American; one-fourth are English; another quarter are Scottish or Irish; with songs from Germany (8 percent), France (4 percent) and other countries comprising the remaining 17 percent. If *Richard Dyer-Bennet 1* lays claim to being both fans' and critics' favorite, the first children's album (*6*) and the album of requests (*5*) are not far behind. Each album, of course, has its particular charms, and one can state with certainty that Dyer-Bennet never released an album that did not live up to his high standards.

In 1977 Vanguard issued a two-LP collection titled *The Essential Richard Dyer-Bennet*. Vanguard is, of course, well known for recording many of America's most popular folk singers, including Joan Baez, Buffy Sainte-Marie, Doc Watson, the Weavers, Mississippi John Hurt, and Paul Robeson. The album features cover art by Eric von Schmidt and includes twenty-seven songs culled from seven of Dyer-Bennet's most popular recordings as follows: *RDB1* (7), *RDB2* (5), *RDB3* (2), *RDB5* (4), *RDB6* (3) *RDB12* (4), *RDB13* (2). Dyer-Bennet's original notes for each song are included. In a short introduction to this career retrospective, Dyer-Bennet neatly summarizes his recorded repertoire to date: "the songs range in time from the 16th to the 20th centuries and deal with birth, love, work, play, and death—the major components of the human experience."[92]

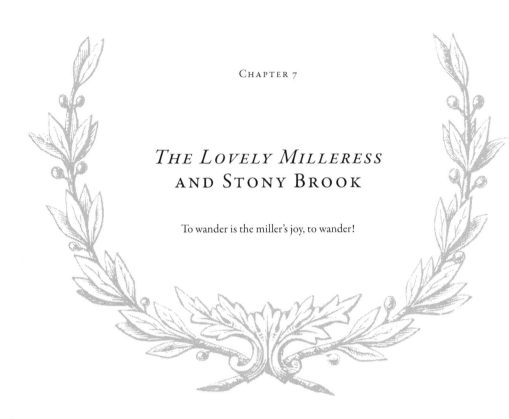

CHAPTER 7

THE LOVELY MILLERESS
AND STONY BROOK

To wander is the miller's joy, to wander!

While perhaps colored by hyperbole, Howard Schneider's description of Dyer-Bennet's career after his 1964 recording was released (*Richard Dyer-Bennet 13*) serves to indicate the minstrel had reached a kind of crossroads. "Then suddenly, and almost mysteriously, he 'disappeared' in the mid-1960s. There were no more records, no more annual concerts at Town Hall. It wasn't unusual to hear radio program directors and folk aficionados ask where Dyer-Bennet was, and whether he was alive or dead."[1] He had, in fact, been working for some time on a translation of the Wilhelm Müller poems that Franz Schubert set to music as the song cycle *Die schöne Müllerin*. Brooke Dyer-Bennet recalls the intensity her father brought to such work. "When he was working on a translation he would be consumed by the task, totally engaged and quite oblivious to anything else going on around him. He'd often have a pack of cigarettes within reach. He'd light one and take one puff and go back to work, letting the cigarette burn until the ash was the full length of the cigarette, and my mother would sometimes have to slide an ashtray under his hand so that the ash wouldn't fall off onto the table!"[2]

In 1967 the translation was published by Schirmer as *The Lovely Milleress*. In his program notes to a 1979 performance of the piece, Dyer-Bennet writes at length about the challenges he faced as translator.

Working on a new translation for one of the most celebrated song cycles it became clear to me what considerations are important in translating a text for purposes of singing. First, the text must be singable; if it is not, all other considerations are meaningless. Second, it must suit the music, or more desirably, it should sound as though the music had been suited to it. Primarily this means evoking poetic images equivalent to those evoked by the original text; it also means that the accented syllables of words, and the stressed words of phrases, must match the music accents and stresses determined by the original text. Third, the rhyme scheme must be kept, for the musical phrases take their shape from the rhyme scheme of the original poetry. And the literal meaning should be kept whenever this can be done without violating the first three considerations. When all four requirements cannot be met, and something must give way, liberties must be taken with the strictly literal meaning.

In approaching the translation I did not devise a set of rules and then attempt to follow them. I worked empirically. Being a singer, I have some sense of what is and what is not singable; a life-long love of good English prose and poetry has given me some ability with my own tongue; and schooling in Germany resulted in a more than academic knowledge of that language. A combination of these three disciplines has enabled me to achieve a singable, modestly poetic, reasonably accurate English version.

. . . The problem then remained of what to call *Die schöne Müllerin* in English? The answer to this became a symbolic key to the entire cycle. Since the words of the title appear several times in the songs, it was necessary to find an English phrase with an identical number of syllables, and with identical accents. My solution was to give the word "miller" a feminine ending. Whether or not this particular word has been previously so transmuted in English prose or poetry, I don't know. Having discovered each other we soon were on friendly terms, and *The Lovely Milleress* has become friendly to my ear and comfortable to my voice.[3]

In a 1964 letter to Conrad Osborne, Dyer-Bennet, then working on the translation, shared his thoughts on the nature of the text.

To what extent is it a "true story" and to what extent a "fantasy?" If the former, the language may tend toward plainness and directness; if the latter, it may be allowed a more poetic form. For me, the key to the cycle is the notion that it lies midway between. It is a fairy tale, and the central character is the brook. Perhaps more accurately, it could be a true story, except for a few touches of magic—one of which is that the brook is a living thing, and at least a central character. The whole thing is one of those dark, delicious, sad fairy tales of which Germans and Austrians are so fond. It is almost as though, having led the young miller into his adventure, the brook regrets his love affair with the milleress, tries to tempt him away (no. 10), fails; but is exultant when the boy is jilted for the hunter, and wins the contest by sad default, by possessing him in the only way water may possess a human.[4]

Whatever perspective he may have brought to the work, Dyer-Bennet's translation is certainly poetic. Compare, for example, a literal translation (left) of the cycle's second song, "Wohin?" with Dyer-Bennet's (right).

I hear a brooklet rushing	*I heard a brooklet rushing*
Right out of the rock's spring,	*As from the rock it sprang*
Down there to the valley it rushes,	*Toward the valley rushing*
So fresh and wondrously bright.	*So fresh and bright it rang.*
I know not how I came here	*I know not what came o'er me*
Nor who gave me the advice;	*Nor why I had to go*
I had to go down there	*But staff in hand I followed*
With my wanderer's staff.	*The water's downward flow.*
Downward and always farther	*Descending and even further*
And always the brook follows after;	*I followed the course it took*
And always rushing crisply	*And ever freshly rustling*
And always bright is the brook.	*And ever sparkling the brook.*
Is this then my road?	*Is this my road to follow?*
O, brooklet, speak, where to?	*Oh, brooklet, tell me where.*
You have with your rushing	*Bewildered by thy murmuring*
Entirely intoxicated my senses.	*I neither know nor care.*
But why do I speak of rushing?	*What say I then of murm'ring?*
That can't really be rushing:	*No murmur do I hear*
Perhaps the water-nymphs	*The water nymphs are singing*
Are singing rounds down there.	*Beneath the ripples clear.*
Let them sing, my friend, let it rush,	*Oh, leave this enchanted singing*
And wander joyously after!	*And wander gaily on!*
Millwheels turn	*The millwheels are a-turning*
In each clear brook.	*In all the brooks that run.*[5]

Along with *Die Winterreise* (1827), *Die schöne Müllerin* remains a masterpiece of the *Lied* genre and is still often performed and recorded. Schubert (1797–1828) discovered Müller's poems in 1823 "at the very period when he must have realized that his own recently contracted syphilis was certainly grave and possibly mortal."[6] The tragic story of a traveling miller who finds and then loses love must have held great appeal for Schubert, for he set to work soon after discovering the text.

Dyer-Bennet had long admired Schubert. In his liner notes to *Richard Dyer-Bennet 11*, for example, he had compared Stephen Foster to the Austrian composer. He had also sometimes performed lieder in concert. As early as 1946, for example, he sang a number of Bach's *Geistliche Lieder* at Town Hall. In 1977 Dyer-Bennet told Raymond Ericson:

> I've long wanted to do Schubert. But my whole career has been spent in the kind of direct communication that comes from singing Elizabethan songs, Scottish border ballads and other folk songs in English. It's a question of "listen! I'm going to tell you this story", because the Müller poems form a melodrama. I couldn't come out and sing it in German. I looked at other translations of the cycle. Did you know that Longfellow did one? But none of them suited me. I had spent two years in Germany, so I was at home with the language, and I'm a singer. I decided to make my own version, I started over a decade ago. Two of my good friends were against it, Paul Ulanowsky, the noted pianist for *lieder* recitals, and Aksel Schiotz, the great Danish tenor. I finished half of it before Paul died, and when I tried it out for him, he thought it would work. Aksel's daughter, who had heard her father sing the cycle all her life, told him that she loved my version and now knew what it was all about![7]

Before performing his translation in public, however, Dyer-Bennet felt he must improve his voice. "I always felt as if I were using only half my voice. About the time I decided to do the Schubert, I discovered a teacher, Cornelius Reid, who was able to develop my voice to its fullest capacity. It's still a light lyric tenor—I can't claim more than that—but I don't have any difficulty with the cycle now."[8] Dyer-Bennet began lessons with Reid in 1968. Reid was a proponent of the bel canto method of singing. While difficult to accurately define, bel canto stresses vocal freedom, characterized by "vitally resonant tones covering a wide pitch range."[9] Dyer-Bennet's decision to seek his help mirrors Reid's belief that while "few are privileged to achieve perfection . . . it is a goal toward which every teacher and student of singing should strive."[10]

Dyer-Bennet had long believed he had succeeded in spite of, not because of, his voice. His dissatisfaction with his instrument sent him to Reid. "At their first session together, Reid made Dyer-Bennet sing to a note on the scale where his voice cracked, at which point the teacher knew he could work with the new pupil—even though the pupil was 58."[11] In his book, Reid quotes Sam Barlow as having written: "An artist is one who has sufficient technique to communicate his vision."[12] It is precisely this "sufficient technique" that Dyer-Bennet felt he lacked at this point in his career. After working with Reid, he was excited about his new ability. "In two years," he told the *Stony Brook News*, "my range increased by an octave and a half, the timbre changed from a weak and semicounter to a full lyric tenor; and I was able to sing a far wider repertoire and to be easily heard in much larger concert halls."[13] He went on to maintain that "existing methods of voice training are clearly inadequate because, quite bluntly, they are based upon false concepts of the nature of the vocal instrument. Such phrases as 'support of the diaphragm,' 'breath control' and 'placing the tone in the masque' are nonsense."

"It was partly as a result of his own vocal development through his work with Reid that Dyer-Bennet hit on a theory concerning the training of the actor's speaking voice."[14] Dyer-Bennet believed that man had "used the voice for cooing and grunting before he used words. If the primary function of this instrument [the voice] is singing, then speech is a secondary function. In training the speaking voice, therefore, you should observe the rules governing the singing voice."[15] Indeed, Dyer-Bennet planned to write a book, *Training the Actor's Voice*. In the extensive notes that exist from the aborted project, Dyer-Bennet writes:

> The basic fault of traditional methods for training the speaking voice is that an attempt is made to solve all problems by dealing with every part of the instrument except that part by which the primary sound is made: the vocal cords themselves and the immediately surrounding voice box. . . . The voice box can produce noise or it can produce tone. When the vocal cords have come close enough together to produce some sound, but not close enough to produce clear pitch, they produce what the acoustical physicist calls "articulated voice." When they come close enough together to produce clear pitch, the acoustical physicist refers to the sounds as "musical tone." . . . It is the distinction between "articulated noise" and "musical tone" and the relationship of musical tone to vowel definition which are the crux of my thesis.[16]

Soon Dyer-Bennet would have occasion to put his theory into practice. In 1968 he attended a student production of *Macbeth* at the Elizabethan Arts and Literature festival in Vermont where he had been lecturing. After the performance, he approached the student cast and offered a few tips on vocal projection he thought might prove helpful. Dyer-Bennet, of course, had experience as an actor. Besides his role in *Second Best Bed*, Dyer-Bennet had also played Feste in two scenes from *Twelfth Night* for Continental's 1952 recording *An Evening with William Shakespeare*. The students he counseled were under the supervision of

Irving Ribner, then chairman of the English department at the State University of New York (SUNY) Stony Brook. "Ribner invited Dyer-Bennet to Stony Brook to meet William Bruehl, chairman of the Theater Department, to discuss his theory of vocal training for actors."[17] This meeting led, in turn, to Dyer-Bennet leading a workshop on campus. Both students and faculty liked what they saw. In the fall of 1970 Dyer-Bennet was offered a position as both artist-in-residence and member of the theatre department. At 57, the Berkeley dropout became Associate Professor Dyer-Bennet.

In a press release titled "Famous Balladeer to Provide Voice Training at Stony Brook Theatre Dept.," the school announced that "Mr. Dyer-Bennet has joined the Department of Theatre Arts at Stony Brook as a lecturer offering a course which will train the human voice—male or female—so that it has a range of three octaves, a dynamic scale from piano to forte throughout, with clear verbal definition."[18] In the release Dyer-Bennet is quoted as saying "There is no school or university in the English speaking world to which a young actor can go with any assurance of learning to use his voice so that he can be clearly heard and understood in even a moderately sized theatre of 500–600 capacity. Where better do this than at a young institution like Stony Brook, starting out freshly and unbound by traditional methods?"

Part of the sixty-four-member state university system, Stony Brook was founded in 1957. The campus is located sixty miles east of New York City and stands on 1,100 wooded acres. In 1970 there were 8,419 full-time students enrolled there. The campus was more than 200 miles from Dyer-Bennet's home in Monterey, however, which resulted in a complicated commute. On Mondays Dyer-Bennet and his wife would drive the 150 miles to New York, where Mel was working. The following day Dyer-Bennet would make the sixty-mile drive to Stony Brook. He kept a regular room at the Three Village Inn where he also ate most of his meals. He taught and held office hours on Tuesdays and Thursdays. On Thursday evenings or Friday mornings Dyer-Bennet drove back into Manhattan to pick up Mel, and together they would head back to Monterey for the weekend.

The 1970–71 Stony Brook Undergraduate Bulletin lists three Dyer-Bennet courses: THR 130 Voice Training for Actors, THR 133 Voice and Diction, and THR 350 The Art of Minstrelsy. The course description for 130 warns that it is "open only to students with a professional commitment to acting or other professional users of the speaking voice."[19] Students are required to arrange weekly tutorials with the instructor. The course is a prerequisite to THR 133. That class will include "methodological reconstruction of habits of articulation and idiomatic usage toward the goal of a cleanly articulated, standard American usage." Lecture, musical illustration, and discussion form the basis of THR 350, which explores the traditions of minstrelsy and "its place in the social context and in the history of the performing arts generally." In 1973–74 the 133 course was renumbered 230 and retitled Voice and Articulation; a new course, Interpreting and Acting with the Voice, was added in the 1974–75 schedule.

Lesl Harker attended Dyer-Bennet's minstrelsy class in 1971 and has vivid memories of the experience she shared with some twenty other students that year.

> He sang a lot to us. He taught us about ballads, and the origins of the broadside ballads. He had everyone doing vocal exercises, and demonstrated the bel canto method of singing which he had of late been learning from Cornelius Reid. In connection with the vocal exercises was a theory he had about ear training, which he knew could benefit anyone, even someone who was tone-deaf. He explained how he was able to teach someone to sing no matter what their ability, using ear training techniques. He told us about his musical career, starting with the great Swedish minstrel Sven Scholander. He taught the basics of minstrelsy, poetry, accompaniment, melody, performance, voice, and guitar. His aim was to elevate folk music to the level of art music and taught us of the Trinity between the poetry, the singing and the accompaniment.
>
> There was a section on guitar work. He saw that several of us did not use classical guitar position when we held the instrument, so he had us working on this. I recall him having me write out a C scale, and then showing me where it was, note by note on his guitar, and me trying to copy him, as he was trying to get my left hand into position. He also gave us specific fingerboard exercises, and told us that if our roommates were sleeping or sick of hearing it we should do them without sounding the strings.
>
> He was a great fan of Joan Baez, who sang in a more classical vein than other folk singers. He criticized the use of tricks and mannerisms in the singing of recorded artists—when the mannerisms were used as a routine way of singing and not as a special effect, he considered it a crutch. As soon as he'd spot one of us doing it, he'd ask us to try our song without the mannerism.[20]

Harker remembers Dyer-Bennet suggesting that she change the keys of several songs in her repertoire. "He said I should take the key of the songs higher, which solved a lot of my trouble. I had never realized that if I raised the pitch I could sing the songs more easily." In addition to such technical assistance, Dyer-Bennet helped Harker prepare for a trip she was going to take to Britain after graduation. "He presented me with a folk music research itinerary, complete with letters of introduction, to Cecil Sharp House, the English Folk Song and Dance Society, and Hamish Henderson at the U of Edinburgh." Dyer-Bennet, she claims, defined her musical direction. Harker applied what she learned with Dyer-Bennet to various musical ventures. In 1975 she became a resident minstrel in the London Tudor Rooms in Leicester Square, a position she held for four years. Upon her return to the United States she formed a Celtic band, Keltia. She sang and played both flute and guitar for the group, whose repertoire included a number of Dyer-Bennet songs. She found chart success in the early 2000s with her interpretation of the traditional song "Lord Franklin." A few years later her cover of W. B. Yeats's "Song of Wandering Aengus" was very popular on the internet. Harker continues to actively pursue her life in music, and in 2006 published a book of flute transcriptions titled *300 Tunes from Mike Rafferty*.

Harker was not the only one pleased with Dyer-Bennet's tutelage. In their course evaluations, other Stony Brook students similarly sang Dyer-Bennet's praises.[21]

"Mr. Dyer-Bennet is the best thing at Stony Brook."

"Richard Dyer-Bennet is one of the sweetest and most patient men I have ever met. He helps everybody on their voice training and is so vibrant and interesting that I really enjoy coming to this voice training course."

"Dyer-Bennet is totally charming. In excellent command of his area and capable of enducing [*sic*] his own interest and enthusiasm into his students."

"Mr. Dyer-Bennet is a delightful man who knows his stuff. He's the type who learns while he teaches and is open to new ideas."

"His criticism is based on an uncanny perception of the problems students have, and it is very helpful."

"Mr. Dyer-Bennet is great. It's just a pleasure coming to see him. I never thought I could feel confident with my voice—he has made it possible."

"Mr. Dyer-Bennet is without a doubt a most valuable asset to the state university. Teachers of his stature in the field of music are rare."

"Mr. Dyer-Bennet is the best teacher I've ever had. I learned more with him than with any other instructor."

"Mr. Dyer-Bennet is a very happy man and makes you happy just to be in his presence."

A few dissenting opinions were, of course, registered.

"I did not realize how much this course would be a course in Mr. Dyer-Bennet's philosophies and opinions (rather than in balladry or folklore). While he was always enthusiastic and interesting, I think that I might not have taken this course if I had understood what it would be like."

Dyer-Bennet quickly found that he was in his element at Stony Brook. "Teaching in Theatre Arts is one of the most exciting things I have ever done. Perhaps that's because it lets me begin to pass on to my students some of the things I have learned myself. I have toured for a quarter of a century. Now I am happy to teach."[22] Numerous friendships blossomed with colleagues and students in a variety of departments. He was closest to Andrew Schulman, who introduced himself to Dyer-Bennet late in his freshman year. "I'd heard that he had a '57 Velazquez guitar. I just wanted to see the guitar," Schulman admits. At first Dyer-Bennet said he had only five minutes to spare, but more than an hour later the two were still talking. Schulman had been playing the guitar since age eight. As a nineteen-year-old he was now playing only rock and rhythm and blues. "He started talking to me about learning to play classical guitar, that it would be great as a foundation for me."[23] By the time Schulman left Dyer-Bennet's office that day he had decided to take his course the following fall. Heeding Dyer-Bennet's advice, Schulman began studying classical guitar with Jerry Willard. He also began taking a series of independent study courses with Dyer-Bennet, including one devoted to the English lutenist/composer John Dowland. Dyer-Bennet was so happy with Schulman's aptitude for music that he made him his teaching assistant and turned over one section of the introductory speaking course to him.

Schulman's assistance proved vital, for in 1972 Dyer-Bennet suffered a cerebral hemorrhage that left him unable to teach his classes for the remainder of the year. The minstrel's ability to play the guitar was also forever diminished. This loss was devastating to Dyer-Bennet, but, typically, he faced the change stoically and soon chose a new musical direction. Schulman was asked to take over Dyer-Bennet's course load. The work was obviously difficult but would prove valuable in Schulman's eventual role as leader of the Abaca String Band, a New York–based quintet. Schulman likens both teaching and leading a group to that of a lion tamer. "If the musicians respect you, you'll get a great show, but if they don't, they'll maul you."[24]

The following year Dyer-Bennet returned to teaching duties and Schulman graduated, quite conscious of the fact that "all the formative work of what became my career" had been a result of his chance meeting with the minstrel. "He was the single most important influence on my career," he recalls. "My career came out of my association with Dyer-Bennet." Schulman credits Dyer-Bennet with far more than encouraging him to take up the classical guitar. "He taught me to make sure my interest in music was well rounded," Schulman says. "I was infatuated with Bach at the time, but he told me 'you know, Andrew, you can't just stay on top of Mount Olympus all the time.'" Schulman began to study other kinds of music at Stony Brook and soon realized that a piece can be appreciated for any number of reasons. "It can be terrific because it's grand, terrific because it's charming, or terrific because it's tremendously silly."

Upon graduation, Schulman was quickly able to find remunerative work in New York City. After serving a brief apprenticeship in Greenwich Village vegetarian restaurants, he landed a steady gig playing his guitar for customers at Windows on the World, the restaurant housed on the top floor of the World Trade Center.

In 1978 he became artist-in-residence at Pacific Lutheran University in Tacoma, Washington, before moving back to New York in 1981 to resume his performing career as a soloist and ensemble player. Part of his solo work, of course, involves storytelling between numbers. Here again, Dyer-Bennet's influence was enormous. "Dyer-Bennet was a tremendous raconteur. Part of his talking was planned out but part he left open for improvisation, for which he had a gift." Schulman recalls that Dyer-Bennet also enjoyed telling long stories in class. "Sometimes he would get on these really long stories, and I was the only person who could interrupt him. The only way to interrupt him was to find a spot where he had to catch a breath. I would get an appropriate question in my mind that would steer us back to wherever we'd been and I'd wait for the perfect moment."

The word Schulman uses most often to describe Dyer-Bennet is "mentor." "He gave me insight into the great music figures of the day, gave me insight into how to carry myself," Schulman claims, before finally noting: "The other influence from Dyer-Bennet was that he was a class act. He was very good at what he did. He had his own style, he was true to himself. He knew who he was. He told me that all really accomplished performers have that. He was comfortable in his own skin, doing what he loved."

By 1974 Dyer-Bennet felt sufficiently recovered from his stroke to return to the stage. With Harry Rubenstein on piano he performed *The Lovely Milleress* in October at Stony Brook. Not until 1977, however, did he feel ready to perform the song cycle for a New York audience. At sixty-three, he realized the chance he was taking. "I know I'm sticking my neck out," he admitted, "but I just had to do it."[25] It was to be his first major New York performance since 1963. Nancy Garniez accompanied Dyer-Bennet on the piano at the concert, held in Alice Tully Hall.

While Dyer-Bennet certainly hoped his return would be a triumphant one, Peter Davis, writing for the *New York Times*, found that the singer's voice "does not have enough body to fill out Schubert's vocal lines satisfactorily, and now, at age 63, he tends to sound extremely fragile and wispy. The dynamic level of his singing was unduly restricted and the tonal coloring virtually on one level throughout, resulting in an inevitable aura of monotony and excessive caution."[26] Davis does, however, praise Dyer-Bennet's translation, calling it "faithful to the original" and "often ingenious in its rhyme scheme." The *New Yorker*'s Andrew Porter found Dyer-Bennet's presentation "unfailingly fresh, youthful, and enthusiastic," but felt his voice "too small for so large and so unresonant a hall" and that his phrasing "lacked the verbal freedom and vividness he brings to 'Lord Rendal' or 'Barbara Allen.'"[27] For his part, Cornelius Reid was pleased with his pupil's performance. "I cannot begin to tell you have [*sic*] pleased and deeply moved Wanda and I were by your performance of The Lovely Milleress. It was both a testament and a statement about life and art and I am pleased that there were so

many present who were aware of that. . . . I put one of your old records on after we
got up to the barn and was surprised to hear the great difference in the strength
and character of your voice. I don't believe you could have gotten through the
Schubert with the old voice, which, as one can hear, was limited in both power
and range."[28]

In the *New York Post*, Speight Jenkins praised Dyer-Bennet's decision to include the prologue and epilogue written by Müller (and not usually performed or
recorded by others), but expressed doubts that a translation was necessary. "Not
because everyone understands German but because the genius of the composer
was such that though every word is set meaningfully, the musical moods of the
songs more clearly convey the emotions of the singer than do the words themselves. Constant concentration to see just how much of the English verse was
comprehensible added little to the cycle's effect. Mueller's verses, after all, would
long ago have sunk into oblivion without Schubert."[29] Jenkins also found fault
with the singing. "Dyer-Bennet sang the songs musically with a voice commensu-
rate with his age, and though he hit almost every pitch, the tone was simply too
quavery to be enjoyable. Further, the sheer feat of getting out the music took so
much energy, there was little dynamic variation in the way he sang, and to [*sic*]
many of the songs seemed the same."

As early as 1967 Dyer-Bennet had contemplated recording Schubert's song
cycle. At that time he had failed to interest CBS Records in taking on the project.
In June 1976 Dyer-Bennet began recording *The Lovely Milleress*, again accompanied by Nancy Garniez, for his own label. They chose as their studio the Temple
of Music in Pittsfield, Massachusetts, where Dyer-Bennet had recorded a number
of his albums in the early 1960s. Recording did not proceed smoothly, however.
First of all, some recording equipment was stolen from the site before the project
had begun. Troubles with microphones followed, and, finally, "an occasional bird
call and wind sigh from the surrounding woods found their way onto our otherwise technically immaculate tapes."[30] Warren Syer served as recording engineer
and eventually surmounted these considerable difficulties. Everyone involved in
the project agreed that there would be no splicing during numbers; the song cycle
was recorded live.

Accompanist Nancy Garniez sheds additional light on the project. "Dick and
I met weekly for a little over a year in my New York studio, usually for about two
hours. There was talk about singing, about teaching, about Schubert, about many
things, and some 30 to 40 minutes of music-making. . . . When a significant difference of opinion arose, we would search in the music for indications of a proper
resolution. My suggestions inevitably reflected a pianist's way of hearing. Dick's
that of a singer. Though quite dissimilar in background, experience, and tempera-
ment, neither of us attempted to dominate the other or dictate in any matter of

music or interpretation. In fact, two separate, intact human beings must be fully present in order to make this music come to life."[31]

The Lovely Milleress is Dyer-Bennet's least distinguished recording. One wonders how greatly the stroke he suffered in 1972 had changed his vocal abilities. Since no recordings of Dyer-Bennet's voice exist between *Richard Dyer-Bennet 13* (1964) and *The Lovely Milleress*, it is impossible to judge the changes to his voice that had resulted from his sessions with Reid. Indeed, given his enthusiasm for the "new" voice that Reid had given him, it is surprising that Dyer-Bennet had not visited the recording studio for so long. While singing the Schubert piece, Dyer-Bennet's voice sounds deeper than on previous recordings. He sounds less comfortable in this new register; his voice seems small and is strained by both high and low notes. These deficiencies are especially apparent in "Giving Thanks to the Brook." "The Inquisitive One" also stands out as sub par. Sadly, one could quote numerous other examples. The voice that struck the listener as so natural on previous recordings here sounds forced and foreign. Perhaps more importantly, it does not sound like the voice of a young, vigorous apprentice miller. This is nowhere more apparent than in "Mine." What should sound triumphant here sounds rather meek. Only near the end of the cycle, on the mournful "Withered Flowers," does Dyer-Bennet's voice show signs of its former stature.

Critic Andrew Porter notes that Dyer-Bennet's voice "certainly doesn't have the variety and resourcefulness that a *complete* account of *Die Schöne Müllerin* needs. The cycle is taken down a semitone, but the tenor has trouble in sustaining the resultant A flats of "Ungeduld"; he can't sweep through the bold arpeggios of "Die böse Farbe" and ring out on the F's. As singers go, sixty-three isn't all that old. Santley made wonderful records in his seventieth year, and Henschel in his seventy-eighth. Those singers don't sound cautious; Dyer-Bennet does."[32] Porter does praise Dyer-Bennet's translation, however, and defends the practice of performing *lieder* in translation.

Undaunted by any criticism he may have heard or read about his performances of the cycle, Dyer-Bennet continued to perform *The Lovely Milleress* until 1979. Friends and family were supportive, not critical. "It was what he wanted to do," says Andrew Schulman. "I don't think anybody liked it, but I wasn't going to tell him that. And the reason that I didn't was that there was no need to." If Dyer-Bennet's performance of the song cycle will fade from memory, his translation may survive the test of time. Indeed, others, including David Tannenbaum in 1983, have used it as their text.

Dyer-Bennet had not entirely abandoned his old repertoire. In 1973 he gave a series of lectures and concerts for the New School in New York. Besides the traditional English and American songs with self-accompaniment, Dyer-Bennet also performed Elizabethan songs on the lute, and pieces by Handel, Purcell, and

Mozart accompanied by Harry Rubenstein on the harpsichord. Besides giving concerts, Dyer-Bennet also advertised himself during this period as willing to speak on a number of topics: "the relationship between performer and repertoire; criteria for development of style; values contributing to the life of a song and to tenure of works in general; aspects of literary and history in relation to music; music and poetry as symbols of meaning beyond their apparent context; and the relationship between a singer's craft and other disciplines." While at Stony Brook, Dyer-Bennet also undertook a number of narration roles that hinted at a forthcoming career change. In 1975, for example, director Amy Kaiser chose him to play the narrator's role in Henry Purcell's rarely performed opera *King Arthur* (1691). (While Purcell's best-known work *Dido and Aeneas* features music uninterrupted by spoken dialogue, it is atypical of his operatic work in this distinction.) Dyer-Bennet reprised the role in a 1979 performance in New York's Buttenweiser Hall. In 1976 Dyer-Bennet narrated both Aaron Copland's *A Lincoln Portrait* and Prokofiev's *Peter and the Wolf* in a Long Island performance. On this occasion Dyer-Bennet told Lawrence van Gelder of the *New York Times* that while he did not anticipate "going back to being primarily a performer ever again,"[33] he likewise did not foresee a time when he would stop performing entirely.

Always ambitious and eager for new projects, Dyer-Bennet planned next to translate and perform Beethoven's song cycle *An die ferne Geliebte*. This venture was abandoned, however, when Dyer-Bennet fell under the spell of another timeless classic, Homer's *Odyssey*.

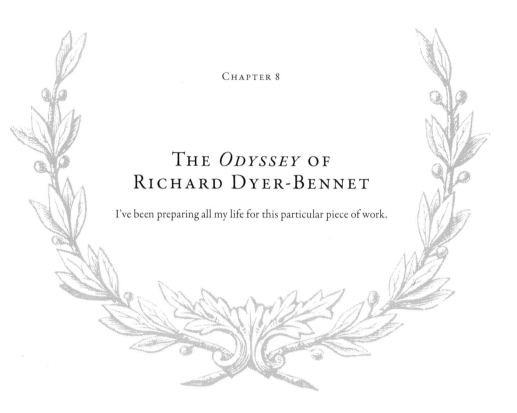

CHAPTER 8

THE *ODYSSEY* OF
RICHARD DYER-BENNET

I've been preparing all my life for this particular piece of work.

In 1961 American poet Robert Fitzgerald (1910–1985) published a modern English blank verse translation of Homer's *Odyssey*. The book won that year's Bollingen Award, an annual prize for the best book written by an American citizen. Born to Irish-American parents, Fitzgerald graduated from Harvard in 1933 and subsequently went to work first for the *New York Herald Tribune* and then *Time*. He went on to teach English at Sarah Lawrence, Princeton, and finally Harvard. A celebrated poet in his own right, Fitzgerald is today best known for his translations of classics such as *Oedipus at Colonus*, *The Iliad*, *The Odyssey*, and *The Aeneid*.

Reviewing Fitzgerald's *Odyssey* for the *Nation*, William Arrowsmith spoke for many critics when he wrote that "Fitzgerald's new *Odyssey* . . . deserves to be singled out for what it is—a masterpiece. It has long been needed. For years now there has been nothing to march beside Lattimore's fine *Iliad*; readers of the *Odyssey* had to make due with . . . prose versions. Fitzgerald makes them all obsolete; there will not be another *Odyssey* as good as this in our generation, and probably not for several generations. Seven years of work went into its completion, and the result is exactly the achievement one might have expected of a translator whose *Oedipus at Colonus* is among the great translations of our age. At last we have an Odyssey worthy of the original. . . . It is as good English as the Greek is wonderful Greek. Translation can do no more."[1]

Ralph Hexter chose Fitzgerald's translation for his 1993 *Guide to the Odyssey*. In his preface he explains his choice. "I had long known, as reader and teacher, that the Fitzgerald translation of *The Odyssey* is astoundingly vivid; it seems to me to capture in English what I appreciate in Homer's Greek. As I worked on the guide, rereading, back and forth, again and again, both Homer and Fitzgerald, I began to appreciate what a truly monumental accomplishment the Fitzgerald translation is, how accurate, how brilliant."[2]

Dyer-Bennet was no less effusive in his praise of the translation. "I really think that Fitzgerald has created what is—within my experience, I can't speak of the whole gamut of literature—within what I have read and heard, Robert has created the finest single piece of verbal material for the solo performer that exists in the English language. And this is not hyperbole; I am not exaggerating my own feeling about this. I think it is a masterpiece. . . . I think if Homer could appear on the scene today, understanding English perfectly and heard Robert's verse Homer would say: 'yes, that man knows what I meant.'"[3]

Dyer-Bennet had always considered himself first and foremost a storyteller. His love of Homer was evident even when he was a boy. One of Dyer-Bennet's earliest memories was hearing a line from *The Iliad*: "And in the ears of Patroclus the din of battle rang no more."[4] One should not forget that his maternal grandfather had been a classicist at Berkeley and that Homer had been read to him as a child. "I dare say these early memories of great voices and noble language are quite accurate indications of influences which were later to shape my life."[5] When he found the time to read Fitzgerald's new translation in 1972, Dyer-Bennet began to form a scheme in his mind. Wasn't Homer's poetry meant to be heard, not read? Why not give the world a spoken *Odyssey*? Dyer-Bennet initially performed a fifteen-minute reading from the epic at the conclusion of a folk song performance at Stony Brook in 1977. "The audience was thunderstruck."[6]

Alice Wilson, a Stony Brook professor who saw that performance, encouraged Dyer-Bennet to pursue his dream. To that end the minstrel visited Fitzgerald at Harvard. By way of introducing himself, Dyer-Bennet knocked upon Fitzgerald's office door and began to recite some passages from memory. "I asked Fitzgerald, 'Do I have the right feeling for this?' . . . He immediately replied, 'Oh, yes.'"[7] Fitzgerald initially thought Dyer-Bennet was interested in recording only excerpts of the epic. When Dyer-Bennet told him he meant to record the work in its entirety, Fitzgerald recalled that Ezra Pound had told him much the same thing as he began his translation: "No excerpts. Let Homer have his way."[8] Fitzgerald gave Dyer-Bennet another piece of advice. "He told me, 'you're a performer. Just follow your instincts as a performer.'"⁹ Dyer-Bennet's enthusiasm grew when he learned that Fitzgerald had always hoped someone would thus offer to be his voice.

The poet's blessing secured, Dyer-Bennet applied for and obtained a two-year National Endowment for the Humanities grant to create a recording of Fitzgerald's glorious translation. The proposal was titled "To Make Audible the Robert Fitzgerald Translation of Homer's Odyssey." Dyer-Bennet asked the organization to fund him so that he could retire from teaching. "I need, in effect, to be brought away from the university for the next five years, with a chance of continued support for another five. Given a free five years I believe I have a fair chance of recording a complete *Odyssey*—something which apparently does not exist anywhere in the world."¹⁰ Essential in his winning the $100,000 award was Dyer-Bennet's personal recital of passages for the grant committee.

In preparation for the monumental project the minstrel read all of Fitzgerald's original poetry to gain a sense of his art and establish a necessary spiritual link with him. These include *Poems* (1935), *A Wreath for the Sea* (1943), *In the Rose of Time* (1956), and *Spring Shade* (1972). To augment his knowledge of Greece, Dyer-Bennet—like Fitzgerald before him—chartered a seventy-five-foot boat and sailed among the Greek islands for three weeks with Mel and ten friends in June 1982. "Almost everyone who spends some time in Greece and writes about it knowingly speaks of a quality of light in the country,"¹¹ Dyer-Bennet said. "That's what I felt I needed to know. It wasn't that I needed to see, specifically, the color of the sea so that I would understand what Homer means by the 'wine dark sea'; it wasn't anything so specific or limited as that. It was just the general feeling of this country." While in Greece Dyer-Bennet declaimed parts of the *Odyssey* in the amphitheater at Delphi, "ran a foot race with a friend at the site of the ancient stadium further up the mountain," and "took delight in swimming ashore from the boat at Odysseus's home island, Ithaca."¹²

Dyer-Bennet estimated it would take him five years to learn to perform *The Odyssey* and then accurately record it onto twenty-four hours of tape. Though the passages declaimed on stage were, of course, memorized, Dyer-Bennet did not set himself the impossible task of memorizing the entire text. "It will not be necessary," he wrote in his grant proposal, "to memorize the whole text. I must become so familiar with it that a glance at a page will enable me to perform it, as in the case of an oft-repeated story read to a child. To this end I shall have each page of the printed text photographically enlarged so that it is easily legible at a distance of ten feet or so." Thanks to filmmakers Susan Fanshel and Jill Godmilow, we are able to observe Dyer-Bennet at work on the project. In the 1970s the Rockefeller Foundation was looking to fund interesting projects in the arts taking place on SUNY campuses. They learned of Dyer-Bennet's project and were immediately intrigued. Godmilow knew Dyer-Bennet from having heard him sing in the late 1950s, so when she and Fanshel were offered the opportunity to make a short documentary film about his project, they readily accepted. The result was *The Odyssey Tapes*, a twenty-seven-minute film shot in and around Dyer-Bennet's Monterey home.

The film has no narration. It consists entirely of Dyer-Bennet's comments on the project and his entire career, supplemented by rare Archie Lieberman footage of the minstrel on tour. On numerous occasions Dyer-Bennet is seen playing a small harp to accompany his reading. "I don't feel I have to hold myself strictly to the stringing of the instrument that Homer used," he says. "But how to use it? Should it be a constant rhythmic line of some sort underlying the voice?" In the end Dyer-Bennet settled for "using it as what you might call an oral paragraph." Luthier Alan Carruth recalls that Dyer-Bennet "was not happy with the sound of a lyre, happened to see a small harp I had built, and so looked me up. He wanted an instrument that would cover about the range of a guitar, and be light enough that he could hold it with his left hand and move around as he played."[13] In all, Dyer-Bennet had six harps built before finding what he considered the right one.

Fitzgerald speculated that the harper telling the tale "must have used the instrument not only for accompaniment but for pitch, and to fill pauses while he took thought for the next turn. No doubt the instrument marked rhythm too."[14] After witnessing one of Dyer-Bennet's declamations, Ron McDonald wrote that Dyer-Bennet uses the harp "as a kind of melodic punctuation, an unobtrusive and often haunting means of pointing the text."[15] Still, not everyone believed the harp enriched the performances. Mel, for example, preferred to hear her husband unaccompanied. She wished that at the time they had known how much Dyer-Bennet's stroke had contributed to what she called his "lack of inventiveness"[16] on the harp. Fitzgerald was excited by the prospect of the harp accompaniment, however, and so Dyer-Bennet persisted in its use.

From 1977 until 1990, Dyer-Bennet (now under contract with the International Concert Musicians Bureau) performed excerpts from the *Odyssey* on more than forty occasions, mainly on college campuses and in performance halls, and once at the Coolidge Auditorium in the Library of Congress. He especially enjoyed performing for classicists in the audience. He kept in touch with Harvard classicist Cedric Whitman and consulted with both him and Fitzgerald on occasion.

In *The Odyssey Tapes*, Dyer-Bennet is shown recording passages in his Monterey home as part of what he viewed as a first step in the process. "This will by no means be a performance, but simply a first reading, to which I can listen reasonably objectively and begin to judge if and where a touch of the harp is suitable."[17] Later on the camera captures him performing passages from Book

22 ("Death in the Great Hall") in the familiar confines of the Village Vanguard, and it is, indeed, a triumphal return for the minstrel. The small club is filled to its limit as Dyer-Bennet holds the crowd spellbound. He plucks the harp from time to time to emphasize certain passages.

> *He drew to his fist the cruel head of an arrow for Antinous*
> *just as the young man leaned to lift his beautiful drinking cup,*
> *embossed, two-handled, golden: the cup was in his fingers:*
> *the wine was even at his lips: and did he dream of death?*
> *How could he? In that revelry amid his throng of friends*
> *who would imagine a single foe—though a strong foe indeed—*
> *could dare to bring death's pain on him and darkness on his eyes?*
> *Odysseus' arrow hit him under the chin*
> *and punched up to the feathers through his throat.*
> *Backward and down he went, letting the wine cup fall*
> *from his shocked hand. Like pipes his nostrils jetted*
> *crimson runnels, a river of mortal red,*
> *and one last kick upset his table*
> *knocking the bread and meat to soak in the dusty blood.*

As Francis Clines wrote after seeing a similar performance, Dyer-Bennet "is not merely reciting, he is weaving voice and glance, tone and meter, shifting himself for each new character in the tale of human wrongs and wanderings and revenge."[18] While reciting *The Odyssey*, Dyer-Bennet injected himself into the piece and made it his own. In this sense he embodies Albert Lord's notion that "The singer of tales is at once the tradition and an individual creator."[19] At the conclusion of the performance, Dyer-Bennet takes a bow, and the Vanguard crowd rises as one for a standing ovation.

In November 1982 Dyer-Bennet performed "A Goddess Intervenes" (Book One), "A Hero's Son Awakens" (Book Two), and, again, "Death in the Great Hall" (Book Twenty-two) at the University of Virginia's Cabell Hall. In the program for that performance Dyer-Bennet writes: "Homer's great epic poem was given form by the voice and not by the pen. Homer spoke it, he did not write it. 'The Odyssey' was meant for the ear, not the eyes. . . . I am memorizing several excerpts for live performance, since that is my way to learn how to perform the material for the recording. I must also become so familiar with Fitzgerald's text that it comes from my lips as though it were my own, and not as some memorized poetry."[20] David Kovacs's review of the performance noted that "The qualities that make the poem great were enhanced by Dyer-Bennett's [sic] skillful recitation, at once leisurely and intense."[21]

Dyer-Bennet hoped his recordings and recitals would "get Homer out of the classroom and into more people's lives."[22] He planned, in fact, to begin work on *The Iliad* upon finishing *The Odyssey*. Between 1985 and 1990 Dyer-Bennet corresponded with the company Books on Tape, discussing the possibility of their producing his work. Ultimately, however, Dyer-Bennet remained dissatisfied with the quality of the recorded work. Unfortunately, the NEH grant was not extended past its original two years. The news was discouraging, but Dyer-Bennet kept working on the project until poor health forced him to cease performing in 1990. The recording, too, was put on hold, the project far from complete. He had joked about the whole project being a "race with senility,"[23] but now it was his body, not his mind, that was beginning to fail him.

One of Dyer-Bennet's last performances was at Meredith College in Raleigh, North Carolina, in October 1990. In addition to performing scenes from *The Odyssey*, Dyer-Bennet held a workshop for students. Evaluations of both were quite positive. "His voice and articulation were clear and enticing,"[24] wrote one student. "He sounded as if he were Homer telling the story," wrote another. "It was a good experience for me—I mean, how many times do we get to hear a minstrel?" After witnessing the reading, student Louise Taylor wrote Dyer-Bennet a letter. "I feel fortunate to have had such a wonderful opportunity."[25]

In attempting to record Homer's epic, Dyer-Bennet was ahead of his time. Today a number of audio book versions of *The Odyssey* are available, read by the likes of actors Ian McKellen and Anthony Quayle. Stanley Lombardo has done them one better by recording his own translation of the work. While such works are commonplace now, they did not exist in the early 1980s.

Never able to satisfy his zest for life, Dyer-Bennet spent his last years studying, reading, and adding to his vast collection of recordings and books. He played tennis as often as his health would allow. A number of projects remained unfinished. One was to write a book about tennis in the same vein as Izaak Walton's *Compleat Angler* (1653). Dyer-Bennet dearly loved the sport; the effect his stroke had on his tennis game was felt just as keenly as his diminished ability to play the guitar. Another project that never came to fruition was a proposed radio program called *A Minstrel's Diary*. Dyer-Bennet described it as a series of radio programs, where the central figure is a minstrel. "He is without name and belongs to no specific country or time. He is the program's narrator and relates stories of a particular historical period, assuming a role in the depiction of these events."[26] A third was an LP dealing with America's song heritage. "There are revealing songs from every period of American history—not just quaint old songs, but songs that give us the feel and smell, the aura, of our fellow humans down through the generations."[27] Finally, the minstrel hoped to make one more recording, "of songs he had never performed publicly. The record was to include Mendelssohn's 'On Wings of Song

Transport Me,' a song his grandmother had taught him when he was about six years old, the first song he ever learned."[28]

In October 1991 Dyer-Bennet was diagnosed with lymphoma. Mel, Bonnie, and Brooke, together with nurses, took care of him at home as best they could until hospitalization was necessary. Mel brought a photograph of Scholander to her husband's hospital room. On one occasion, as Mel fed him a spoonful of hot cereal, he looked at her, held her eyes, and said, "that's enough." In December Dyer-Bennet slipped into a coma. Mel moved into his hospital room and stayed with him day and night. The minstrel died on December 14, 1991, aged seventy-eight.

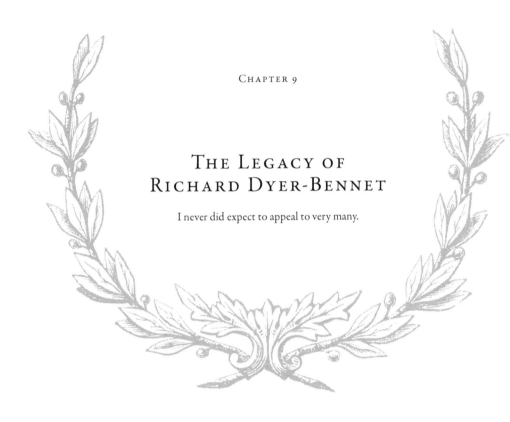

CHAPTER 9

THE LEGACY OF
RICHARD DYER-BENNET

I never did expect to appeal to very many.

If Richard Dyer-Bennet modeled himself on Sven Scholander, there has been no one who has taken up his mantle. Joan Baez came as close as anyone, but her vision was quite different from Dyer-Bennet's. Baez began her career singing and recording traditional folk songs, some hundreds of years old. Indeed, in a cover story for *Time* in 1962, she is described as singing "with an ethereal grace that seems to have been caught and stopped in passage over the 18th-century Atlantic."[1] Fearing that she would be pigeonholed as someone who sang only "old" songs, however, Baez soon began championing the works of Bob Dylan and other 1960s songwriters, as well as writing her own material. Dyer-Bennet certainly admired her singing. "She has the loveliest voice. When I first heard her I thought she had the makings of an extraordinary performer. But in the end she really doesn't take you directly into the scene of the song, the heart, the action. She isn't another Scholander."[2] Certainly Dyer-Bennet would take exception to a statement she makes in the *Time* article. "I don't care very much about where a song came from or why—or even what it says. All I care about is how it sounds and the feeling in it."[3] Dyer-Bennet, along with Theodore Bikel, is described in the same article as an artist who will "sing anything from anywhere with a lofty and cosmopolitan distinction."[4]

Artists such as Will Holt, Andrew Schulman, Ruth Buell, and Lesl Harker were heavily influenced by Dyer-Bennet, but were not able to establish a lasting presence in the recording industry's mainstream. A number of professional performers shared Dyer-Bennet's approach to folk, and some of them became quite well known for a time. William Clauson, sometimes called "the Viking troubadour," had a fine, trained voice and recorded two albums of Bellman songs. He enjoyed a successful career that included a performance at Carnegie Hall. William Elliott, a tenor, sang "in the contemporary minstrel-troubadour vein of Richard Dyer-Bennet" and apparently "won that well-known performer's earnest endorsement."[5] Elliott's ultimate lack of success may have been due to what Robert Shelton called "a quality of bloodless antiquarianism that even his musical attainments could not overcome."[6]

Shelton also compared Carolyn Hester's (born 1937) early recordings to Dyer-Bennet's. The English counter-tenor Alfred Deller (1912–1979) was similar to Dyer-Bennet in that he sang folk songs in a cultured style, but apparently neither artist influenced the other. Austrian-born soprano Martha Schlamme (née Haftel, 1923–1985) worked with Will Holt on the off-Broadway show *The World of Kurt Weill* and also recorded many albums of folk songs. Due to her genteel approach to folk music, she was sometimes described as a "lady Richard Dyer-Bennet."[7] Her star, too, has long since faded. In 1963, John Winn was described as a performer who "could very well inherit the mantle of Richard Dyer-Bennet as 'the 20th-century minstrel."[8] Winn had come to folk music after beginning in opera and choral singing. "I certainly was aware of Mr. Dyer-Bennet's artistry. I did some similar material in my early 'Troubadour' years."[9] Like so many others, though, Winn eventually gravitated to contemporary material and continues to write and perform his own songs to this day.

Yet even if someone had wanted to emulate Dyer-Bennet, it would have been a formidable task. Quite simply, Dyer-Bennet's art was unique and highly individual. As Daniel Sheehy, director and curator of Smithsonian Folkways, wrote in his liner notes to *Richard Dyer-Bennet 2*, "Ironically, it is this same singularity of style that made it difficult for others to follow in his musical footsteps. As a consequence, today he is among the least recognized of the most significant folk-revival figures."[10] He certainly was not merely a Scholander clone, yet his adherence to minstrelsy probably limited his appeal. Some of his material was too obscure to the casual listener, but he never compromised his vision. Certainly he desired neither fame nor wealth. In 1956 he noted in a letter to his mother that he was down to a few dollars, but that he had been in similar straits many times before. "I could have chosen a financially more rewarding path even in my own profession,"[11] he wrote. "I did not do so and have no right to complain about lack of money. I have other satisfactions and will make enough for the important things in the long run."

It is important to remember that many of Dyer-Bennet's contemporaries who eventually found fame had champions who promoted their work. Woody Guthrie's songs, for example, were not widely known until first Pete Seeger, then the Weavers, and finally Bob Dylan expressed their admiration for them and began including "This Land Is Your Land", "So Long It's Been Good to Know You," and others in performance and on recordings. The same can be said for Lead Belly, whose "Goodnight Irene" became famous in the hands of the Weavers shortly after his death. The Weavers, while very much a group act, showcased Seeger's talent and enthusiasm. Originally a rather rough-hewn group, they were "cleaned up" by producer Gordon Jenkins in order to appeal to a wider audience. Seeger's gift for composition also sets him apart from Dyer-Bennet. While Dyer-Bennet was a fine songwriter, he wrote very few songs, and his pieces lacked the universal appeal of Seeger's "Where Have All the Flowers Gone?" or "Turn, Turn, Turn."

Certainly some disliked, or at least did not approve of Dyer-Bennet's so-phisticated approach to his material. These critics described his style as "sissi-fied" or "precious." While individual members of the highly influential Almanac Singers might have admired Dyer-Bennet as a person, the only form of material they found acceptable was "no-fancy-stuff folk music."[12] "They held the likes of John Jacob Niles in utter contempt and used to go around mockingly imitating him. Richard Dyer-Bennet was acceptable only for 'Waltzing Matilda.'"[13] In his book *Folk Music USA*, Ronald Lankford is similarly disparaging. "Richard Dyer-Bennet, a prissy singer with classical training, specialized in arty folk songs that drove the ladies wild."[14] As Pete Seeger correctly points out, "I think it's all a mat-ter of taste. Some people like a hard-bitten kind of a voice, like Woody Guthrie's or Doc Boggs."[15]

Roger Butterfield addresses the question in another way. "I really don't know what folk music is, unless it is any kind of music that catches the fun and sadness and adventurousness and ultimate hopes of a whole lot of people, in a form that is not too contrived or sophisticated or smooth."[16] It is exactly Dyer-Bennet's "so-phisticated or smooth" approach that alienated some folk music fans.

Dyer-Bennet's performances were sometimes described as "art songs." Indeed, Studs Terkel once described him as "an art singer who sang folk songs as well."[17] Oscar Brand wrote that "Dyer-Bennet sang folk songs as if they were art songs."[18] Dyer-Bennet never used the term "art song" to describe his style, however, and given its definition, this is appropriate: "a song of serious artistic purpose, written by a professional composer, as opposed to a traditional or folk song."[19] From his recorded repertoire, only the Schubert songs can be accurately classified as art songs.

Yet Dyer-Bennet never considered himself a folk singer either. "Civilization has doomed the true folk singer, who by definition depends on direct oral tradition for his music,"[20] he wrote in 1961. "This distinction between folk singing and minstrelsy is more than a mere semantic quibble. If you are born and raised among rural people who know the songs, and if you can carry the tunes, and do, you are a folk singer, like it or not. If you are born and raised in the city, you may copy the intonation and accent of a true rural folk singer, but you will be, at best, an imitation of the real thing. What you can become is a minstrel."[21]

A number of writers characterized Dyer-Bennet as belonging to another time. Ross Altman, for example, describes him as "a man out of his time, on loan to us from an old past" before adding "and radiant with that ancestral glow which allows each new age to see from whence it has come."[22] Others, like Howard Schneider, identified Dyer-Bennet as an anachronism. In a 1944 *Newsweek* article Dyer-Bennet is described as "a minstrel without a court to sing to" and having "no royal patron."[23] While the article goes on to observe that "he has found a substitute in the concert-going public" it is now clear that the public eventually found others in whom they were more interested.

Perhaps compared to some of his peers, Dyer-Bennet lacked professional ambition. His unwillingness to sacrifice his family life also contributed to his lack of fame today. Dyer-Bennet's decision to leave New York for Aspen in 1947, for example, certainly slowed his career's momentum at a central time in its development. Coupled with his subsequent blacklisting, it is hardly surprising that, even if his existing fan base continued to delight in his annual Town Hall concerts, he was winning over few new fans as the 1960s dawned. At age forty-seven, he was probably deemed "too old" by many a new, young folk music enthusiast. And even if Dyer-Bennet possessed the ability to evoke the color and mood of a former age, fans were beginning to appreciate and demand more contemporary "folk songs."

In 1963, for example, Bob Dylan released *The Freewheelin' Bob Dylan*, an album whose songs reflected the Zeitgeist. "Blowin' in the Wind" gave no answers but posed vital questions; "Masters of War" shook a scolding finger at politicians and generals; "Talking World War III Blues" used black comedy to portray cold war paranoia; "Oxford Town" protested the University of Mississippi's refusal to allow James Meredith, a negro, to register for classes. Perhaps the album's most important track, however, was "A Hard Rain's A-Gonna Fall," a song that—while inspired in part by the old ballad "Edward"—warns of forthcoming doom in a new, quasi-poetic, and often cryptic way. Inspired by Dylan, a host of new "singer-songwriters" appeared on the scene to give their take on the times that were indeed, a-changing. As the sixties and seventies progressed, however, Dyer-Bennet, as we have seen, looked not forward but back—first to nineteenth-century Germany, and finally to classical Greece.

Dyer-Bennet often was referred to in the press as "the twentieth century minstrel." Lesl Harker remembers, however, that in class at Stony Brook he sometimes dubbed himself "the last minstrel,"[24] and as the twenty-first century dawns it is hard to disagree with that assessment. In 1963 Nat Hentoff titled his profile of Dyer-Bennet "The Last Minstrel." There he notes: "The young audiences that eagerly attend the appearances of such equally young singers as Joan Baez and Bob Dylan consider Dyer-Bennet too 'sophisticated' and removed from folk 'roots.'"[25] When asked by Hentoff about the chances of his own audience increasing, Dyer-Bennet is realistic. "A certain percentage may eventually get dissatisfied with the narrowness of repertory of some of their current favorites. They may also become bored with hearing just tonic, dominant, and subdominant chords in a couple of keys as the background to folk singing. If that happens, they will move in the direction of more challenging music and will acquire wider tastes. A few may even discover minstrelsy. I say a few because I never did expect to appeal to very many."

As far as comparing his success with that other singers achieved, Dyer-Bennet wrote in a letter to friend Bob Cooper: "I don't believe I resent the success of any other performers. Perhaps I would if my own career were diminished by others' success, but this has not been the case. Though a number of individuals and groups are now reaching larger audiences than I ever or will ever reach, the fact is that my own career has maintained an unspectacular but steady advance."[26] Concerning an artist's inevitable regrets, Dyer-Bennet admitted in the same letter that he never achieved his "boyhood dream of singing as well as McCormack and playing as well as Segovia! But then, I doubt that Dowland himself ever achieved such mastery of both techniques." While realizing he might never attain such heights, Dyer-Bennet was quite happy that "the attempt seems to keep me meaningfully and gainfully employed."

Dyer-Bennet cared deeply about how performers approached folk materials. "In the cities, towns and villages of America today," he wrote in 1947, "people who love music can listen to Heifetz, Horowitz, Toscanini, Anderson, Segovia, etc. Why should they listen to any performer less skilled in his own art? The novelty of the rediscovered material may intrigue them for a year or two, but they are going to become more demanding as they hear more performers. Do not make the mistake of underestimating the judgment of a mass audience. And most important of all, remember that folksongs are the dearly loved, hand polished creations of generations of human beings—as such they merit the greatest respect and highest art with which a performer can serve them."[27]

Dyer-Bennet recognized that his recorded work might well become his legacy. "No matter how limited my appeal may become, if I do nothing else, I can leave behind a sizable body of my material as it was performed. . . . I don't want to leave it only in books, where the music cannot live. . . . I may well not be the most skillful possible representative of my way of singing, but these albums will indicate what a minstrel could do in the twentieth century. . . . If I didn't leave some such record, who would know what minstrelsy was?"[28]

Dyer-Bennet's two songbooks, published in 1946 and 1971, are valuable for the documentation of his accompaniments. As John Raymond wrote in his review of the 1971 publication, *The Richard Dyer-Bennet Folk Song Book*, "learning exactly how an artist of the caliber of Dyer-Bennet works out an accompaniment on the guitar can help advance a student beyond the monotonous um-dum-dum strums that most amateurs never get beyond."[29] Artist Rodney Shackell supplied beautiful black-and-white illustrations for each of the fifty songs featured in the publication. The book includes piano arrangements by Harry Rubinstein and guitar accompaniments and fingering indications by Dyer-Bennet. Mindful that the keys in which he sings are too high for most voices, Dyer-Bennet sets the songs in more moderate keys. In the introduction to this work, Dyer-Bennet provides enlightening comments on his approaches to accompaniment and interpretation. As a final reminder to the reader, Dyer-Bennet quotes Scholander: "Make each song your own. If you do not, no amount of printed or spoken direction will help you, and the song will remain dead in your heart and dry upon your lips."[30]

Not until 1995 were listeners able to experience Dyer-Bennet's take on minstrelsy in the industry's current medium, the compact disc. That year the Center for Folklife and Cultural Heritage, under the auspices of Smithsonian Folkways, acquired the rights to reissue all fourteen albums released by Dyer-Bennet Records. Founded in 1988, Smithsonian Folkways' mission statement is to play an active role in "supporting cultural diversity and increased understanding among peoples through the documentation, preservation, and dissemination of sound."[31] It may be easier, however, to describe the company as the continuation of Moses Asch's (1905–1986) old Folkways label. In 1987 the Smithsonian acquired Folkways from the Asch estate. Under the capable leadership and boundless enthusiasm of its Russian-born founder, Folkways released more than 2,000 LPs between its founding in 1948 and Asch's death. The company's most popular performers are Woody Guthrie, Lead Belly, Pete Seeger, and Ella Jenkins, though literally hundreds of other important folk acts were recorded by Asch. Following Asch's death, the Smithsonian Institution Center for Folklife and Cultural Heritage in Washington, D.C., acquired the Folkways recordings and—as a stipulation of the purchase—agreed to keep each and every recording Asch had made available in perpetuity.

Smithsonian Folkways has built upon Asch's considerable legacy by acquiring the Ralph Rinzler Archives, Collector Records (founded by Dyer-Bennet's contemporary Joe Glazer in 1970), Cook Records (begun by Emory Cook), the FastFolk Musical Magazine Collection, Monitor Records (which produced albums from Russia and Eastern Europe), and Paredon Records (founded by Irwin Silber and Barbara Dane), as well as numerous photographic archives.

Richard Dyer-Bennet 1 became available for purchase on CD in 1997. *Richard Dyer-Bennet 6 (2000), 2* (2001), and *5* (2001) followed. The other albums in the numbered series are available on demand. The appearance of *Richard Dyer-Bennet 1* on CD elicited a number of interesting reviews. Writing for the Los Angeles *New Times*, Keven McAlester raised a topic long familiar to Dyer-Bennet fans: whether or not his style was suitable to folk songs. "So uncommon is the combination of Dyer-Bennet's un-self-conscious, high-pitched vocals and his classical-guitar strumming style that it can seem alternately droll and unsettling. Such was not his aim, of course; his singing is virtually flawless, his presentation completely without irony. But in a medium that generally rewards raspy authenticity, his precision can hit you like an unexpected bucket of ice water. That's a large part of his charm: the idea of singing unassailable melodies of 'The Vicar of Bray' or 'The Lonesome Valley' in a near-perfect countertenor sounds almost audacious today, but it was just common sense to Dyer-Bennet. It speaks well of his talent and intellect that on *Richard Dyer-Bennet 1* he ends up sounding more like a modern minstrel than the stylistic train wreck that one would reasonably expect."[32]

Andrew Pincus was more straightforward in his praise. "In an era when folk music means belting out amplified ballads over thumping guitars, it is good to be reminded that a single unamplified voice, accompanying itself with an acoustic guitar, can create an entire world."[33] Music critic Greg Sandow recalls the effect hearing the newly rereleased *Richard Dyer-Bennet 1* had on him. "I slipped the disk into my CD player and discovered a voice the poet Keats would have loved, full of truth and beauty."[34] What higher praise can be awarded a singer? Scholander would certainly have been proud of his pupil.

Indeed, Dyer-Bennet's life was a brilliant success. He sought and found truth and beauty in both his professional and personal life. "He loved life," Andrew Schulman remembers. "He had a great smile. He actually had a twinkle in his eye. He really did."[35] To Pete Seeger, Dyer-Bennet was "not only one of the most honest artists, but truly a thoughtful artist, looking into ancient times in old England for what he felt were the most beautiful songs he could sing, for the most important songs he could sing. He reached thousands of us with his beautiful versions of the English ballads."[36]

Harvey Cort describes Dyer-Bennet as "a unique performer. He was not a folk singer. He really didn't consider himself a folk singer. He took folk material and the term he used was that he 'transmuted' it into what might be called an art song. I don't know of any other artist who did that."[37] Studs Terkel spoke for many when he wrote: "my life has been enriched by Richard Dyer-Bennet's artistry. His wondrous lyric tenor and marvelously singular accompaniments must never be forgotten."[38]

Writing in 1961, Dyer-Bennet claimed: "the way to performances that will always ring true is shaped by the words and music of the songs themselves and has nothing to do with transient taste or stylistic mannerism. All great singers of songs find this way for themselves, and the young aspirant will do himself and his art justice only if he searches until he finds it."[39] Richard Dyer-Bennet was one such singer. He found songs that had permanence and introduced them to an entirely new audience. He was inspired by tradition, but never became its slave. Beckman and Scholander set him on his way, but the road Richard Dyer-Bennet traveled was very much his own.

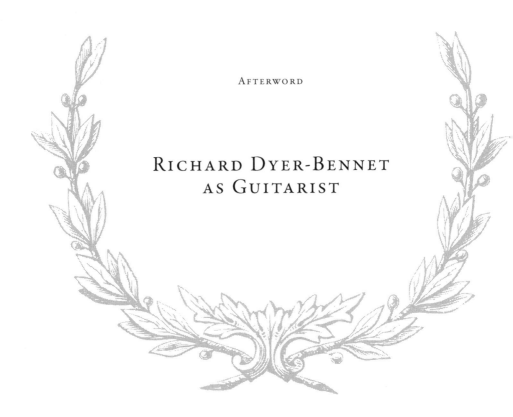

RICHARD DYER-BENNET
AS GUITARIST

I first heard about Richard Dyer-Bennet in 1971 at the end of my freshman year at Stony Brook University. One of my guitar friends told me there was this faculty member who taught a course in voice training for actors in the theater department, was once a famous folk singer, and had this really great guitar made by the Puerto Rican guitar maker Manuel Velazquez. I had started playing the guitar at age eight and it had been at the center of my life since that time, and knowing there was a great guitar nearby was reason enough to make the trip to the other side of the sprawling Stony Brook campus where the theater department was located, to visit the guitar and its owner.

I got to his office late in the afternoon of a beautiful spring day in May 1971 and knocked on the door. It opened and there was Richard Dyer-Bennet as I will always remember him, wearing his tan corduroy sport jacket with elbow patches, a friendly smile, and a warm welcome to a student he had never met before.

I quickly explained that I was a guitarist and had heard that his Velazquez guitar was an excellent instrument, and asked if I could see it. He was about to leave for the day and told me that yes, I could see the guitar, but that he had to leave in five minutes. I said that would be fine, entered the office, and ninety minutes later we both left his studio having started an enduring relationship, mentor and protégé.

First, about the guitar: it was indeed a beauty. Built in 1957 for Dick by Velazquez, the soundboard is made of German spruce, the back and sides of Brazilian rosewood, and the neck of Spanish cedar—the preferred woods for most concert guitarists. Although he added his own ideas, the building design Velazquez used, specifically the bracing pattern, was based on guitars made by three illustrious predecessors: Antonio de Torres Jurado and Santos Hernández of Spain, and Hermann Hauser Sr. of Germany.

What this produced was what Dyer-Bennet needed: a first-rate concert instrument with sparkling trebles and warm basses, an instrument better than he had ever had. And he had realized he needed to deal with an important issue that was a problem of traditionally made guitars: intonation, or the degree to which an instrument plays in tune. What he had used before the Velazquez was not producing a level of intonation that satisfied him, especially as Dyer-Bennet had an excellent ear and sang so very well in tune. Velazquez was one of the mid-twentieth-century luthiers (the traditional term for guitar makers, originally used for lute makers, now also used in general for builders of all stringed instruments) who was concerned with the proper intonation of a guitar, basically building the instrument so that it played well in tune. The science of this aspect of guitar making would make a really big jump in the 1970s, particularly with the work of American luthier John Gilbert, but Manuel Velazquez had made good progress as a result of his intuitive sense and his meticulous craftsmanship, and his 1957 guitar was a big step up for Dyer-Bennet.

I think the reason that our first meeting, five minutes that became ninety, is that Dyer-Bennet instantly recognized in me a kindred spirit; as much as he was a singer, he was also a born guitarist. I first began to play the guitar at age eight and started out with folk music, but after less than a year's lessons my folk guitar teacher—a lovely nineteen-year-old beret-wearing beatnik named Jane—suggested I study classical guitar. My initial classical guitar studies lasted for about a year; I learned to play scales, Carcassi etudes, and some easy Bach and Spanish pieces, but I eventually grew weary of the required practice diligence. And more importantly, the Beatles arrived in America! So, it was off into pop music, and then when I got to college, jazz studies.

So there I was, in Dyer-Bennet's office, playing this marvelous classical guitar, and I think what happened was that he sensed where I could go with the guitar. He started talking about the great Spanish guitarist, Andres Segovia, whom he knew because among other things they were both on the roster of famous impresario Sol Hurok, and his two friends, the other great classical guitarists of the day, Julian Bream and John Williams. I told him of my classical studies when I was a

child, and played the famous *Little Prelude in D minor* by J. S. Bach, which had
stayed in my memory and fingers.

The semester was essentially over and Dick suggested I take his course, "Theater
130: Voice Training for Actors" in the fall semester. I did, and he eventually asked
me to be his teaching assistant. In the fall semester of my junior year, November
1972, he had a stroke and I was asked to take over his course load so his students
could finish out the semester.

Richard Dyer-Bennet became one of my three main career influences, the other two being my father, Sydney Schulman, a photographer who taught me about
professionalism, and the guitar professor at Stony Brook, Jerry Willard, who led
me into the world of serious guitar study and performance. As Paul Jenkins has
written here, the great influence on Dyer-Bennet was Sven Scholander, not only
because of his singing and repertoire, but because of his use of the "Swedish lute,"
also called "lute-guitar," to accompany himself. This instrument, similar to the
guitar, was a perfect vehicle for the self-accompanied singer.

Dyer-Bennet was essentially self-taught as a player, but recognized the draw-
backs to this approach and eventually studied classical guitar with the renowned
Cuban-American guitarist Rey de la Torre, who in turn was the most eminent
disciple of Miguel Llobet. Llobet was the foremost student of Francisco Tarrega
(1852–1909). So Dyer-Bennet was able to immerse himself in the great tradition
of the modern classical guitar, a perfect means to achieve the quality in accompaniment that he had so long strived for in his singing.

This quality of performance is heard throughout his recordings and is made
manifest in several ways. Of course, the most obvious aspect is the clarity and
consistency of the guitar playing. But in order to achieve the crucial aspect of variety that programming needs, especially a solo performance, several things need
to be done. After all, solo voice accompanied by solo guitar was the essence of a
Dyer-Bennet concert or recording.

The first two aspects of variety in programming are the choice of tempo and
key. Both require in their own ways a solid technique. Obviously a fast tempo
requires the ability for the fingers to move quickly, both in terms of harmonic
support, changing chords precisely, and also for melodic counterpoint. A slow
tempo demands the ability to play smoothly, what is called legato. And it is the
change from song to song in tempo and key that is so important in establishing
variety, and therefore sustaining interest in the program. This variety in tempo
and keys is ever present in Dyer-Bennet's programming.

The next thing in establishing variety in the kind of performance he did is the
ability to use different types of accompaniment. Several types of accompaniment
can be heard in most of Dyer-Bennet's arrangements. A typical accompaniment,

the most common with guitar playing, is referred to as chordal accompaniment. A chord on the guitar can involve up to six notes (there are six strings on the standard classical guitar, which is what Dyer-Bennet used), and can be played in a variety of ways. It can be strummed, as is often heard in folk music, which means that the notes of the chord, for example the six notes of an E major chord in the first position—from bass to treble, E, B, E, G#, B, E—are played in order from the lowest note to the highest, and, although not simultaneously, still very quickly. Dyer-Bennet did not use a guitar pick, the small plastic (originally tortoise shell) object often used on guitars, mandolins, citterns, etc. He played with a classical technique using the right-hand fingers for plucking the notes; in a strum the thumb alone is often used, although various combinations of right-hand fingers can also be employed. That same chord, however, can be strummed in the opposite direction, from highest to lowest notes. An example of this type of chord playing can be heard in the opening moments of "The Quaker Lover," "Three Fishers," "Lord Rendal," and "Fine Flowers in the Valley."

Another type of chordal accompaniment is the use of arpeggiation, which involves the separate playing of each note of a chord, in a rhythm. This is a very common type of accompaniment used for centuries in art song and popular music as well as folk music. Examples of the use of arpeggios can be heard in "Greensleeves," "Venezuela," and "The Joys of Love."

A more sophisticated type of accompaniment is the ability to play polyphonically, as a pianist would. This involves playing self-sustaining lines: a melody line acting as a countermelody to the vocal line, and a bass line. It is possible to even have two or three melodic lines moving on the guitar, depending on the complexity. And this is where Dyer-Bennet understood he would need to study classical guitar; it is a much more difficult type of playing than strumming a chord. You can hear this style in "Pedro," "Barbara Allen," and "I Once Loved a Girl."

Two more things that make for first-rate accompaniment are tone color and synchronicity. Tone color is one of the great strengths of the classical guitar, the ability to manipulate the right hand when it is plucking the strings so that the sound can vary in timbre. I have often heard this considered one of the most sophisticated of instrumental techniques. It is this variation in tone color to match the emotion established by the words, and to match the color of the singer's voice, that makes it so important. Dyer-Bennet was a master at doing this.

The idea of synchronicity of voice and accompaniment speaks for itself. It takes a great accompanist to get it really right, in part because the accompanist must follow the lead of the singer; among other things, the singer does not always sing the song the same way. It does help if you are accompanying your own singing; you know exactly how you are phrasing the melody!

Finally, a crucial and often overlooked aspect to making a song arrangement, and playing it to greatest effect, is the attention paid to the bass line. What Johannes Brahms once said—that the way he composed was by writing the melody and bass line first and then filling in the rest—is true of many composers. The bass line is the most important counterpoint to the melody. Dyer-Bennet was always conscious of that, and the bass line in his arrangements, and the way he played them, was always highly musical.

Richard Dyer-Bennet was a terrific arranger and accompanist. He was quite expert at all the elements that I have enumerated. As I look back on those years I will say that I think he knew that he was good at doing these things, but he never said so in so many words. In this and all other respects, Richard Dyer-Bennet was a true gentleman.

And now for a little irony. As I have already said, Dyer-Bennet was my mentor, and all these years later I am glad to be part of this well-deserved biography. As a result many memories have come back to me, happy memories in a personal way, and a realization of how much of my career as a professional musician was shaped by his influence. The irony is this: the focus of his energy back then was about guiding me, his student/protégé, as it was with all of the other young people that were fortunate enough to come into his circle. It was not about him, it was about you. And as a result, although I knew many things about what he had done, I did not really know his work as a singer/guitarist. I never attended any of his concerts, and did not have any of his recordings.

So, as a result of Paul Jenkins asking me to write about his guitar playing and arrangements, I have immersed myself in his recordings. And lo and behold, more than a student/protégé, I am now . . . a fan!

ANDREW SCHULMAN
DECEMBER 2008

DISCOGRAPHY

Albums are listed in chronological order by recording date. Many thanks to Thomas Stern for his assistance.

BALLADS AND FOLK SONGS SUNG BY RICHARD DYER-BENNET. 1941. Three 12" 78 r.p.m. Recorded and released privately by Frederick C. Packard Jr.
> The Charleston Merchant/Come All Ye/The Golden Vanity/Cockle Shells/The Lincolnshire Poacher/Early One Morning/Lord Rendal/Brigg Fair/The Leprechaun

RICHARD DYER-BENNET, LUTE SINGER. 1941. Three 10" 78 r.p.m. Keynote 108.
> The Lincolnshire Poacher/The Derby Ram/The Golden Vanity/The House Carpenter/The Swag Man/Hullabaloo Belay/What Shall We Do with the Drunken Sailor/The Charleston Merchant

BABES OF THE ZOO. 1944. Two 10" 78 r.p.m. Russian War Relief. Musicraft RWR-5134.

SCOTTISH SONGS (SCHOTTISCHE LIEDER). 1946. Four 12" 33 r.p.m. Concert Hall CHC-13.
> Faithfu' Johnie/O Sweet Were the Hours/O How Can I Be Blithe and Glad/The Lovely Lass of Inverness/Could This Ill World Have Been Contriv'd/Sunset/Again My Lyre/On the Massacre at Glencoe/The British Light Dragoons/O Mary at Thy Window Be/Bonny Laddie, Highland Laddie

IRISH SONGS. 1946. Three 12" 78 r.p.m. Concert Hall.
> Once More I Hail Thee/The Return to Ulster/Oh! Who, My Dear Dermot/The Morning Air Plays on My Face/The Pulse of an Irish/Morning a Cruel Turmoiler Is

LOVE SONGS. 1946. Three 10" 78 r.p.m. Disc 609.
> Two Maidens Went Milking One Day/Westryn Wynde/Venezuela/As I Was Going to Ballynure/Blow the Candles Out/Brigg Fair

MINSTREL SONGS OF THE USA. 1947. Four 10" 78 r.p.m. Vox Records 632.
> Blue Mountain Lake/Colorado Trail/Lass from the Low Country/Old Bangum/Quaker Lover/Turkish Reverie/Were You There?

MINSTREL SONGS OF GERMANY. 1947. Four 10" 78 r.p.m. Vox Records 633.
> Song of Reproach (Minnelied)/The Three Tailors/Secret Love/Jan Hinnerk/The Ghost of Basel/Phyllis and Her Mother/Moonrise/Where To?

RICHARD DYER-BENNET, TWENTIETH-CENTURY MINSTREL. 1949. 33 r.p.m.
Decca DL79102.
> The Devil and the Farmer's Wife/The Eggs and Marrowbone/The Willow Tree/Villikens and
> His Dinah/Lolly Toodum/Mo Mary/The Swapping Song/The Old Maid/Early One Morning/
> Greensleeves/Oh Sally My Dear/Fain Would I Wed a Fair Young Maid

RICHARD DYER-BENNET, TWENTIETH-CENTURY MINSTREL. 1949. 10" 33 r.p.m.
Decca DLP5046.
> The Devil and the Farmer's Wife/ Eggs and Marrowbone /The Willow Tree/Villikens and His
> Dinah/ Swapping Song /The Old Maid/Early One Morning/ Greensleeves/Oh Sally My Dear

FOLK SONGS. 1951. 33 r.p.m. Remington RLP-199-34. Note: Same as Continental 2011.
> Lord Randall/The White Lily*/Kitty My Love/The Rising of the Moon/The Wife Wrapt in
> Sheepskin/My Good Old Man/Lowlands/John Henry/The Golden Vanity/Greensleeves/Bonnie
> Dundee/Pull Off Your Old Coat*/Binnorie/The Laird O' Cockpen/The Lonesome Dove/The Kerry
> Recruit
> *listed on the album, but not actually included.

AN EVENING WITH WILLIAM SHAKESPEARE. 1952. Two 12" 33 r.p.m. Continental
Records.
> Dyer-Bennet sings three songs, "Fain Would I Wed," "O Mistress Mine," and "Come Away Death." He
> also plays the part of Feste in Act I, Scene 5 and Act II, Scene 2 of *Twelfth Night*.

FOLKSONGS OF THE BRITISH ISLES. 1953. 45 r.p.m. Vox VIP 30,120.
> The Ash Grove/ The Bold Fenian Men/David of the White Rock/The Bonny Earl of Murray

RICHARD DYER-BENNET 1. 1955. 33 r.p.m. Dyer-Bennet Records DYB 1000.
> Oft in the Stilly Night/Molly Brannigan/Down by the Sally Gardens/The Bold Fenian Men/Three
> Fishers/The Bonnie Earl of Morey/Fine Flowers in the Valley/The Vicar of Bray/So We'll Go No
> More A-Roving/Phyllis and Her Mother/The Joys of Love/I'm a Poor Boy/Pull Off Your Old Coat/
> Down in the Valley/Pedro/The Lonesome Valley

RICHARD DYER-BENNET 2. 1956. 33 r.p.m. Dyer-Bennet Records DYB 2000.
> When Cockleshells Turn Silverbells/Corn Rigs Are Bonnie/The Garden Where the Praties Grow/
> The Bailiff's Daughter of Islington/Two Maidens Went Milking/Who Killed Cock Robin?/Veillée de
> Noel/Jan Hinnerk/Woman! Go Home!/Blow the Candles Out/Eggs and Marrowbones/The Beggar
> Man/The Turkish Reverie

RICHARD DYER-BENNET 3. 1957. 33 r.p.m. Dyer-Bennet Records DYB 3000.
> The Lady's Policy/Dinah and Villikens/Fain Would I Wed/Willie Taylor/Charlie is My Darling/Lilli
> Bulero/The Beloved Kitten/Spottlied auf Napoleons Rückzug Aus Russland 1812/The Lass from the
> Low Country/The Swapping Song/The House Carpenter/The Lady Who Loved a Swine/Go Down,
> Moses

RICHARD DYER-BENNET 4. 1957. 33 r.p.m. Dyer-Bennet Records DYB 4000.
> A May Day Carol/The Rising of the Moon/The Kerry Recruit/Searching for Lambs/The Bonnets of
> Bonnie Dundee/The Spanish Lady in Dublin City/The Three Ra'ens/Song of Reproach/The Three
> Tailors/The Swagman/The Foggy, Foggy Dew/The Fox/Drill, Ye Tarriers, Drill

RICHARD DYER-BENNET 5. 1958. 33 r.p.m. Dyer-Bennet Records DYB 5000.
> Greensleeves/The "Golden Vanity"/The White Lily/Lord Rendal/Westryn Wynde/Barbara Allen/
> Venezuela/The Quaker Lover/John Henry/Spanish Is the Loving Tongue/I Ride an Old Paint/Edward

RICHARD DYER-BENNET 6. 1958. 33 r.p.m. Dyer-Bennet Records DYB 6000.
Come All Ye/Old Bangum/Three Jolly Rogues of Lynn/Aunt Rhody/Frog Went a Courting/John
Peel/The Leprechaun/The Piper of Dundee/Bow Down/The Tailor and the Mouse/I Went Out One
Morning in May/Green Corn/Buckeye Jim/Little Pigs/Three Crows/The Hole in the Bottom of the Sea

RICHARD DYER-BENNET 7. 1958. 33 r.p.m. Dyer-Bennet Records DYB 7000.
Faithfu' Johnie/On the Massacre of Glencoe/Bonnie Laddie, Highland Laddie/Sunset/The Lovely
Lass of Inverness/The Pulse of an Irishman/Once More I Hail Thee/Morning a Cruel Turmoiler Is/The
Morning Air Plays on My Face/The Return to Ulster/Oh! Who My Dear Dermot/Again, My Lyre

RICHARD DYER-BENNET 8. 1959. 33 r.p.m. Dyer-Bennet Records DYB 8000.
Agincourt Song/Come Live with Me/Come Away, Death!/I Care Not for These Ladies/Flow,
My Tears/All in a Garden Green/Henry Martin/All Mein Gedanken/Die Bekehrte Schäferin/
Kränzelkraut/Jagabenteur/Warnung/Le Brave Marin/Aminte

RICHARD DYER-BENNET 9. 1960. 33 r.p.m. Dyer-Bennet Records DYB 9000.
The Laird o' Cockpen/The Two Sisters of Binnorie/Early One Morning/The Pride of Petravore/
Gently, Johnny, My Jingalo/The British Light Dragoons/Schneiders Höllenfahrt/Der Tod von Basel/
Le Joli Tambour/The Buffalo Skinners/John Riley/The Cherry Tree Carol

AKSEL SCHIØTZ, BARITONE, SINGING SCHUBERT, BELLMAN, WOLF,
BRAHMS. 1960. 33 r.p.m. Dyer-Bennet Records DYBXS 2.[Richard Dyer-Bennet accompanies
Schiøtz on guitar.]
Liebesbotschaft/Ganymed/Der Wanderer am den Mond/An die Laute//Fredman's epistles. No. 25,
Blåsen nu alla!/Fredman's song. No. 31, Opp, Amaryllis!/Fredman's epistles. No. 30, Drick ur ditt
glass/Heb auf dein blondes Haupt/ Der Tambour/Verschwiegene Liebe/Auf dem grünen Balkon/
Anakreons Grab/An die Nachtigall/Salamander/Im Waldeseinsamkeit/Mein Mädel

RICHARD DYER-BENNET 10. 1962. 33 r.p.m. Dyer-Bennet Records DYB 10000.
The Lincolnshire Poacher/Lowlands/I Once Loved a Girl/She Moved Thro' the Fair/The Seven
Little Pigs/O Speak Then, My Love/Le Véritable Amour/The Unfortunate Troubadour/The Reaper's
Ghost/ Two Comments/Go 'Way, Old Man/The Wife Wrapped in Wether's Skin/My Good Old
Man/No Hiding Place

MORE SONGS BY THE 20TH-CENTURY MINSTREL. 1962. 33 r.p.m. Stinson Records
SLP60.
The Three Tailors/Song of Reproach/Colorado Trail/Quaker Lover/Come All Ye/Where To
Schubert/Eggs and Marrowbone/The Charleston Merchant/Moonrise/Secret Love/Blue Mountain
Lake/Lass from the Low Country/Early One Morning/Swapping Song

A RICHARD DYER-BENNET CONCERT. 1962. 33 r.p.m. Stinson SLP61.
Phyllis and Her Mother/Old Bangum/Oh No John/The Leprechaun/Lord Randal/The Ghost of
Basel/Jan Hinnerk/The Three Rogues/The Lincolnshire Poacher/Cockle Shells

RICHARD DYER-BENNET 11. 1962. 33 r.p.m. Dyer-Bennet Records.
Linger in Blissful Repose/Gentle Annie/Come with Thy Sweet Voice Again/If You've Only Got a
Moustache/Jeanie with the Light Brown Hair/For Thee, Love, For Thee/Ah! May the Red Rose Live
Always!/Beautiful Dreamer/Sweetly She Sleeps, My Alice Fair/There Are Plenty of Fish in the Sea/
Open Thy Lattice Love/Come Where My Love Lies Dreaming

1601. 1962. 33 r.p.m. Dyer-Bennet Records DYBS 1601.
    1601 (spoken)/Old Joe Clark/The Old She-Crab/The Tailor's Boy/The Eer-i-e Canal/There Was a
Friar in Our Town/The Gatherin' o' the Clan

RICHARD DYER-BENNETT SINGS BALLADS [*sic*]. 1963. 33 r.p.m. Stinson SLP35.
    Spanish Is the Loving Tongue/Gently Johnny, My Jingalo/I Once Loved a Girl/John Henry/
Greensleeves/Barbara Allen/The Three Ravens/The Willow Tree/The Devil and the Farmer's Wife

RICHARD DYER-BENNET 12. 1964. 33 r.p.m. Dyer-Bennet Records.
    Shallow Brown/The Drunken Sailor/The Eddystone Light/Hullabaloo Belay/The Mermaid/The
Willow Tree/The Charleston Merchant/Peter Gray/The Roving Gambler/Billy Barlow/Australian
Girls/Hanging Johnny/The Derby Ram/Plain Language from Truthful James

RICHARD DYER-BENNET 13. 1964. 33 r.p.m. Dyer-Bennet Records.
    The Soldier and the Lady/The Tale of the Tales (spoken)/The Man Who Was Full of Fun (spoken)/
The King of the Noise (spoken)/The Devil and the Farmer's Wife/The Old Gray Goose/ The Wolf
Who Was a Friend (spoken)/The Fox and the Geese

THE ASCH RECORDINGS, 1939–1945. Vol. 2. 1967. Two 33 r.p.m. Asch (Folkways) AA 1-2
and AA3-4.
    Two Maidens Went Milking One Day

AMERICA'S MUSICAL HERITAGE. 1971. Two 33 r.p.m. American Heritage DL 734856/DL
734857.
    Villikens and His Dinah

THE ESSENTIAL RICHARD DYER-BENNET. 1977. Two 33 r.p.m. Vanguard VSD 95-96.
Rereleased in 1991 on compact disc as THE ART OF RICHARD DYER-BENNET.
    Blow the Candles Out/Down by the Sally Gardens/The Lonesome Valley/Come All Ye/The Bonnie
Earl of Morey/Pull Off Your Old Coat/John Peel/The Swapping Song/Venezuela/The Lass from
the Low Country/The Devil and the Farmer's Wife/Hanging Johnny/The Drunken Sailor/Westryn
Wynde/The Soldier and the Lady/Greensleeves/Two Maidens Went Milking/Molly Brannigan/The
Leprechaun/Peter Gray/Hullabaloo Belay/Eggs and Marrowbone/Who Killed Cock Robin?/Phyllis
and Her Mother/Edward/The Garden Where the Praties Grow/So We'll Go No More A-Roving

THE LOVELY MILLERESS (DIE SCHÖNE MÜLLERIN). 1978. Two 33 r.p.m. Dyer-
Bennet Records 33674/33675.

RICHARD DYER-BENNET IN A PROGRAM OF DRAMATIC DECLAMATION OF
THREE EXCERPTS FROM HOMER'S THE ODYSSEY. 1979. One sound tape reel. Library
of Congress.

THE ODYSSEY TAPES. 1980. 3/4" videocassette. Research Foundation, SUNY/The Arts on TV.

A PROGRAM OF POETRY, TRANSLATIONS, AND MUSIC IN MEMORY OF
ROBERT FITZGERALD, CONSULTANT IN POETRY, 1984–1985. 1985. Excerpts from
the *Odyssey* read by Richard Dyer-Bennet.

THE ART OF RICHARD DYER-BENNET. 1991. CD. Vanguard Classics OVC 6007.
Originally released in 1977 as THE ESSENTIAL RICHARD DYER-BENNET. For song titles
see above.

FOLK SONG AMERICA: A TWENTIENTH-CENTURY REVIVAL. 1991. Smithsonian.

Greensleeves

RICHARD DYER-BENNET 1. 1997. CD. Smithsonian-Folkways SF 40078. For song titles, see
listing above for RICHARD DYER-BENNET 1.

RICHARD DYER-BENNET 6. 2000. CD. Smithsonian-Folkways SF 45053. For song titles, see
listing above for RICHARD DYER-BENNET 6.

RICHARD DYER-BENNET 2. 2001. CD. Smithsonian-Folkways SF 40142. For song titles, see
listing above for RICHARD DYER-BENNET 2.

RICHARD DYER-BENNET 5. 2001. CD. Smithsonian-Folkways SF 40143. For song titles, see
listing above for RICHARD DYER-BENNET 5.

RECORDINGS WITH UNKNOWN RECORDING DATES

BALLADS. 78 r.p.m. Stinson. 364.
O No John/Three Jolly Rogues/Come All Ye/The Frog and the Mouse/John Peel/Eddystone Light/
Little Pigs/Molly Malone

BALLADS. 33 r.p.m. Asch Records. 560.
Spanish Is the Loving Tongue

FOLK SONGS. 33r.p.m. Continental Records CST-2011.
Lord Randall/Kitty, My Love/The Rising of the Moon/The Wife Wrapt in Sheepskin/My Good Old
Man/Lowlands/John Henry/The Golden Vanity/Greensleeves/Bonnie Dundee/Binnorie/The Laird
O' Cockpen/The Lonesome Dove/The Kerry Recruit

FOLK SONGS. 7" 45 r.p.m. Remington REP-1.
Lord Randall/The Wife Wrapt in Sheepskin/My Good Old Man/John Henry

RICHARD DYER-BENNET. 45 r.p.m. Dyer-Bennet Records.
Greensleeves/John Henry/Joys of Love/Lonesome Valley

RICHARD DYER-BENNETT [sic]. 33 r.p.m. Archive of Folk Music FM-103.
Spanish Is a Loving Tongue/Gently Johnny My Jingalo/I Once Loved a Girl/John Henry/
Greensleeves/Barbara Allen/The Three Ra'ens/The Willow Tree/The Devil and the Farmer's Wife

RICHARD DYER-BENNET AND TOM GLAZER SING OLDEN BALLADS. 33 r.p.m.
Mercury MG 2007.
The Golden Vanity/The Lincolnshire Poacher/The Derby Ram/The Swag Man/The House
Carpenter/The Charleston Merchant/Hullabaloo Belay/What Shall We Do with the Drunken Sailor

Glazer's side includes: Twelve Days of Christmas/The Sheeling Song/Hush Little Baby/Sixteen Come
Sunday/Green Sleeves/Waly Waly/Uncle Reuben/Blow the Candles Out/Black-Eyed Susie/ Go 'Way
From My Window

RICHARD DYER-BENNET: 20TH-CENTURY MINSTREL. 33 r.p.m. Stinson SLP 2.
Blow the Candles Out/Venezuela/The Frog and the Mouse/Little Pigs/Molly Malone/Two Maidens
Went Milking One Day/As I Was Going to Ballynure/Westryn Wynde/John Peel/Brigg Fair/
Eddystone Light

RICHARD DYER-BENNET: BALLADS. Three 12" 78 r.p.m. Asch/Stinson 461.
Barbara Allen/I Once Loved a Girl/The Three Ra'ens/John Henry/Gently Johnny!

REPERTOIRE

Key
1,2,3 etc: Dyer-Bennet Records numbered albums.
1601: 1601
461: Ballads (Asch 78 rpm)
560: Ballads (Asch)
609: Love Songs
CHC 13: Scottish Songs
CHIR: Irish Songs
Concert: performed in concert, but never recorded.
CST-2011: Folk Songs (Continental)
D45: Richard Dyer-Bennet (45 rpm)
DL734856: America's Musical Heritage
DL79102: Richard Dyer-Bennet: 20th Century Minstrel (Decca)
DLP5046: Richard Dyer-Bennet: 20th Century Minstrel (Decca 10")
FM-103: Richard Dyer-Bennett [sic] Archives of Folk Music
K108: Richard Dyer-Bennet Lute Singer
MER: Richard Dyer-Bennet and Tom Glazer Sing Olden Ballads
OWI: Office of War Information Broadcasts or Recordings
Packard: Ballads and Folk Songs Sung by Richard Dyer-Bennet
REM: Folk Songs (Remington)
REP: Folk Songs (Remington, 45rpm)
S364: Ballads (Stinson)
Shake: An Evening with William Shakespeare
SLP 2: Richard Dyer-Bennet: 20th-Century Minstrel
SLP 35: Richard Dyer-Bennett [sic] Sings Ballads
SLP 60: More Songs by the 20th Century Minstrel
VAN: The Essential Richard Dyer-Bennet
Vox 30 120: Folk Songs of the British Isles
VOX 632: Minstrel Songs of Germany
VOX 632: Minstrel Songs of the USA

Song	Album 1	Album 2	Album 3	Album 4	Album 5	Album 6	Album 7	Origin
Again, My Lyre	7	CHC-13						English
Agincourt Song	8							English
Ah! May the Red Rose Live Alway! (Foster)	11							American
All in a Garden Green	8							English
All mein Gedanken	8							German
Amarilli	Concert							Italian
Aminte	8							French
Annie Laurie	Concert							Scottish
As I Was Going to Ballynore	SLP2	609						Irish
Ashgrove, The	Vox 30 120							Welsh
Australian Girls	12							American
Bailiff's Daughter of Islington, The	2							English
Barbara Allen	5	FM-103	SLP35	461				English
"Barber of Seville" aria	Concert							Italian
Battle of Bismarck Sea, The	OWI							Dyer-Bennet
Beautiful Dreamer	11							American
Beggarman, The	2							Irish
Beloved Kitten, The	3							German
Billy Barlow	12							American
Billy Boy	Concert							American
Black Is the Color of My True Love's Hair	Concert							American
Black Jack Gypsy	Concert							English

Blow the Candles Out	2	SLP2	VAN	609		English
Blow Ye Winds of the Morning	Concert					American
Blue Mountain Lake	SLP60	VOX 632				American
Bold Fenian Men, The	1	Vox 30 120				Irish
Boll Weevil, The	Concert					American
Bonnets of Bonnie Dundee, The (a.k.a. Bonnie Dundee)	4	CST-201	REM			Scottish
Bonnie Doon	Concert					Scottish
Bonnie Earl of Morey, The	1	VAN	Vox 30 120			Scottish
Bonny Laddie, Hieland Laddie	7	CHC-13				Scottish
Bow Down	6					English
Brave Hollanders, The	OWI					Dyer-Bennet
Brennan on the Moor	Concert					Irish
Brigg Fair	SLP2	609	Packard			Irish
Bristol Belle and the Pride of Madrid	Concert					English
British Light Dragoons, The (Scott)	9	CHC-13				Scottish
Buckeye Jim	6					American
Buffalo Skinners	9					American
Careless Love	Concert					American
Charleston Merchant, The	K108	MER	SLP60	12	Packard	American
Charlie Is My Darling	3					Scottish
Cherry Tree Carol, The	9					American
Coasts of High Barbary, The	Concert					American
Cock Robin	2	VAN				English

Title								Origin
Colorado Trail, The	SLP60	VOX 632						American
Come Again, Sweet Love (Dowland)	Concert							English
Come All Ye	6	SLP60	S364	VAN	Packard			Irish
Come Away, Death! (Shakespeare)	8	Shake						English
Come Live with Me	8							English
Come Where My Love Lies Dreaming (Foster)	11							American
Come With Thy Sweet Voice Again (Foster)	11							American
Corn Rigs Are Bonnie (Burns)	2							Scottish
Could This Ill World Have Been Contrived	CHC-13							Scottish
Cow, The	OWI							Dyer-Bennet
Dark as a Dungeon	Concert							American
David of the White Rock	Vox 30 120							Welsh
Der Tod von Basel	9	SLP6	VOX 633					German
Derby Ram	12	K108	MER					English
Devil and the Farmer's Wife, The	13	DL70192	VAN	FM-103	DLP5046			American
Die bekehrte Schäferin	8							German
Dinah and Villikens (a.k.a. Villikens and His Dinah)	3	DL70192	DLP5046	DL734856				English
Douce Dame Jolie	Concert							French
Down by the Sally Gardens (Yeats)	1	VAN						Irish
Down in the Valley	1							American
Drill, Ye Tarriers, Drill	4							American
Drink to Me Only with Thine Eyes (Jonson)	Concert							English
Drunken Sailor, The	12	K108	MER	VAN				English

Title		DL79102	SLP60	Packard	DLP5046	
Early One Morning	9					English
Eddystone Light, The	12	SLP2	S364			English
Edward	5	VAN				Scottish
Eggs and Marrowbone	2	DL79102	SLP60	VAN	DLP5046	Irish
Erie Canal, The	1601					American
Fain Would I Wed	3	Shake				English
Faithfu' Johnie	7	CHC-13				Scottish
Famine Song (Irish Famine Song)	Concert					Irish
Fascists Are Getting Uneasy, The	OWI					Dyer-Bennet
Fascists Bray, The	OWI					Dyer-Bennet
Fine Flowers in the Valley	1					Irish
Finland Rise Again	OWI					Dyer-Bennet
Fish Hooks	OWI					Dyer-Bennet
Flow My Tears (Dowland)	8					English
Foggy, Foggy Dew	4					American
For Thee, Love, For Thee (Foster)	11					American
Fox, The (a.k.a. The Fox and the Geese)	4	13				American
Frog Went A-Courtin' (The Frog and the Mouse)	6	S364	SLP2			English
Garden Where the Praties Grow, The	2	VAN				Irish
Gatherin' o' the Clan, The	1601					Scottish
Gentle Annie (Foster)	11					American
Gently Johnny, My Jingolo	9	FM-103	SLP35	461		English
Go Down, Moses	3					American

Go Tell Aunt Rhodie	6						American
Go Way from My Window (Niles)	Concert						American
Go 'Way, Old Man	10						American
Golden Vanity, The	5	CST-2011	K108	MER	Packard		English
Green Broom	Concert						English
Green Corn (Lead Belly)	6						American
Greensleeves	5	CST-2011	D45	DL-79102	DLP5046	VAN	English
Grey Wolf of the Sea, The	OWI						Dyer-Bennet
Hanging Johnny	12	VAN					American
Henry Martin	8						Scottish
High Germany	Concert						English
Highway Man, The	Concert						English
Hole in the Bottom of the Sea	6						American
Hood and the Bismarck, The	OWI						Dyer-Bennet
House Carpenter, The	3	K108	MER	Packard			American
How Hell Busted Loose Up at Blue Mountain Lake	Concert						American
How Should I Your True Love Know?	Concert						English
Hullabaloo Belay	12	K108	MER	VAN			American
I Attempt from Love's Sickness to Fly (Purcell)	Concert						English
I Care Not for These Ladies	8						English
I Once Loved a Girl	10	FM-103	SLP35	461			American
I Ride an Old Paint	5						American
If You've Only Got a Mustache (Foster)	11						American

I'm A Poor Boy	1							American
Jag Vill Ga Vall	4							Swedish
Jagdabenteuer	8							German
Jan Hinnerk	2	SLP61	VOX 63					German
Jeanie with the Light Brown Hair (Foster)	11							American
Jennie Jenkins	Concert							American
John Anderson My Jo (Burns)	Concert							Scottish
John Henry	5	CST-2011	D45	FM-103	REM	REP	461	American
John Peel	6	VAN	S364	SLP2				English
John Riley	9							English
Johnny Has Gone for a Soldier	Concert							American
Joys of Love, The	1							French
Keeper, The	Concert							English
Kerry Recruit, The	4	CST-2011	REM					Irish
King Herod and the Cock	Concert							English
Kitty My Love	CST-2011	REM						Irish
Kränzelkraut	8							German
Lady Who Loved a Swine, The	3							English
Lady's Policy, The	3							English
Laird o' Cockpen, The	9	CST-2011	REM					Scottish
Lasciatemi Morire	Concert							Italian
Lass from the Low Country, The	3	SLP60	VAN	VOX 632				English
Le Brave Marin	8							French

Title							Language
Le Joli Tambour	9						French
Le Roi a fait battre Tambour	Concert						French
Le Veritable Amour	10						French
Der Leiermann (Schubert)	Concert						German
Leprechaun, The	6	VAN	SLP61	Packard			Irish
Les Sabots	Concert						French
Lied der Landsknechte	Concert						German
Lilli Bulero	3						English
Lincolnshire Poacher, The	10	K108	SLP61	Packard			English
Linger in Blissful Repose (Foster)	11						American
Little Pigs	6	S364	SLP2				Scottish
Lolly Toodum	DL79102						American
Londonderry Air (My Gentle Harp)	Concert						Irish
Lonesome Dove	REM	CST-2011					American
Lonesome Valley	1	VAN	D45				American
Lord Rendal (Lord Randall)	5	REM	SLP61	CST-2011	Packard	REP	Scottish
Lovely Lass of Inverness, The (Burns)	7						Scottish
Lowlands	10	REM	CST-2011				English
Mark How the Glorious Morning	Concert						Unknown
Mary Had a Baby	Concert						American
May Day Carol, The	4						English
McArthur the Rattler	OWI						Dyer-Bennet
Mermaid, The	12						American

Title					Nationality
Miller's Will, The	Concert				American
Mo Mary	DL79102				Irish
Modern Merchant Seaman	OWI				Dyer-Bennet
Molly Brannigan	1	VAN			Irish
Molly Malone	SLP2	S364			Irish
Moonrise	SLP60	VOX 633			German
Morning a Cruel Turmoiler Is	7	CHIR			Irish
Morning Air Plays on My Face	7	CHIR			Irish
Motherless Child	Concert				American
My Father's Cook	Concert				Dyer-Bennet
My Gentle Harp (Londonderry Air)	Concert				Irish
My Good Old Man	10	REM	CST-2011	REP	American
My Mind to Me a Kingdom Is	Concert				English
My Old Gray Mare	Concert				American
Next Market Day, The	Concert				American
Nightingale, The	Concert				English
No Hiding Place	10				Irish
Norway Resistance Song	OWI				American
O Cease Plaguing (O cessate di piagarmi--Scarlatti)	Concert				Dyer-Bennet
O Mary, at Thy Window Be	CHC-13				Italian
O Mistress Mine (Shakespeare)	Shake				Scottish
O Speak Then, My Love	10				English
Oft in the Stilly Night (Thomas Moore)	1				Portuguese
					Irish

Oh How Can I Be Blithe and Glad	CHC-13				Scottish
Oh Sweet Were the Hours	CHC-13				Scottish
Oh! Who, My Dear Dermot	7	CHIR			Irish
Oh, No, John	S364	SLP61			English
Oh, Sally My Dear	DL79102	DLP5046			English
Oh, Sleep (Handel)	Concert				English
Old Bangum	6	VOX 632	SLP61		American
Old Gray Goose, The	13				American
Old Joe Clarke	1601				American
Old Maid, The	DL79102	DLP5046			English
Old She-Crab, The	1601				American
On the Massacre of Glencoe (Scott)	7	CHC-13			Scottish
Once More I Hail Thee (Burns)	7	CHIR			Irish
One Morning in May	6				American
Open Thy Lattice, Love (Foster)	11				American
Ozymandias (Shelly)	Concert				English
Passing By (Purcell)	Concert				English
Passive Resistance	OWI				Dyer-Bennet
Pedrillo's Serenade from The Magic Flute	Concert				German
Pedro	1				Dyer-Bennet
Peter Gray	12	VAN			American
Phyllis and Her Mother	1	SLP61	VAN	Vox 633	German
Pick a Bale of Cotton	Concert				American

Title				Origin
Piper of Dundee, The	6			Scottish
Plain Language from Truthful James (Crane)	12			American
Praties They Grow Small, The	Concert			Irish
Pride of Petravore, The	9			Irish
Pull Off Your Old Coat	1	REM	VAN	American
Pulse of an Irishman, The	7	CHIR		Irish
Quaker Lover, The	5	SLP60	VOX 632	American
Reaper's Ghost, The	10			Dyer-Bennet
Return to Ulster, The (Scott)	7	CHIR		Irish
Riddle Song, The	Concert			American
Rising o' the Moon, The	4	CST-2011	REM	Irish
Rommel the Fox	OWI			Dyer-Bennet
Roving Gambler, The	12			American
Rugelied	Concert			German
Saucy Sailor, The	Concert			English
Schneiders Höllenfahrt	9			German
Searching for Lambs	4			English
Secret Love	SLP60	VOX 633		German
Seven Little Pigs	10			Irish
Shallow Brown	12			American
She Moved Thro' the Fair	10			Irish
Shepherd Boy, The	Concert			Unknown
Sigh No More, Ladies	Concert			English

Sir Patrick Spens	Concert					English
Snowy Breasted Pearl, The	Concert					Irish
So We'll Go No More A-Roving (Byron)	1	VAN				English
Soldier and the Lady, The	13	VAN				American
Soldiers Three	Concert					English
Some People Think Hitler's Dead	OWI					Dyer-Bennet
Song of Reproach	4	SLP60	VOX 633			German
Song of Willow	Concert					English
Spanish is the Lovin' Tongue	5	FM-103	SLP35	560		American
Spanish Lady of Dublin City, The	4					Irish
Sportlied auf Napoleons Rückzug Aus Russland 1812	3					German
Streets of Laredo, The	Concert					American
Sunset (Scott)	7	CHC-13				Scottish
Swapping Song, The	3	DL-79102	SLP60	VAN	DLP5046	English
Sweetly She Sleeps, My Alice Fair (Foster)	11					American
Tailor and the Mouse, The	6					English
Tailor's Boy, The	1601					English
Take This Hammer	Concert					American
Lovely Lass of Inverness, The	7	CHC-13				Scottish
There Are Plenty of Fish in the Sea (Foster)	11					American
There Was a Friar in Our Town	1601					English
Three Crows	6					Scottish
Three Fishers	1					English

Title						Nationality
Three Jolly Rogues of Lynn	6	S364	SLP61			English
Three Ravens	4	FM-103	SLP35	461		English
Three Tailors	4	SLP60	VOX 633			German
Tribute to Chiang Kai-shek	OWI					Dyer-Bennet
Turkish Reverie	2	VOX 632				American
Turn Ye to Me	Concert					Scottish
Two Comments	10					Greek
Two Maidens Went Milking One Day	2	VAN	609	SLP2	Asch	English
Binnorie	9	REM	CST-2011			Scottish
Unfortunate Troubadour, The	10					Dyer-Bennet
Upon Julia's Clothes (Herrick)	Concert					English
Veillee de Noel	2					French
Venezuela (Niles)	5	SLP2	VAN	609		American
Vicar of Bray, The	1					English
Viens dans ce bocage	Concert					French
Visan om Drängen	Concert					Swedish
Waltzing Matilda (The Swagman)	4	MER	K108			Australian
Warnung	8					German
Wee Cooper O' Fife, The	Concert					Scottish
Were You There?	VOX 632					American
Westryn Wynde	5	VAN	SLP2	609		English
When Cockleshells Turn Silverbells	2	SLP61	Packard			English
When to Her Lute Corinna Sings (Campion)	Concert					English

When That I Was and a Little Tiny Boy	Concert				English
Where To (Schubert)	SLP60	VOX 633			German
White Lily (Jonson)	5	REM			English
Who Enters Russia by the Sword	OWI				Dyer-Bennet
Wife Wrapped in the Wether's Skin, The	10	REM	CST-2011	REP	American
Willie Taylor	3				English
Willow Tree, The	12	FM-103	DL79102	DLP5046	American
With Rue My Heart Is Laden	Concert				English
Woman! Go Home	2				Austrian
World's Too Small for Fascists, The	OWI				Dyer-Bennet
Ye Banks and Braes o' Bonnie Doon	Concert				Scottish

Notes

Introduction

1. Ellen J. Steckert, "Cents and Nonsense in the Urban Folksong Movement: 1930–1966," in Neil V. Rosenberg (ed.), *Transforming Tradition* (Chicago: University of Chicago Press), 96.
2. Ibid., 97.
3. Ibid., 98.
4. Ibid.
5. Ibid., 99.
6. Ibid.

Chapter 1. Master and Pupil

1. Richard Dyer-Bennet, "A New Age of Minstrelsy," *Hi-Fi Stereo Review* (July 1961): 33.
2. Program Notes for Concert at Gustavus Adolphus College. November 20, 1968.
3. Dyer-Bennet, "A New Age of Minstrelsy," 33.
4. Jill Godmilow and Susan Fanshel. *The Odyssey Tapes*. Video recording. New York: Odyssey Tapes, 1981.
5. Oscar Brand, telephone conversation with author, January 31, 2007. Mel Dyer-Bennet disputes this story.
6. Richard Shelton, "A Jousting Minstrel," *New York Times*, November 18, 1962.
7. Thomas Percy. *Reliques of Ancient English Poetry* (London: J.M. Dent, 1906), 9.
8. Ibid., 11.
9. Ibid., 25.
10. Richard Barnfield, poem VIII in *The Passionate Pilgrim*.
11. Elizabeth Blair, "Sting's 'Labyrinth': 16th Century Pop Music," npr.org/templates/story/story .php?storyId=6263882. Retrieved March 6, 2008.
12. Stanley Sadie, ed. *New Grove Dictionary of Music and Musicians* (London: MacMillan, 2001), 213.
13. Carl Michael Bellman. *Fredman's Epistles and Songs. A Selection in English with a Short Introduction by Paul Britten Austin* (Stockholm: Proprius Förlag, 1999), xiv.
14. Ibid.
15. Leif Bergman, "Sven Scholander: ett porträtt av vår förste moderne trubadur," *Sumlen*, 1977, 125–67. ("Sven Scholander: A Portrait of Our First Modern Troubadour," unpublished translation by Liz Slaughter, 2007, 10.)
16. Ibid., 13.
17. Ibid., 13.
18. Ibid., 12.
19. Ibid., 15.
20. Ibid., 15.

21. Ibid., 29.
22. Ibid., 22.
23. Ibid., 23.
24. Ibid., 25.
25. Ibid., 26.
26. Ibid., 27.
27. Ibid., 27.
28. Ibid., 31.
29. Ibid., 29.
30. Ibid., 33.
31. Dyer-Bennet, "A New Age of Minstrelsy," 33.
32. Studs Terkel, taped conversation with Richard Dyer-Bennet. WFMT radio. Original date unknown; rebroadcast December 19, 1991.
33. Gordon T. Ledbetter. *The Great Irish Tenor* (London: Duckworth, 1977), 108.
34. J. C. Reid to Richard Dyer-Bennet, 1959.
35. Bette Seigerman, "Shakespeare and the Quality of Sound," source and date unknown.
36. Richard Dyer-Bennet to Miriam Dyer-Bennet Sr., September 27, 1938.
37. Miriam Dyer-Bennet Jr., e-mail message to author, November 29, 2007.
38. Richard Dyer-Bennet, "Biographical Notes," unpublished manuscript, 1960.
39. Ibid.
40. Michael R. Jones. "The Passion of Adam von Trott: The Heroic Stance of the Foreign Minister of the German Resistance." *In Heroism and Passion in Literature: Studies in Honour of Moya Longstaff*, ed. Graham Gargett (New York: Rodopi, 2004), 189.
41. A. V. Shirk, "Richard Dyer-Bennet: The Classical Folksinger," *Sing Out!* 43, no. 2 (Fall 1998): 57.
42. Dyer-Bennet, "A New Age of Minstrelsy," 33.
43. Gertrude Wheeler Beckman. *Tools for Speaking and Singing* (New York: Schirmer, 1955), 8.
44. Ibid., iii.
45. Ibid, 115.
46. Bonnie Dyer-Bennet, "A Biographical Essay on Richard Dyer-Bennet" booklet accompanying *Richard Dyer-Bennet 1* (Smithsonian Folkways, 1997), 5.
47. Dyer-Bennet, "A New Age of Minstrelsy," 33.
48. Dyer-Bennet, "Biographical Notes."
49. Ibid.
50. Ibid.
51. Dyer-Bennet, "A New Age of Minstrelsy," 33.
52. Hentoff.
53. Richard Dyer-Bennet to Miriam Dyer-Bennet Sr., September 9, 1935.
54. Richard Dyer-Bennet to Miriam Dyer-Bennet Sr., September 3, 1935.
55. *The Odyssey Tapes.*
56. Bonnie Dyer-Bennet, "A Biographical Essay," 5.
57. Frank Kelly, "Dyer-Bennet: A Painter in Song," publication unknown, September 26, 1945.
58. Richard Dyer-Bennet to Miriam Dyer-Bennet Sr., November 27, 1935.
59. John M. Conly, "Minstrel on a Peninsula," *Atlantic* (February 1960): 104.
60. Dyer-Bennet, "A New Age of Minstrelsy," 34.
61. Richard Dyer-Bennet to Miriam Dyer-Bennet Sr., September 9, 1935.
62. Dyer-Bennet, 34.
63. Ibid., 34–35.
64. Molly Bliss, "Dyer-Bennet Sings Homer to the Super Bowl," *Centre Daily Times*, January 22, 1980.

65. Edward Prime-Stevenson. Source unknown.

66. Ibid.

67. Richard Dyer-Bennet to Miriam Dyer-Bennet Sr., April 4, 1939.

68. Richard Dyer-Bennet to Miriam Dyer-Bennet Sr., May 17, 1939.

69. Richard Dyer-Bennet to Miriam Dyer-Bennet Sr., July 2, 1941.

Chapter 2. New York

1. A. V. Shirk, "Richard Dyer-Bennet: The Classical Folksinger," *Sing Out!* 43, no. 2 (Fall 1998): 60.

2. Max Gordon. *Live at the Village Vanguard* (New York: Da Capo, 1982), 55.

3. Pete Seeger to Richard Dyer-Bennet, April 13, 1989.

4. Melvene Dyer-Bennet, telephone conversation with author, June 26, 1995.

5. Ronald D. Cohen. *Rainbow Quest: The Folk Music Revival and American Society, 1940–1970.* (Amherst: University of Massachusetts Press, 2002), 54.

6. Shirk, 59.

7. Gordon, 58.

8. Ibid.

9. James Gavin. *Intimate Nights: The Golden Age of New York Cabaret* (New York: Grove Weidenfeld, 1991), 47.

10. Gordon, 3.

11. Gordon, 2.

12. Gordon, 55.

13. Ibid.

14. Gordon, 56.

15. Dyer-Bennet, "A New Age of Minstrelsy," 34.

16. Richard Dyer-Bennet to John Dyer-Bennet, January 26, 1955.

17. Gordon, 55.

18. Ibid.

19. Gordon, 58.

20. Shirk, 60.

21. Ibid.

22. Louis Biancolli, "Dyer-Bennet in Folk Songs," *New York World Telegram*, March 6, 1944.

23. "Dyer-Bennet Gives Ballad Program," *New York Times*, March 5, 1944. (Author listed only as R.L.)

24. Dyer-Bennet, "A New Age of Minstrelsy," 34.

25. *New York Herald Tribune*, April 21, 1945.

26. Paul Bowles, "Dyer-Bennet Recital," *New York Herald Tribune*, December 31, 1945.

27. Martin Bernheimer, "Dyer-Bennet Gives a Ballad Concert Here," *New York Herald Tribune*, November 13, 1960.

28. *New York Times*, May 10, 1962.

29. Virgil Thomson, "Music," *New York Herald Tribune*, November 8, 1948.

30. Ibid.

31. *New York Times*, December 16, 1991.

32. Dyer-Bennet, "A New Age of Minstrelsy," 32.

33. Conrad L. Osborne, "The Voice of a Genuine Original," essay accompanying *Richard Dyer-Bennet 1* (Smithsonian-Folkways, 1991), 16.

34. Harriet Johnson, *New York Post*, March 3, 1946.

35. *The Odyssey Tapes.*

36. Hentoff.

37. Walter Winchell, *New York Times*, November 18, 1944.
38. *New York Times*, November 19, 1944.
39. Sol Hurok Agency. Promotional material. Date unknown.
40. Harlow Robinson. *The Last Impresario* (New York: Viking, 1994), xvi–xvii.
41. Ibid., xxii.
42. Dyer-Bennet, "A New Age of Minstrelsy," 34.
43. Greg Sandow, "On Disk: Folk Pioneer," *Wall Street Journal*, February 18, 1998.
44. Melvene Dyer-Bennet, interview with author, December 29, 2007.
45. Kathleen Smith. *God Bless America: Tin Pan Alley Goes to War* (Lexington: University Press of Kentucky, 2003), 51.

CHAPTER 3. EARLY RECORDINGS

1. Richard Dyer-Bennet to Miriam Dyer-Bennet Sr., May 17, 1939.
2. Howard Taubman, "Records: Carl Sandburg," *New York Times*, November 23, 1941.
3. *New York Times*, "Records: Morton Gould Album," May 21, 1944.
4. John Ward, liner notes to *Love Songs*, Disc Company of America, 1946.
5. Newspaper article, August 9, 1946. No author or source identified.
6. Howard Taubman, "Records: Fighting Songs," *New York Times*, September 1, 1946.
7. Philip Lieson Miller, liner notes to *Irish Songs*, Concert Hall, 1946.
8. Miller, liner notes to *Scottish Songs*, Concert Hall, 1946.
9. Ibid.
10. Maynard Solomon. *Beethoven* (New York: Schirmer, 1998), 388.
11. Hugh Douglas. *Robert Burns: The Tinder Heart* (Gloucestershire: Alan Sutton Publications, 1996), 281.
12. Richard Dyer-Bennet, liner notes to *Richard Dyer-Bennet 7*, Dyer-Bennet Records, 1958.
13. Barry Cooper. *Beethoven's Folksong Settings* (Oxford: Clarendon, 1994), 71.
14. Ibid., 70.
15. Howard Taubman, "Records: Concert Hall," *New York Times*, October 5, 1947.
16. Richard Dyer-Bennet, *Folk Song Book*, 41.
17. Richard Dyer-Bennet, liner notes to *Richard Dyer-Bennet 3*, Dyer-Bennet Records, 1957.
18. Richard Dyer-Bennet. *Richard Dyer-Bennet: The 20th-Century Minstrel* (New York: LeedsMusic, 1946), 22.
19. Richard Dyer-Bennet, *Folk Song Book*, 107.
20. Alan Lomax, liner notes to *Richard Dyer-Bennett* [sic]: *Twentieth-Century Minstrel*, Decca, 1949.
21. Richard Dyer-Bennet, liner notes to *Richard Dyer-Bennet 2*, Dyer-Bennet Records, 1956.
22. Richard Dyer-Bennet, *Folk Song Book*, 86.
23. Pete Seeger, telephone conversation with author, September 24, 2008.
24. Richard Dyer-Bennet, liner notes to *Richard Dyer-Bennet 3*, Dyer-Bennet Records, 1957.
25. *New York Times*, "Miscellany of Mozart's Best Scores," July 15, 1951.
26. Richard Dyer-Bennet, liner notes to *Richard Dyer-Bennet 10*, Dyer-Bennet Records, 1962.
27. Dyer-Bennet, *Folk Song Book*, 94.

CHAPTER 4. ASPEN INTERLUDE AND LIFE ON THE ROAD

1. Brochure, Dyer-Bennet Studio: The Summer Course in Aspen Colorado, 1947.
2. Will Holt, telephone conversation with author, December 6, 2006. All subsequent quotes from Holt are from this conversation.
3. Gertrude Wheeler Beckman, diary entries, summer, 1948.

4. Val Sigstedt, telephone conversation with author, August 12, 2007. All subsequent quotes from Sigstedt are from this conversation.

5. Uncle Ruthie (Ruth Buell), "From the East to the West," *FolkWorks* (July-August 2004): 20.

6. Austin Stevens, "Aspen Sets Sights for Cultural Role," *New York Times*, July 17, 1949.

7. Dyer-Bennet, "A New Age of Minstrelsy," 35.

8. Richard Kaplan, "Minstrel in White Tie," *Coronet* (May 1958): 104.

9. Ann Marshall, "He Sings of Life: Birth, Love, Death," *Savannah Morning News*, October 24, 1965.

10. Ibid.

11. Richard Dyer-Bennet to Bob Cooper, November 2, 1962.

12. Richard Dyer-Bennet to Mel Dyer-Bennet, January 18, 1952.

13. Brooke Dyer-Bennet, e-mail to author, September 11, 2008. All subsequent quotes from Brooke are from this message.

14. Bonnie Dyer-Bennet, e-mail to the author, September 12, 2008. All subsequent quotes from Bonnie are from this message.

15. Richard Dyer-Bennet to Mel Dyer-Bennet, September 30, 1960.

16. Richard Dyer-Bennet, "Alaska," unpublished journal, 1961. All subsequent quotes on the Alaska tour are from this journal.

17. Richard Dyer-Bennet to Mel Dyer-Bennet, May, 1953.

18. Richard Dyer-Bennet to Mel Dyer-Bennet, May 9, 1961.

CHAPTER 5. THE BLACKLIST

1. Pete Seeger, telephone conversation with author, September 24, 2008.

2. Richard Reuss with JoAnne C. Reuss. *American Folk Music and Left-Wing Politics* (Langham, MD: Scarecrow Press, 2000), 4–5.

3. Cohen, 17.

4. Pete Seeger, telephone conversation with author, September 24, 2008.

5. Ibid.

6. Booklet accompanying *Wasn't That a Time*, Vanguard, 1993, 8.

7. Pete Seeger, introduction to *People's Songs* newsletter, no. 1, 1946.

8. Reuss, 139.

9. Reuss, 235.

10. David Dunaway. *How Can I Keep from Singing?* (New York: Da Capo, 1981), 105.

11. Pete Seeger, telephone conversation with author, September 24, 2008.

12. *Red Channels; the report of Communist influence in radio and television*. (New York: American Business Consultants, 1950), 1.

13. Ibid., 2.

14. John Dyer-Bennet to Secretary of the Army, July 28, 1955.

15. Richard Dyer-Bennet to John Dyer-Bennet, July 30, 1954.

16. Richard Dyer-Bennet to John Dyer-Bennet, January 26, 1955.

17. United States Congress. Senate Committee on the Judiciary. *Subversive Infiltration of Radio, Television and the Entertainment Industry*. (Washington: U.S. Government Printing Office, 1952), 208.

18. Ibid., 209.

19. Ibid.

20. Ibid., 214.

21. Ibid., 220.

22. Ibid.

23. Ibid.

24. Pete Seeger, "Review of Sea Songs," *Sing Out!* 15, no.5 (Winter 1957): 21.

25. Irwin Silber, "Burl Ives Sings a Different Song," *Sing Out!* 3, no.2 (1952): 2.

26. Victor Navasky. *Naming Names* (New York: Penguin, 1991), xii–xiii.

27. Eric Bentley (ed.). *Thirty Years of Treason: Excerpts from Hearing Before the House Committee on Un-American Activities.* (New York: Viking, 1971), 696.

28. R. Serge Denisoff. *Great Day Coming: Folk Music and the American Left* (Urbana: University of Illinois Press, 1971), 87.

29. David Caute. *The Fellow Travelers: A Postscript to the Enlightenment* (London: Weidenfeld and Nicolson, 1973), 325.

30. Booklet accompanying *Wasn't That a Time*, Vanguard, 1993, 21.

31. Ibid.

32. Ibid., 22.

33. Ibid.

34. Oscar Brand. *The Ballad Mongers* (New York: Funk & Wagnall's, 1962), 139.

35. Ibid., 136.

36. Richard Dyer-Bennet to John Dyer-Bennet, August 11, 1954.

37. Richard Dyer-Bennet to John Dyer-Bennet, January 27, 1955.

38. Pete Seeger, telephone conversation with author, September 24, 2008.

39. Harvey Cort, telephone conversation with author, October 2, 2008.

40. Oscar Brand, telephone conversation with author, January 31, 2007.

CHAPTER 6. DYER-BENNET RECORDS

1. Richard Dyer-Bennet to Miriam Dyer-Bennet Sr., 1956.

2. Bonnie Dyer-Bennet, "A Biographical Essay," 10.

3. Ibid.

4. Harvey Cort, telephone conversation with author, October 2, 2008.

5. Ibid.

6. Ibid.

7. Ibid

8. Ibid.

9. Richard Dyer-Bennet, liner notes to *Richard Dyer-Bennet 1*, Dyer-Bennet Records, 1955.

10. Edward D Ives. *The Bonnie Earl of Murray* (Chicago: University of Illinois Press, 1997), xvi.

11. Richard Dyer-Bennet, liner notes to *Richard Dyer-Bennet 1*, Dyer-Bennet Records, 1955.

12. Dyer-Bennet, *Folk Song Book*, 131.

13. Ibid., 135.

14. Ibid., 53.

15. Richard Dyer-Bennet, liner notes to *Richard Dyer-Bennet 1*, Dyer-Bennet Records, 1955.

16. Norman Pellegrini, e-mail message to author, October 7, 2007.

17. Richard Dyer-Bennet, liner notes to *Richard Dyer-Bennet 1*, Dyer-Bennet Records, 1955.

18. Dyer-Bennet, *Folk Song Book*, 111.

19. Kenneth Goldstein, "Review of *Richard Dyer-Bennet 1*," *The Record Changer*, date unknown.

20. John M. Conly, "Dyer-Bennet: Song Recital," *Atlantic* (June 1956): 91.

21. Max De Schaunsee, review of *Richard Dyer-Bennet 1*, *Philadelphia Bulletin*, date unknown.

22. Elinor Hugh, review of *Richard Dyer-Bennet 1*, *Boston Herald*, April 29, 1956.

23. A. V. Shirk, "Richard Dyer-Bennet: The Classical Folksinger," *Sing Out!* 43, no. 2 (Fall 1998): 61.

24. Schwann Long Playing Record Catalog, 1956.

25. This quote is listed on the back of the booklet accompanying the CD release of *Richard Dyer-Bennet 1*. I have not been able to find the original source.

26. Richard Dyer-Bennet, liner notes to *Richard Dyer-Bennet 2*, Dyer-Bennet Records, 1956.

27. Dyer-Bennet, *Folk Song Book*, 77.

28. Ibid., 45.

29. John M. Conly, review of *Richard Dyer-Bennet 2*, *Atlantic* (April 1957): 98.

30. Howard La Fey, review of *Richard Dyer-Bennet 2*, *High Fidelity* (1956).

31. *Chicago Heights Star*, review of *Richard Dyer-Bennet 2*, February 26, 1957.

32. *Billboard*, review of *Richard Dyer-Bennet 2*, February 16, 1957.

33. Dyer-Bennet, *Folk Song Book*, 104.

34. Ibid., 81.

35. Richard Dyer-Bennet, liner notes to *Richard Dyer-Bennet 3*, Dyer-Bennet Records, 1957.

36. *Christian Science Monitor*, review of *Richard Dyer-Bennet 3*, date unknown.

37. *New York Folk Quarterly*, review of *Richard Dyer-Bennet 3*, date unknown.

38. John M. Conly, review of *Richard Dyer-Bennet: Folksongs*, *Atlantic* (December 1957): 188.

39. Edward Randal, "Folk Music," *High Fidelity* (February 1958).

40. Robert Sherman, review of *Richard Dyer-Bennet 3*, *Hi Fi Music at Home* (February 1958).

41. Richard Dyer-Bennet, liner notes to *Richard Dyer-Bennet 4*, Dyer-Bennet Records, 1957.

42. Ibid.

43. Ibid.

44. Ibid.

45. Ibid.

46. Dyer-Bennet, *Folk Song Book*, 68.

47. Robert Sherman, review of *Richard Dyer-Bennet 4*, *American Record Guide* (April 1958).

48. John M. Conly, review of *Richard Dyer-Bennet 4*, *Atlantic* (1958).

49. Dyer-Bennet, *Folk Song Book*, 91.

50. Ibid., 59.

51. Nat Hentoff, review of *Richard Dyer-Bennet 5*, *The Reporter*, date unknown.

52. Don Noel, "Dyer-Bennett [sic] Record Reveals His Virtuosity," *Hartford Times*, 1959.

53. Paul Little, "Music in the Groove," *Chicago Heights Star*, date unknown.

54. Richard Dyer-Bennet, liner notes to *Richard Dyer-Bennet 6*, Dyer-Bennet Records, 1958.

55. Emma Dickson Sheehy, review of *Richard Dyer-Bennet 6*, *Parents Magazine*, date unknown.

56. Richard Perry, "Some Fine Voices for Spring," *The Citizen's Weekly*, April 16, 2000.

57. Alfred Frankenstein, "Review of *Richard Dyer-Bennet 7*," *San Francisco Chronicle*, 1958.

58. John M. Conly, "Beethoven: Twelve Scottish and Irish Songs," *Atlantic* (February 1959): 113.

59. Carolyn Sanford, "Lead-In Groove," *Orange County Daily News*, date unknown.

60. *Hartford Times*, "Review of *Richard Dyer-Bennet 8*," December 1960.

61. Richard Dyer-Bennet, liner notes to *Richard Dyer-Bennet 8*, Dyer-Bennet Records, 1959.

62. Ibid.

63. John M. Conly, "Richard Dyer-Bennet 8," *Atlantic* (April 1960): 105.

64. Alfred Frankenstein, "Richard Dyer-Bennet 8," *San Francisco Chronicle*, date unknown.

65. *New York Times*, review of Richard Dyer-Bennet 8, September 11, 1960.

66. Nash had written the part of a ballad seller in the play especially for Dyer-Bennet. On stage Dyer-Bennet played "Greensleeves" and several other songs. The play was not well received, but in his review Lewis Nichols singles out Dyer-Bennet as "the one performer who keeps a clean reputation" ("Annie Shouldn't Live Here," *New York Times*, June 4, 1946).

67. Harvey Cort, telephone conversation with author, October 2, 2008.

68. *Hartford Times*, review of *Richard Dyer-Bennet 10*, date unknown.

69. Richard Dyer-Bennet, liner notes to *Richard Dyer-Bennet 11*, Dyer-Bennet Records, 1962.

70. Ibid.

71. Alfred Frankenstein, "Dyer-Bennet Records Foster's Songs as He Wrote Them," *San Francisco Sunday Chronicle*, December 16, 1962.

72. Ibid.

73. Evelyn Foster Morneweck to Richard Dyer-Bennet, August 20, 1969.

74. John S. Kohn, "Mark Twain's 1601," *Princeton University Library Chronicle* 18 (1957): 49.

75. Richard Dyer-Bennet, liner notes to *1601*, Dyer-Bennet Records, 1962.

76. Richard Dyer-Bennet, liner notes to *Richard Dyer-Bennet 5*, Dyer-Bennet Records, 1958.

77. Richard Dyer-Bennet, liner notes to *1601*, Dyer-Bennet Records, 1962.

78. Ibid.

79. Harvey Cort, telephone conversation with author, October 2, 2008.

80. Henrietta Yurchenko, review of *1601*, *The American Record Guide* (January 1963).

81. Everett Helm, review of *1601*, *Musical America*, date unknown.

82. Stephanie Gervis, Review of *1601*, *Village Voice*, date unknown.

83. O. B. Brummel, Review of *1601*, *High Fidelity*, date unknown.

84. Richard Dyer-Bennet, liner notes to *Richard Dyer-Bennet 12*, Dyer-Bennet Records, 1964.

85. Nat Hentoff, "Richard Dyer-Bennet 12," *Hi-Fi Stereo Review* (March 1965).

86. Richard Dyer-Bennet, liner notes to *Richard Dyer-Bennet 13*, Dyer-Bennet Records, 1964.

87. George and Helen Papashvily. *Yes and No Stories* (New York: Harper and Brothers, 1946), 5.

88. *High Fidelity*, review of *Richard Dyer-Bennet 13* (March 1965).

89. E. B. White to Richard Dyer-Bennet, May 30, 1966.

90. Richard Dyer-Bennet, liner notes to *Aksel Schiøtz, baritone, singing Schubert, Bellman, Wolf, Brahms*, Dyer-Bennet Records, 1960.

91. *High Fidelity*, review of *Aksel Schiøtz, baritone, singing Schubert, Bellman, Wolf, Brahms*, date unknown.

92. Richard Dyer-Bennet, liner notes to *The Essential Richard Dyer-Bennet*, Vanguard, 1977.

CHAPTER 7. *THE LOVELY MILLERESS* AND STONY BROOK

1. Howard Schneider, "Richard Dyer-Bennet Was an Anachronism—a 20th-Century Minstrel," *Denver Post*, April 8, 1973.

2. Brooke Dyer-Bennet, e-mail message to author, September 11, 2008.

3. Richard Dyer-Bennet, program notes, September 18, 1979.

4. Richard Dyer-Bennet to Conrad Osborne, October 2, 1964.

5. Richard Dyer-Bennet. *The Lovely Milleress* (New York: Schirmer, 1967).

6. Maurice J. E. Brown. *The New Grove Schubert* (New York: Norton, 1983), 94.

7. Raymond Ericson, "Dyer-Bennet Meets Schubert at Tully Hall," *New York Times*, January 21, 1977.

8. Ibid.

9. Cornelius Reid. *Bel Canto: Principles and Practices* (New York: Coleman-Ross, 1950), 19.

10. Ibid., 28.

11. Joe Plummer, "How Do You Find a New Voice at 58?" *Sunday Record*, April 27, 1975. Dyer-Bennet was actually 55 when he started working with Reid in 1968.

12. Reid, 15.

13. *Stony Brook News*, "Famous Balladeer to Provide Voice Training at Stony Brook Theatre Dept." Date unknown.

14. Bonnie Dyer-Bennet, "A Biographical Essay," 11.

15. Ibid., 11–12.

16. Richard Dyer-Bennet, "Training the Actor's Voice," unpublished manuscript, date unknown.

17. Bonnie Dyer-Bennet, 12.

18. *Stony Brook News.*

19. State University of New York at Stony Brook. Undergraduate Bulletin, 1970.

20. Lesl Harker, e-mail message to author, November 20, 2007.

21. These comments were provided by F. Jason Torre, SUNY Stony Brook archivist.

22. Bette Seigerman, "Shakespeare and the Quality of Sound," source and date unknown, 2.

23. Andrew Schulman, e-mail message to author, October 2, 2007. All subsequent quotes from Schulman are from this e-mail.

24. Ibid.

25. Ericson.

26. Peter G. Davis, "Dyer-Bennet Sings His Own Translation of Schubert," *New York Times*, January 24, 1977.

27. Andrew Porter, "Song in Green," *New Yorker* (February 28, 1977): 98.

28. Cornelius Reid to Richard Dyer-Bennet, January 16, 1977.

29. Speight Jenkins, "Dyer-Bennet Sings Schubert," *New York Post*, date unknown.

30. Richard Dyer-Bennet, liner notes to *The Lovely Milleress*, Dyer-Bennet Records, 1978.

31. Nancy Garniez, "Schubert Wallah," liner notes to *The Lovely Milleress*.

32. Andrew Porter, "*Lieder* in English?" *High Fidelity* (April 1979).

33. Lawrence van Gelder, "Dyer-Bennet Back on Stage," *New York Times*, March 21, 1976.

CHAPTER 8. THE *ODYSSEY* OF RICHARD DYER-BENNET

1. William Arrowsmith, review of Fitzgerald's *Odyssey*, *The Nation*, July 1, 1961.

2. Ralph Hexter. *A Guide to the Odyssey* (New York: Vintage, 1993), xi.

3. *The Odyssey Tapes.*

4. Bonnie Dyer-Bennet, "A Biographical Essay," 3.

5. Richard Dyer-Bennet, "Biographical Notes."

6. H. J. Kirchhoff, "A Storyteller and His Odyssey," *Globe and Mail*, October 29, 1988.

7. Francis X. Clines, "An Epic Reading out of an Epic Life," *New York Times*, December 5, 1978.

8. Ron McDonald, "When Homer Has His Way . . . ," *Smith Alumnae Quarterly* (February 1981).

9. Kirchhoff.

10. Richard Dyer-Bennet, "To Make Audible the Fitzgerald Translation of Homer's Odyssey." Grant proposal to the National Endowment for the Humanities, 1978.

11. Godmilow.

12. Bonnie Dyer-Bennet, 14.

13. Alan Carruth, e-mail message to author, November 7, 2007.

14. Robert Fitzgerald. *The Odyssey* (New York: Farrar, Strauss, and Giroux, 1998), 491.

15. McDonald.

16. Melvene Dyer-Bennet, telephone conversation with author, June 26, 1995.

17. Richard Dyer-Bennet, "To Make Audible."

18. Clines.

19. Albert B. Lord. *The Singer of Tales* (Cambridge, MA: Harvard University Press, 1960), 4.

20. Richard Dyer-Bennet, program notes for a performance of excerpts from the *Odyssey* at the University of Virginia, November 4, 1982.

21. David Kovacs, "Selections from Odyssey Keep Audience Spellbound," *Charlottesville Daily Progress*, November 4, 1982.

22. Catherine Fox, "A Tale for the Telling," *Maclean's* (November 19, 1979): 202.

23. Ibid.

24. Handwritten comments from attendees.

25. Louise Taylor to Richard Dyer-Bennet, October 24, 1990.

26. Dyer-Bennet, "A Minstrel's Diary."

27. Richard Dyer-Bennet, "Notes for a Projected LP Recording and Booklet Dealing with America's Song Heritage," unpublished manuscript, date unknown.

28. Bonnie Dyer-Bennet, 14.

Chapter 9. The Legacy of Richard Dyer-Bennet

1. *Time*, "Sibyl with Guitar" (November 23, 1962): 54.

2. Howard Schneider, "Richard Dyer-Bennet was an Anachronism—a 20th Century Minstrel," *Denver Post*, April 8, 1973.

3. *Time*, "Sibyl with Guitar" 56.

4. Ibid., 60.

5. Robert Shelton, "Folk Recital Given by William Elliott," *New York Times*, December 23, 1965. In the program notes for Elliott's December 22, 1965, performance, Dyer-Bennet gave his endorsement to the young performer. "To combine poetry, melody, and accompaniment into one complex sound is the difficult task of the self-accompanied singer. There have been few masters since the time of John Dowland, and I have wondered whether the present renaissance of interest in traditional songs might produce a new school of such singers. A rare bit of evidence that this could happen is the emergence of William Elliott. He has voice, instrumental technique, the ability to compose good accompaniments, and above all, musical taste and intelligence. He should be widely heard, and I hope he will be."

6. Ibid.

7. *Time*, "The Welcome Interloper" (June 21, 1963): 46.

8. Robert Shelton, "Guitarist, 18, Charms Audience," *New York Times*, July 13, 1963.

9. John Winn, e-mail to the author, July 25, 2008.

10. Daniel Sheehy, essay accompanying CD rerelease of *Richard Dyer-Bennet 2*, Smithsonian-Folkways, 2001.

11. Richard Dyer-Bennet to Miriam Dyer-Bennet Sr., 1956.

12. Agnes Cunningham and Gordon Friesen. *Red Dust and Broadsides* (Amherst: University of Massachusetts Press, 1999), 223.

13. Ibid.

14. Ronald D. Lankford. *Folk Music U.S.A.: The Changing Voice of Protest*. (New York: Schirmer, 2005), 2.

15. Pete Seeger, telephone conversation with author, September 24, 2008.

16. Roger Butterfield, "Turkeys in the Straw," *Saturday Review of Literature* (January 31, 1948): 56.

17. Studs Terkel, taped conversation with Richard Dyer-Bennet.

18. Oscar Brand. *The Ballad Mongers*.

19. *Norton/Grove Concise Encyclopedia of Music*. Stanley Sadie, ed. (New York: Norton, 1988), 33.

20. Dyer-Bennet, "A New Age of Minstrelsy," 35.

21. Ibid., 32.

22. Ross Altman, "Richard Dyer-Bennet: A Minstrel Out of Time," *Pipe Dream* (March 18, 1975).

23. *Newsweek*, "Twentieth-Century Bard," March 13, 1944.

24. Lesl Harker, e-mail to author, November 20, 2007.

25. Hentoff, 52.

26. Richard Dyer-Bennet to Bob Cooper, November 2, 1962.

27. Richard Dyer-Bennet, unpublished manuscript, February 10, 1947.
28. Hentoff, 52.
29. John Raymond, "Minstrel Keeps Folksong Alive," *Atlanta Constitution*, December 5, 1971.
30. Dyer-Bennet, *Folk Song Book*, 11.
31. folkways.si.edu/about_folkways/history_mission.html. Retrieved March 6, 2008.
32. Keven McAlester, "Tenor Madness," *Los Angeles New Times*, January 8, 1998.
33. Andrew Pincus, "Great Berskshire Voices Sound Again on New CDs," *The Berkshire Eagle*, January 11, 1998.
34. Greg Sandow, "On Disk: Folk Pioneer," *Wall Street Journal*, February 18, 1998.
35. Andrew Schulman, e-mail to author, October 2, 2007.
36. Pete Seeger, telephone conversation with author, September 24, 2008.
37. Harvey Cort, telephone conversation with author, October 2, 2008.
38. Studs Terkel, quoted on booklet accompanying CD release of *Richard Dyer-Bennet 1*, Smithsonian-Folkways, 1997.
39. Dyer-Bennet, "A New Age of Minstrelsy," 35.

References

Altman, Ross. 1975. Richard Dyer-Bennet: A Minstrel Out of Time. *Pipe Dream*, March 18.

American Business Consultants. 1950. *Red Channels; the report of Communist influence in radio and television*. New York: American Business Consultants.

Arrowsmith, William. 1961. Review of *The Odyssey*, by Robert Fitzgerald. *Nation*, July 1.

Austin, Paul Britten. 1967. *The Life and Songs of Carl Michael Bellman*. Malmö: Allhem Publishers.

Barlow, S. L. M. 1961. *The Astonished Muse*. New York: John Day.

Beckman, Gertrude Wheeler. 1948. Personal journal.

———. 1955. *Tools for Speaking and Singing*. New York: Schirmer.

Bellman, Carl Michael, 1999. *Fredman's Epistles & Songs. A Selection in English with a short introduction by Paul Britten Austin*. Stockholm: Proprius Förlag.

Bentley, Eric, ed. 1971. *Thirty Years of Treason: Excerpts from Hearings Before the House Committee on Un-American Activities*. New York: Viking.

Bergman, Leif. 1977. Sven Scholander: ett porträtt av vår förste moderne trubadur. *Sumlen*, 125–67, Unpublished trans. Liz Slaughter. [Sven Scholander: A Portrait of Our First Modern Troubadour], 2007.

Bernheimer, Martin. 1960. Dyer-Bennet Gives a Ballad Concert Here. *New York Herald Tribune*, November 13.

Biancolli, Louis. 1944. Dyer-Bennet in Folk Songs. *New York World Telegram*. March 6.

Billboard. 1957. Review of *Richard Dyer-Bennet 2*. February 16.

Blair, Elizabeth. Sting's "Labyrinth": 16th Century Pop Music. www.npr.org/templates/story/story.php?storyId=6263882.

Bliss, Molly. 1980. Dyer-Bennet Sings Homer to the Super Bowl. *Centre Daily Times*, January 22.

Bowles, Paul. 1945. Dyer-Bennet Recital. *New York Herald Tribune*, December 31.

Brand, Oscar. 1962. *The Ballad Mongers*. New York: Funk & Wagnalls.

Brown, Maurice J. E. 1983. *The New Grove Schubert*. New York: Norton.

Brummel, O. B. Date unknown. Review of *1601*. *High Fidelity*.

Buell, Ruth. 2004. From the East to the West. *FolkWorks*, July-August.

Butterfield, Roger. 1948. Turkeys in the Straw. *Saturday Review of Literature*, January 31.

Caute, David. 1973. *The Fellow Travelers: A Postscript to the Enlightenment*. London: Weidenfeld and Nicolson.

Chicago Heights Star. 1957. Review of *Richard Dyer-Bennet 2*. February 26.

Christian Science Monitor. 1957. Review of *Richard Dyer-Bennet 3*.

Clines, Francis X. 1978. An Epic Reading, out of an Epic Life. *New York Times*, December 5.

Cohen, Ronald, and Dave Samuelson. 1996. *Songs for Political Action*. (Book accompanying box set of recordings.) Hamburg: Bear Family Records.

Cohen, Ronald D. 2002. *Rainbow Quest: The Folk Music Revival and American Society, 1940–1970*. Amherst: University of Massachusetts Press.

Conly, John M. 1956. Dyer-Bennet: Song Recital. *Atlantic*, June, 91.

———. 1957. Review of *Richard Dyer-Bennet 2. Atlantic*, April, 98.

———. 1957. Richard Dyer-Bennet: Folksongs. *Atlantic*. December, 188.

———. 1958. Review of *Richard Dyer-Bennet 4*. *Atlantic*, April, 104.

———. 1959. Beethoven: Twelve Scottish and Irish Songs. *Atlantic*, February, 113.

———. 1960. Minstrel on a peninsula. *Atlantic*, February, 102–5.

———. 1960. Richard Dyer-Bennet 8. *Atlantic*, April, 105.

Cooper, Barry. 1994. *Beethoven's Folksong Settings*. Oxford: Clarendon.

Cunningham, Agnes, and Gordon Friesen. 1999. *Red Dust and Broadsides*. Amherst: University of Massachusetts Press.

Davis, Peter G. 1977. Dyer-Bennet Sings His Own Translation of Schubert. *New York Times*, January 24.

Denisoff, R. Serge. 1971. *Great Day Coming: Folk Music and the American Left*. Urbana: University of Illinois Press.

De Schaunsee, Max. [1956?] Review of *Richard Dyer-Bennet 1*. *Philadelphia Bulletin*.

Douglas, Hugh. 1996. *Robert Burns: The Tinder Heart*. Gloucestershire: Alan Sutton Publications.

Dunaway, David. 1981. *How Can I Keep from Singing: Pete Seeger*. New York: Da Capo.

Dyer-Bennet, Bonnie. A Biographical Essay on Richard Dyer-Bennet. *Richard Dyer-Bennet 1*, Smithsonian-Folkways, 1997.

Dyer-Bennet, Richard. 1946. *Richard Dyer-Bennet: The 20th Century Minstrel*. Leeds Music Corporation.

———. 1961. A New Age of Minstrelsy. *Hi-Fi/Stereo Review*, July, 31–35.

———. 1971. *The Richard Dyer-Bennet Folk Song Book*. New York: Simon and Schuster.

Ericson, Raymond. 1977. Dyer-Bennet Meets Schubert at Tully Hall. *New York Times*, January 21.

Fitzgerald, Robert, trans. 1998. *The Odyssey*. New York: Farrar, Strauss, and Giroux.

Fox, Catherine. 1979. A Tale for the Telling. *Maclean's*, November 19.

Frankenstein, Alfred. 1958. Review of Richard Dyer-Bennet 7. *San Francisco Chronicle*.

———. [1959?] Richard Dyer-Bennet 8. *San Francisco Chronicle*.

———. 1962. Dyer-Bennet records Foster's songs as he wrote them. *San Francisco Sunday Chronicle*. December 16.

Gavin, James. 1991. *Intimate Nights: The Golden Age of New York Cabaret*. New York: Grove Weidenfeld.

Gervis, Stephanie. [1962?] Review of *1601*. *Village Voice*.

Godmilow, Jill, and Susan Fanshel. 1981. *The Odyssey Tapes*. VHS. New York: Odyssey Tapes.

Goldstein, Kenneth. [1957?] Review of *Richard Dyer-Bennet 1*. *The Record Changer*.

Gordon, Max. 1982. *Live at the Village Vanguard*. New York: Da Capo.

Hartford Times. 1960. Review of *Richard Dyer-Bennet 8*. December.

Hartford Times. [1962?] Review of *Richard Dyer-Bennet 10*.

Helm, Everett. [1962?] Review of *1601*. *Musical America*.

Hentoff, Nat. [1958?] Review of *Richard Dyer-Bennet 5*. *The Reporter*.

———. 1963. The Last Minstrel. *The Reporter*, January 31.

———. 1965. *Richard Dyer-Bennet 12*. *Hi Fi Stereo Review*, March.

Hexter, Ralph. 1993. *A Guide to the Odyssey*. New York: Vintage.

High Fidelity. [1960?] Review of *Aksel Schiøtz*.

High Fidelity. 1965. Review of *Richard Dyer-Bennet 13*. March.

Hugh, Elinor. 1956. Review of *Richard Dyer-Bennet 1*. *Boston Herald*, April 29.

Ives, Edward D. 1997. *The Bonnie Earl of Murray*. Chicago: University of Illinois Press.

Jenkins, Speight. [1977?] "Dyer-Bennet Sings Schubert." *New York Post*.

Johnson, Harriet. Concert review. *New York Post*. March 3, 1946.

Jones, Michael R. 2004. The Passion of Adam von Trott: The Heroic Stance of the Foreign Minister of the German Resistance. In *Heroism and Passion in Literature: Studies in Honour of Moya Longstaff*, ed. Graham Gargett, 185–96. New York: Rodopi.

Kaplan, Richard. 1958. Minstrel in white tie. *Coronet*, May.

Kirchhoff, H. J. 1988. A Storyteller and His Odyssey. *The Globe and Mail*. October 29.

Kohn, John S. Van E. 1957. Mark Twain's 1601. *Princeton University Library Chronicle*.

Kovacs, David. 1982. Selections from Odyssey Keep Audience Spellbound. *Charlottesville Daily Progress*, November 4.

La Fey, Howard. 1956. Review of *Richard Dyer-Bennet 2*. *High Fidelity*.

Lankford, Ronald D. 2005. *Folk Music USA: The Changing Voice of Protest*. New York: Schirmer.

Ledbetter, Gordon T. 1977. *The Great Irish Tenor*. London: Duckworth.

Leicester City Council. Population of Leicester. www.leicester.gov.uk/index.asp?pgid=7911.

Little, Paul. [1958?] Music in the Groove. *Chicago Heights Star*.

Lomax, Alan. 1949. Liner notes to *Richard Dyer-Bennett* [sic]: *Twentieth-Century Minstrel*. Decca DL79102.

Lord, Albert B. 1960. *The Singer of Tales*. Cambridge: Harvard University Press.

Marshall, Ann. 1965. He Sings of Life: Birth, Love, Death. *Savannah Morning News*, October 24.

McAlester, Keven. 1998. Tenor Madness. *Los Angeles New Times*, January 8.

McDonald, Ron. 1981. When Homer Has His Way . . . *Smith Alumnae Quarterly*, February.

Miller, Philip Lieson. 1946. Liner notes to *Irish Songs*. Concert Hall.

———. 1946. Liner notes to *Scottish Songs*. Concert Hall CHC-13.

Navasky, Victor. 1991. *Naming Names*. New York: Penguin.

New York Folklore Quarterly. [1957?] Review of *Richard Dyer-Bennet 3*.

New York Herald-Tribune. 1945. Review of Dyer-Bennet Town Hall concert. April 21.

New York Times. 1944. Dyer-Bennet Gives Ballad Program. March 5.

———. 1944. Records: Morton Gould Album. May 21.

———. 1944. Bennet Sings to Capacity Crowd. November 19.

———. 1951. Miscellany of Mozart's Best Scores. July 15.

———. 1960. Review of *Richard Dyer-Bennet 8*. September 11.

———. 1962. Review of Dyer-Bennet concert. May 10.

———. 1991. Obituary. Richard Dyer-Bennet. December 16.

Newsweek. 1944. Twentieth-century bard. March 13.

Nichols, Lewis. 1946. Annie Shouldn't Live Here. *New York Times*, June 4.

Noel, Don. 1959. Dyer-Bennett [sic] Records Reveal His Virtuosity. *Hartford Times*.

Opera and Concert. 1946. A Modern Minstrel: Richard Dyer-Bennett [sic. August.

Osborne, Conrad L. 1997. The Voice of a Genuine Original. *Richard Dyer-Bennet 1*, Smithsonian-Folkways.

Percy, Thomas. 1906. *Reliques of Ancient English Poetry*. London: J. M. Dent.

Perry, Richard. 2000. Some Fine Voices for Spring. *The Citizen's Weekly*, April 16.

Pincus, Andrew. 1998. Great Berkshire Voices Sound Again on New CDs. *The Berkshire Eagle*, January 11.

Plummer, Joe. 1975. How Do You Find a New Voice at 58? *Sunday Record*, April 27.

Porter, Andrew. 1977. Song in Green. *New Yorker*, February 28.

———. 1979. *Lieder* in English? *High Fidelity*. April.

Randal, Edward. 1958. Folk Music. *High Fidelity*, February.

Raymond, John. 1971. Minstrel Keeps Folksong Alive. *Atlanta Constitution*, December 5.

Reid, Cornelius L. 1950. *Bel Canto: Principles and Practices*. New York: Coleman-Ross.

Reuss, Richard, with JoAnne C. Reuss. 2000. *American Folk Music and Left-Wing Politics*. Langham, MD: Scarecrow Press.

Robinson, Harlow. 1994. *The Last Impresario*. New York: Viking.

Sadie, Stanley, ed. 1988. *Norton/Grove Concise Encyclopedia of Music*. New York: Norton.

———. 2001. *New Grove Dictionary of Music and Musicians*. London: MacMillan.

Sandow, Greg. 1998. On Disk: Folk Pioneer. *Wall Street Journal*, February 18.

Schneider, Howard. 1973. Richard Dyer-Bennet was an anachronism—a 20th-Century minstrel. *Denver Post*. April 8.

Seeger, Pete. 1957. Review of *Sea Songs*. *Sing Out!*, Winter.

———. 1965. Johnny Appleseed Jr. *Sing Out!*, November.

Shakespeare, William. 1939. The Passionate Pilgrim. New York: C. Scribner's Sons.

Sheehy, Daniel. 2001. Liner notes to *Richard Dyer-Bennet 2*. Smithsonian-Folkways.

Sheehy, Emma Dickson. [1958?] Review of *Richard Dyer-Bennet 6*. *Parents Magazine*.

Shelton, Robert. 1962. A Jousting Minstrel. *New York Times*. November 18.

———. 1963. Guitarist, 18, Charms Audiences. *New York Times*, July 13.

———. 1965. Folk Recital Given by William Elliott. *New York Times*, December 23.

Sherman, Robert. 1958. Review of *Richard Dyer-Bennet 3*. *Hi Fi Music at Home*, February.

———. 1958. Review of *Richard Dyer-Bennet 4*. *American Record Guide*, April.

Shirk, A. V. 1998. Richard Dyer-Bennet: The Classical Folksinger. *Sing Out*, Fall.

*Silber, Irwin. 1952. Burl Ives Sings a Different Song *Sing Out!* 3 (2).

Slominsky, Nicolas, ed. 1992. *Baker's Biographical Dictionary of Musicians*. New York: Macmillan.

Smith, Kathleen E. R. 2003. *God Bless America: Tin Pan Alley Goes to War*. Lexington: University Press of Kentucky.

Solomon, Maynard. 1998. *Beethoven*. New York: Schirmer.

Stekert, Ellen J. 1993. Cents and Nonsense in the Urban Folksong Movement: 1930–1966. In *Transforming Tradition*, ed. Neil V. Rosenberg, 84–106. Chicago: University of Chicago Press.

Stevens, Austin. 1949. Aspen Sets Sights for Cultural Role. *New York Times*, July 17.

Stony Brook News. [1972?] Famous Balladeer to Provide Voice Training at Stony Brook Theatre Dept.

Taubman, Howard. 1941. Records: Carl Sandburg. *The New York Times*, November 23.

———. 1946. Records: Fighting Songs. *The New York Times*, September 1.

———. 1947. Records: Concert Hall. *The New York Times*, October 5.

Thomson, Virgil. 1948. Music. *New York Herald-Tribune*, November 8.

Time. 1962. Sibyl with Guitar. November 23, 54–60.

———. 1963. The Welcome Interloper. June 21, 46.

United States Congress. 1952. Senate Committee on the Judiciary. *Subversive Infiltration of Radio, Television and the Entertainment Industry*. Washington: U.S. Government Printing Office.

Van Gelder, Lawrence. 1976. Dyer-Bennet Back on Stage. *The New York Times*, March 21.

Ward, John. 1946. Liner notes to *Love Songs*, Disc Company of America.

The Weavers. 1993. *Wasn't That a Time* (booklet accompanying music recording). Santa Monica, CA: Vanguard.

Winchell, Walter. 1944. Review of Richard Dyer-Bennet concert. *New York Times*. November 18.

Yurchenko, Henrietta. 1963. Review of *1601*. *The American Record Guide*. January.

INDEX

Abaca String Band, 112

Abbott, Dolly 47, 86

"Again, My Lyre," 46

"Agincourt Song," 29, 32, 92

"Ah, May the Red Rose Bloom Always," 97

Aksel Schiøtz, Baritone, 102

Albeniz, Isaac, 30

"All in a Garden Green," 93

"All mein Gedanken," 93

Almanac Singers, The, 24, 37, 67, 126

Altman, Ross, 127

American Business Consultants, 68

American Student Union, 70

American Youth for Democracy, 69

American-Russian Institute, 69

"Aminte," 94, 100

An die ferne Geliebte, 116

Anderson, Marion, 29

Andersson, Dan, 10

Andrews Sisters, The, 48, 60

Ann Summers Management, 65

"Annie Laurie," 31, 32

Anschütz, Ernst, 94

Armour, Richard, 66

Armstrong, Louis, 48

Arne, Thomas, 92

Arrowsmith, William, 117

"As I Was Going to Ballynure," 32

Asch, Moses, 129

Aspen, Colorado, 54–55

Associated Artists, Ltd., 65

Auer-Herbeck, Ida, 18

Austen Riggs Center, 36

"Australian Girls," 100

Babes of the Zoo, 42

Bach, Johann Sebastian, 57, 107, 133, 134

Bacon, Sir Francis, 98

Baez, Joan, 4, 43, 82, 93, 95, 103, 110, 124, 128

Bailey, Pearl, 27

"Bailiff's Daughter of Islington, The," 34, 86

Baillie, Joanna, 45

"Ball of Kerrimuir, The," 99

Ballads, 47, 51

Ballads and Folksongs Sung by Richard Dyer-Bennet, 40–41

"Barbara Allen," 25, 30, 34, 91, 93, 113, 135

Barlow, Sam, 108

Barnfield, Richard, 6

Basie, Count, 48

"Beautiful Dreamer," 97

Becket, Wheeler, 15, 16

Beckman, Gertrude Wheeler, 18, 55–58, 60, 86, 90, 131

Beethoven, Ludwig van, 44–45, 57, 100, 116

"Beggarman, The," 86

Bellman, Carl Michael, 7–12, 102

"Beloved Kitten," 32, 87–88

Berg, Alban, 56

Berkeley, California, 15

Bernstein, Jascha, 45

Bernstein, Leonard, 69

Bikel, Theodore, 76, 124

"Billy Barlow," 100

"Binnorie," 29, 52, 91, 94

Björklund, Edward, 8

"Black Is the Color of My True Love's Hair," 33, 43

"Black Jack Gypsy, The," 34

"Blackbirds and Thrushes," 50

"Blow the Candles Out," 29, 33, 43, 85

"Blowin' in the Wind," 127

Boggs, Doc, 126

"Bold Fenian Men, The" ("Down by the
  Glenside"), 81

Boleyn, Anne, 50

"Bonnie Dundee," 52, 89

"Bonnie Earl of Morey, The," 81–82, 85, 100

"Bonnie Lad That's Far Awa', The," 46

"Bonnie Laddie, Hieland Laddie," 46, 100

Books on Tape, 122

Boswell, Alexander, 45, 52

"Bow Down," 34, 52, 91

Bowles, Paul, 31

Brahms, Johannes, 19, 102, 136

Brand, Oscar, 5, 67, 77, 126

Bream, Julian, 7, 133

"Brigg Fair," 41, 43

"British Light Dragoons, The," 46, 94

Brock, Alfred, 19

Bruehl, William, 109

Brummel, O. B., 100

"Buckeye Jim," 91

Buell, Ruth (née Becker), 58–59, 125

"Buffalo Skinners, The," 95

Bundles for Britain, 71

Burns, Robert, 44–46, 82, 85–86, 99

Butterfield, Roger, 126

Byron, George Gordon, 82

Caccini, Guilio, 19

Caldara, Antonio, 19

Camera Three, 100

Campion, Thomas, 30, 50, 92–93

Carcassi, Matteo, 133

Carissimi, Giacomo, 19

Carnegie Hall, 33–35

Carruth, Alan, 120

Caruso, Enrico, 13

Casey, John Keegan, 51

Chaliapin, Feodor, 13

Chaplin, Ralph, 67

"Charleston Merchant, The," 34, 41–42, 100

"Charlie Is My Darling," 87

Charlotte's Web, 102

Chaucer, Geoffrey, 98

"Cherry Tree Carol," 93, 95

Chilliwack, British Columbia, 14

China Aid, 71

Civil Rights Congress, 69

Clancy Brothers and Tommy Makem, The, 51

Clapp, Edward Bull, 15

Clapp, May Wolcott, 15, 123

Clauson, William, 125

Clines, Francis, 121

"Coast of High Barbary," 34

"Cock Robin" ("Who Killed Cock Robin?"), 86

Collins, Fletcher, 42, 47, 91, 99, 101

Collins, Judy, 4

"Colorado Trail, The," 47

"Come All Ye," 29, 41, 48, 91

"Come All You Fair and Tender Maidens," 47

"Come Away, Death," 92

"Come Live With Me," 92

"Come Where My Love Lies Dreaming," 97

"Come With Thy Sweet Voice Again," 97

Communist Party of America, 69

Concert Hall (recording company), 40, 44, 92

Congress of Soviet-American Friendship, 69

Conly, John, 85, 87, 88, 90, 92, 94

Continental Records, 40, 51

Cook, Emory, 130

Cook Records, 130

Cooper, Bob, 128

Cooper, George, 97

Copland, Aaron, 29, 69, 116

"Corn Rigs are Bonnie," 32, 85–86

Cort, Harvey, 77, 79, 80, 85, 89, 95, 99, 130

"Could This Ill World Have Been Contrived,"
  46, 92

Coward, Noel, 26

Cowper, William, 96

"Cruel Mother, The," 82

Cullinan, Ralph, 94

Cunningham, Sis, 24

Dane, Barbara, 130

Davis, Peter, 113

de Gorgoza, Emilio, 13

de la Torre, José Rey, 30, 56, 134

de Schaunsee, Max, 85

Deane School (Santa Barbara, California), 16

Decca (recording company), 40, 48, 51, 76

Dehr, Rick, 59

Deller, Alfred, 125

"Der Tod von Basel," 32, 94–95

"Derby Ram, The," 41, 100

"Devil and the Farmer's Wife, The," 29, 49, 101

Dido and Aeneas, 116

"Die Bekehrte Schäferin," 93

Die Schöne Müllerin, 65, 102, 104, 106–7

Die Winterreise, 106

Dietrich, Marlene, 26

"Dinah and Villikens," 15, 49, 87

Dowland, John, 6, 7, 30, 93, 112, 128

"Down by the Sally Gardens," 29, 80

"Down in the Valley," 83, 85

"Drill Ye, Tarriers, Drill," 29, 34, 90

"Drink to Me Only with Thine Eyes," 31, 32

"Drunken Sailor, The," 42, 100

Duncan, Isadora, 35

Durgin, Cyrus W., 99

Dyer, Frederick Stewart Hotham, 12

Dyer-Bennet, Bonnie, 36, 54, 63, 78, 91, 123

Dyer-Bennet, Brooke, 36, 54, 63, 78, 91, 104, 123

Dyer-Bennet, Christopher, 13, 55

Dyer-Bennet, Fred, 13, 16, 70

Dyer-Bennet, John, 13, 16, 17, 20, 55, 69, 70

Dyer-Bennet, Melvene, 24–26, 35–36, 54–60, 75, 109, 119, 120, 123

Dyer-Bennet, Miriam, Jr., 13, 15, 16, 69–70

Dyer-Bennet, Miriam Wolcott Clapp, 12, 14, 15, 16, 17, 55, 69–70

Dyer-Bennet, Richard: Alaska, tour of, 63–65; Beckman, meeting with, 17–18; blacklist, appearance on, 68–77; childhood of, 12–15; death of, 123; Dyer-Bennet Records, founding of, 79; Germany, time spent in, 16–17; *Lovely Milleress*, recording of,

114–15; marriage of (first), 20; marriage of (second), 35–36; *Odyssey*, recitation and recording of, 118–22; OWI, work for, 36–38; recordings rereleased on CD, 129–30; Scholander, meeting with, 3–4, 19; School of Minstrelsy, founding of, 54–60; *Schöne Müllerin*, translation of, 104–6; SUNY Stony Brook, professor at, 109–12; tennis, love of, 62, 122; Town Hall, concerts at, 29–32; UC Berkeley, attendance of, 17–18, 20

Dyer-Bennet, Richard Stewart, 12, 14, 15

Dylan, Bob, 43, 126, 127, 128

"Early One Morning," 41, 50, 94

Eastman, Charles, 97

"Eddystone Light, The," 48, 100

"Edward," 90–91, 127

"Eer-i-e Canal, The," 99

"Eggs and Marrowbone," 49, 85

Einstein, Albert, 63

Elizabeth I, Queen of England, 98

Elliott, William, 125

Ericson, Raymond, 107

Erikson, Erik, 36

Eskin, Sam, 56, 83, 99

Essential Richard Dyer-Bennet, The, 103

Evening with William Shakespeare, An, 108

Everly Brothers, The, 100

"Fain Would I Wed a Fair Young Maid," 34, 50, 87

"Faithful Johnie," 45–46

Fanshel, Susan, 119–20

"Fine Flowers in the Valley," 82, 135

"Finland Rise Again," 37

Fitzgerald, Robert, 117–19

Flaherty, David, 91

"Flow My Tears," 93

"Foggy Dew, The," 29, 34, 90

Folk Songs, 51

"For Thee, Love, For Thee," 97

Foster, Stephen, 96–97, 107

"Fox, The" ("The Fox and the Geese"), 90, 101
Frankenstein, Alfred, 20, 92, 94, 96, 97
Franz, Robert, 20
Freewheelin' Bob Dylan, The, 127
Frenkel, Stefan, 45
"Frog Went A-Courting," 48, 91

Galli-Curci, Amelita, 13
"Garden Where the Praties Grow, The," 27, 86
Garniez, Nancy, 113–15
Garrison, David Lloyd, 42, 96, 100
"Gathering of the Clan, The," 99
Geer, Will, 23
Geistliche Lieder, 107
"Gentle Annie," 97
"Gently, Johnny, My Jingalo," 32, 94
Gervis, Stephanie, 100
Gideon, Miriam, 56
Gilbert, John, 133
Gilbert, Ronnie, 76
Gildea, John Rose, 27
Gillespie, Dizzy, 29
Glasgow Rangers Football Club, 16
Glazer, Joe, 130
Gluck, Christoph Willibald, 19
"Go Away from My Window," 43
"Go Down Moses," 5, 88
"Go Tell Aunt Rhody," 25, 91
"Go 'Way Old Man," 96
Godmilow, Jill, 119–20
Goethe, Johann Wolfgang von, 93
Goethe Festival, 59
"Going to Ballynure," 43
"Golden Vanity, The," 25, 29, 41, 47, 52
Goldstein, Ken, 51, 84
Gooding, Cynthia, 4
"Goodnight, Irene," 126
Gordon, Max, 27, 28, 60
Göttingen, Germany, 16
Gould, Joseph Ferdinand, 27
Graham, John (Viscount Dundee), 52
Granados, Enrique, 30
Grant, Mrs. Anne, 46

"Green Corn," 26, 91
Greene, Plunkett, 53
Greensborough, North Carolina, 22
"Greensleeves," 29, 50, 52, 135
Gropper, William, 69
Grundy, Sydney, 82
Guthrie, Woody, 4, 23, 25, 47, 67, 126, 129

Hammet, Dashiell, 69
Handel, George Frederick, 19, 115
"Hanging Johnny," 100
Hansel and Gretel, 15
"Hard Rain's A-Gonna Fall, A," 127
"Hares on the Mountain," 50
Harker, Lesl, 110–11, 125, 128
Harte, Brett, 100–1
Hartnett, Vincent K., 77
Hauser, Hermann, 133
Heifetz, Jascha, 128
Hellerman, Fred, 67
Hellman, Lillian, 69
Helm, Everett, 99
Henderson, Hamish, 110
"Henry Martin," 93
Henry VIII, King of England, 50
Henschel, George, 115
Hentoff, Nat, 91, 101, 128
Hernandez, Santos, 133
Hester, Carolyn, 125
Hexter, Ralph, 118
Hill, Joe, 67
Himmel, Friedrich Heinrich, 93
Hitler, Adolf, 17
Hogg, James, 46
"Hole in the Bottom of the Sea, The," 91–92
Holiday, Billie, 29, 48
Holm, Hanya, 36
Holt, Gordon, 88
Holt, Will, 56, 59, 60, 125
Holzman, Jac, 85
Homer, 116
"Hood and the Bismarck, The," 37
Hoover, J. Edgar, 68

Horowitz, Vladimir, 128
"House Carpenter, The," 41, 87
House Committee on Un-American Activities
    (HUAC), 72–77
Houston, Cisco, 24
"How Hell Busted Loose Up at Blue Mountain
    Lake," 33, 47
Hugh, Elinor, 85
Hughes, Herbert, 43
Hughes, Langston, 69
"Hullabaloo Belay," 42, 100
Hullah, John, 81
Hurok, Sol, 35, 55, 58, 59, 60, 65, 133
Hurt, Mississippi John, 103
Hutchins, Robert M., 59

"I Care Not for These Ladies," 92–93
"I Once Loved a Girl" ("I Once Loved a Boy"),
    21, 93, 95, 135
"I Ride an Old Paint," 90, 91
"I Went Out One Morning in May," 91
"If All the Young Girls," 50
"If You've Only Got a Moustache," 97
Iliad, The, 117–18, 122
"I'm a Poor Boy," 83
Independent Progressive Party, 69
International Concert Musicians Bureau, 120
International Workers of the World (IWW or
    Wobblies), 66–67
Irish Songs, 44–45
"It Ain't Me, Babe," 43
Ives, Burl, 24, 25, 27, 28, 43, 47, 58, 59, 68, 69,
    72–75, 77, 91, 100
Ives, Edward, 81

Jackson, Aunt Molly, 24
Jackson, Walker, 80
Jacoby, Herbert, 26–28
"Jag Vill Ga Vall," 89–90
"Jagabenteur," 94
"Jan Hinnerk," 16, 32, 86
"Jeanie with the Light Brown Hair," 97
Jenkins, Ella, 129

Jenkins, Gordon, 126
Jenkins, Speight, 114
"Jennie Jenkins," 34
"John Henry," 5, 34, 52, 91
"John Peel," 48, 91
"John Riley," 32, 93, 95
Johnson, Harriet, 32
Joint Anti-Fascist Refugee Committee, 69, 71
Jones, Nic, 88
Jonson, Ben, 98
"Joys of Love, The" ("Plaisir d'amour"), 83, 135
Jurado, Antonio de Torres, 133

Kaiser, Amy, 116
Kalischer, Clemens, 79
Kearney, Peadar, 81
Keats, John, 130
"Keeper, The," 29
"Kerry Recruit, The" 33, 52–53, 89
Keynote Records, 67
King Arthur (Purcell), 116
"King Arthur's Sons," 48
"King of the Noise, The," 101–2
Kingsley, Charles, 81
"Kitty My Love," 51
Kleber, Henry, 97
Kovacs, David, 121
"Kränzelkraut," 94

La Fey, Howard, 87
Labor Youth League, 69
"Lady Who Loved a Swine, The," 88
"Lady's Policy, The," 87
"Laird of Cockpen, The," 32, 52, 94, 100
Lampell, Millard, 24
Lankford, Ronald, 126
"Lass from the Low Country," 47, 87
"Last Night I Had the Strangest Dream," 99
Laurence, Paula, 26
"Le Brave Marin," 10, 94
"Le Joli Tambour," 95
Le Ruban Bleu, 26–27
"Le Veritable Amour," 10, 95

Lead Belly (Huddy Ledbetter), 4, 24–26, 47, 67, 76, 84, 91, 101, 126, 129
Lee, Gypsy Rose, 69
Leicester, England, 12
Lenya, Lotte, 26
"Leprechaun, The," 41
Leventhal, Harold, 76
Lewis, Elaine Lambert, 26
Library of Congress, 120
Lichter, Charles, 42
Lieberman, Archie, 120
"Lilli Bulero," 87
Lilly, Josiah, 97
Lincoln Portrait, A, 116
"Lincolnshire Poacher, The," 41, 95
"Linger in Blissful Repose," 97
"Little Pigs," 48, 91
Llobet, Miguel, 30, 134
"Lolly-To-Dum-Day," 29, 34, 49
Lomax, Alan, 48, 69
Lomax, Bess, 24
Lomax, John, 24, 48
Lombardo, Stanley, 122
"Londonderry Air" ("My Gentle Harp"), 31, 32
"Lonesome Dove, The," 52
"Lonesome Valley, The," 33, 79, 84, 93, 100, 130
Lopez, Trini, 60
Lord, Albert, 121
"Lord Randall" ("Lord Rendal"), 25, 29, 41, 51, 91, 113, 135
Lotti, Antonio, 19
Love Songs, 42, 51
Lovely Milleress, The, 104–7, 113–15
Lovely Milleress, The (recording), 115
"Lowlands," 52, 95

"MacArthur the Rattler," 37
MacBeth, 108
MacMurrough, Dermot, 45
Magg, Fritz, 92
Magg, Natasha, 92
"Maids of the Mourne Shore, The," 80
Makem Brothers, The, 53

"Man Who Was Full of Fun, The," 101
Marais and Miranda, 56, 57
Marlowe, Christopher, 92
Marshall Plan, 69
Martin, David Stone, 42, 51
Mason, Redfern, 21
"Masters of War," 127
May, Kenny, 70
"May Day Carol, The," 89
Maynor, Dorothy, 59
McAlester, Keven, 130
McCarthy, Joseph, 69, 73, 77
McCarthy, William H., 97
McCormack, John, 13, 80, 81, 95, 128
McCurdy, Ed, 99
McDonald, Ron, 120
McGee, Brownie, 24
McKellen, Ian, 122
Mendelssohn, Felix, 122
Mercury (recording company), 40
Meredith College, 122
"Mermaid, The," 100
"Midnight Special, The," 26
Midnight Special, The (radio show), 84
Milan, Luis, 30, 95
Miller, Arthur, 69
Miller, Philip, 44
Minstrel's Diary, A, 122
Mitropoulos, Dimitri, 59
"Mo Mary," 29, 49
"Molly Brannigan," 80
"Molly Malone," 48
Monitor Records, 130
Monterey, Massachusetts, 78
Monteverdi, Claudio, 19, 65
"Moonrise," 32
Moore, Thomas, 80
More Songs by the 20th-Century Minstrel, 47
Morneweck, Evelyn Foster, 97
"Morning A Cruel Turmoiler Is," 45
"Morning Air Plays on My Face, The," 45
Morris, George, 97
Mostel, Zero, 69

Mozart, Wolfgang Amadeus, 19, 57, 116
Müller, Wilhelm, 104, 107, 114
"My Good Old Man," 51–52, 95

Napoleon I, Emperor of France, 46, 88
Nash, N. Richard, 94
National Endowment for the Humanities, 119
National Sharecroppers Organization, 69
NATO, 69
Nichols, Mike, 84
"Nightingale, The," 32
Niles, John Jacob, 34, 43, 47, 67, 126
"No Hiding Place," 96
Noel, Dan, 91
"Nymph's Reply, The," 92

"O Speak Then, My Love," 95
Odyssey, The, 116–22
Odyssey Tapes, The, 120–21
Office of War Information (OWI), 36–38, 56
"Oft in the Stilly Night," 80
"Oh, Can You Sew Cushions," 46
"Oh, How Can I Be Blithe and Glad?," 46, 92
"Oh, Mary, At Thy Window Be," 46, 92
"Oh, No, John," 48
"Oh, Sally, My Dear," 50
"Oh, Sweet Were the Hours," 46, 92
"Oh, Who, My Dear Dermot," 45
"Old Bangum," 47, 91
"Old Crab, The," 99
"Old Gray Goose, The," 101
"Old Joe Clark," 99
"Old Maid, The," 49–50
Oliphant, Carolina (Lady Nairne), 52
O'Lochlainn, Colin, 51
"On the Massacre of Glencoe," 46, 100
"On Wings of Song Transport Me," 122–23
"Once More I Hail Thee," 45
"Open Thy Lattice, Love," 97
Osborne, Conrad, 105
"Over There," 37
"Oxford Town," 127

Packard, Frederick, 40
Paepcke, Walter, 54, 59
Paisiello, Giovanni, 19
Papashvily, George and Helen, 101–2
Paredon Records, 130
Parker, Charlie, 29
Parker, Dorothy, 69
"Passionate Shepherd to His Love, The," 92
"Passive Resistance," 37
Pavlova, Anna, 35
"Pedro," 83–84, 135
Pellegrini, Norman, 84
People's Songs, 67–69
Pepper, Elizabeth (Bebe) Hoar, 20, 22
Pepys, Samuel, 50, 63, 98
Percy, Thomas, 6
Pergolesi, Giovanni Batista, 19
Perry, Richard, 92
Peter, Paul, and Mary, 60
Peter and the Wolf, 116
"Peter Gray," 100
"Phyllis and Her Mother," 32, 82
Pincus, Andrew, 130
"Piper of Dundee, The," 32, 91
"Plain Language from Truthful James," 100–1
Pontyprid, Wales, 19
Porter, Andrew, 113, 115
Porter, Cole, 26
Pound, Ezra, 118
"Pride of Petravore," 94
Prime-Stevenson, Edward, 21
Prokofiev, Sergei, 116
Puget, Loisa, 95
"Pull Off Your Old Coat," 32, 51, 83
"Pulse of an Irishman, The," 45
Purcell, Henry, 19, 93, 115, 116

"Quaker Lover, The," 47, 135
Quayle, Anthony, 122
Quill, Mike, 28

Raleigh, Sir Walter, 52, 92, 98
Randall, Edward, 88

Raymond, John, 129

"Reaper's Ghost, The," 95–96

Reardon, Caspar, 26

Red Channels, 68–69, 72, 76–77

Reid, Cornelius, 103, 107–8, 113–14

Reid, J. C., 13–14

Remington (recording company), 40, 51

"Return to Ulster, The," 45

"Reuben, Reuben, I've Been Thinking," 87

Ribner, Irving, 109

Rice, Elmer, 76

Richard Dyer-Bennet: Lute Singer, 41

*Richard Dyer-Bennet: The Twentieth-Century
    Minstrel,* 51

Richard Dyer-Bennet 1, 60, 79–85, 103

Richard Dyer-Bennet 2, 43, 47, 49, 85–87, 101,
    103

Richard Dyer-Bennet 3, 47, 49, 50, 87–88, 103

Richard Dyer-Bennet 4, 41, 52, 88–90

Richard Dyer-Bennet 5, 43, 47, 51, 52, 90–91, 103

Richard Dyer-Bennet 6, 47, 48, 52, 91–92, 103

Richard Dyer-Bennet 7, 44–46, 92

Richard Dyer-Bennet 8, 92–94

Richard Dyer-Bennet 9, 50, 52, 94–95

Richard Dyer-Bennet 10, 41, 51, 95–96

Richard Dyer-Bennet 11, 96–97, 107

Richard Dyer-Bennet 12, 48, 49, 100–1, 103

Richard Dyer-Bennet 13, 49, 101–2, 103, 104, 115

*Richard Dyer-Bennet and Tom Glazer Sing
    Olden Ballads,* 41

Richard Dyer-Bennet Folk Song Book, The, 47,
    50, 52–53, 129

*Richard Dyer-Bennett (sic): Twentieth-Century
    Minstrel,* 48–49

Rinzler, Ralph, 130

"Rising of the Moon, The," 51, 89

Robeson, Paul, 29, 103

Robinson, Earl, 24

Robinson, Edward G., 69

"Rommel the Fox," 37

Rosenzweig, Betty, 101

Rosenzweig, Martin, 100

Rossi, Urico, 92

"Round and Round Hitler's Grave," 67

"Roving Gambler, The," 32, 100

Rubenstein, Harry, 96–98, 113, 116, 129

Saaringen, Eero, 59

Sainte-Marie, Buffy, 103

Sandburg, Carl, 29, 90, 95

Sandow, Greg, 130

Sanford, Carolyn, 92

Santley, Charles, 115

Saslow, George, 55

Scarlatti, Alessandro, 19

Scarlatti, Domenico, 19

Schiøtz, Aksel, 102, 107

Schipa, Tito, 13

Schlamme, Martha, 125

Schneider, Howard, 104, 127

"Schneiders Höllenfahrt," 94

Scholander, F. W., 8, 9

Scholander, Sten, 27

Scholander, Sven, 3, 4, 8–12, 18–20, 27, 33, 35, 41,
    55, 82, 86, 88, 90, 94, 95, 100, 110, 123, 124,
    129, 130, 131, 134

Schubert, Franz, 19, 57, 65, 102, 106–7, 127

Schulman, Andrew, 112–13, 125, 130

Schumann, Robert, 19

Schweitzer, Albert, 59

Scientific and Cultural Conference for World
    Peace, 69, 74

Scott, Sir Walter, 45, 46

Scotti, Antonio, 13

Scottish Songs, 44–45, 92, 94

"Searching for Lambs," 89

Second Best Bed, 94, 99, 108

Seeger, Charles, 24

Seeger, Pete, 4, 24, 25, 47, 50, 66–69, 75–77,
    126, 129, 130

Segovia, Andres, 29, 128, 133

Seldes, Gilbert, 25

"Seven Little Pigs," 95

Shackell, Rodney, 129

Shakespeare, William, 50, 92, 94, 98

"Shallow Brown," 100

Sharp, Cecil, 87, 89
"She Moved Through the Fair," 95
Sheehy, Daniel, 125
Sheehy, Emma Dickson, 92
Shelton, Robert, 125
Sherman, Robert, 88, 90
Sigstedt, Val, 58, 60
Silber, Irwin, 68, 75, 130
Simon and Garfunkel, 100
Simonds, Simon, 82
1601 (recording), 63, 98–100
Smithsonian Folkways, 129–30
Smyth, William, 45–46
"So Long, It's Been Good to Know You," 126
"So We'll Go No More A-Roving," 82, 100
"Soldier and the Lady, The," 29, 101
"Some People Think Hitler is Dead," 37
"Song of Reproach," 89
Songs for John Doe, 67
"Spanish Lady, The," 28, 89
"Spottlied auf Napoleons Rückzug Aus Russland 1812," 88
"St. Patrick's Day," 45
Stalin, Joseph, 68
Stein, Gertrude, 43
Stern, Arthur, 24
Sting, 7
Stinson (recording company), 40, 47, 48, 51
Strasvogel, Ignace, 45
Stuart Little, 102
Sullivan, Maxine, 26
"Sunset," 46
SUNY Stony Brook, 109–12, 118, 128, 132
"Swapping Song, The," 34, 49, 87
"Sweet Betsy from Pike," 49
"Sweetly She Sleeps, My Alice Fair," 97
Syer, Warren, 65, 114

"Tailor and the Mouse, The," 91
"Tailor's Boy, The," 99
"Tale of the Tales," 101
"Talking World War III Blues," 127
Tannenbaum, David, 115

Tarrega, Francisco, 134
Taubman, Howard, 42, 43, 46
Taylor, Louise, 122
Taylor, Telford, 75
Temple of Music, 96, 114
Terkel, Studs, 84, 85, 126, 131
Terry, Sonny, 24
"There Are Plenty of Fish in the Sea," 97
"There Was a Friar in Our Town," 99
"This Land Is Your Land," 23, 126
Thomson, George, 44, 100
Thomson, Virgil, 31
"Three Crows," 26, 91
"Three Fishers," 29, 81, 135
"Three Jolly Rogues of Lynn," 48, 91
"Three Ravens" ("Three Ra'ens"), 29, 89
"Three Tailors," 90
Toscanini, Arturo, 128
Town Hall (New York concert venue), 29–32, 61
Trachtenberg, Alexander, 69
Training the Actor's Voice, 108
Trott zu Solz, Adam von, 17
"Turkish Reverie, The," 25, 47, 85
"Turn, Turn, Turn," 126
"Twa' Sisters, The," 52
Twain, Mark, 98–100
Twelfth Night, 108
Twichell, Joseph Hopkins, 98
"Two Comments," 96
"Two Maidens Went Milking One Day," 33, 43, 85

Ulanowsky, Paul, 102, 107
"Unfortunate Troubadour, The," 96
University of California, Berkeley, 17, 20
University of Virginia, 121
USO (United Service Organizations), 70, 72

van Gelder, Lawrence, 116
van Gelder, Rudy, 79
Vanguard Records, 103
"Veillée de Noël," 86
Velazquez, Manuel, 132–33

"Venezuela," 34, 43, 91, 135
"Vicar of Bray, The," 82, 85, 130
Village Vanguard, The, 26–28, 56, 60, 121
von Damen, Hermann, 89
von Schmidt, Eric, 103
Vox (recording company), 40, 46–47
Vox Presents Richard Dyer-Bennet Singing Minstrel Songs of the USA, 46–47

Wagner, Charles, 21
Walton, Izaak, 122
"Waltzing Matilda" ("The Swagman"), 41, 89, 100, 126
Ward, John, 42–43, 50, 56, 57, 87, 93, 95
Waterloo, Battle of, 46
Watson, Doc, 103
WCBS-TV, 100
Weavers, The, 24, 48, 68, 76, 99, 103, 126
"Wee Cooper of Fife, The," 29
Welles, Orson, 29, 69
Wells, Barnard, 96
"Were You There?," 47
"Westryn Wind," 43
WFMT, 84
"What Shall We Do With the Drunken Sailor?," 42
Wheeler, B. Clark, 55
"When Cockleshells Turn Silverbells," 29, 41, 47, 85
When Dalliance Was in Flower, 99
"Where Have All the Flowers Gone?," 126

White, E. B., 102
White, Josh, 24, 47, 68
"White Lily, The," 28, 29, 33, 35, 51
Whitman, Cedric, 120
"Who Enters Russia by the Sword," 37
"Wife Wrapped in Wether's Skin, The," 32, 51, 95
Wigman, Mary, 35
Willard, Jerry, 112, 134
Williams, John, 133
Williams, Tennessee, 25
"Willie Taylor," 34, 87
"Willow Tree, The," 49, 100
Wilson, Alice, 118
Winchell, Walter, 34
Winn, John, 125
Wolf, Hugo, 19, 102
"Wolf Who Knew How to Be a Friend, The," 102
"Woman, Go Home," 32, 86
Wood, Ellen, 20
"World's Too Small for Fascists, The," 37

"Yankee Doodle," 37
Yeats, William Butler, 29, 80
Yes and No Stories, 101–2
Young Communist League, 70
Yurchenko, Henrietta, 99

Zittel, Ted, 28–29
Zuccalmaglio, Anton Wilhelm von, 94